LOSING POWER

LOSING POWER

AFRICAN AMERICANS AND RACIAL POLARIZATION IN TENNESSEE POLITICS

SEKOU M. FRANKLIN AND
RAY BLOCK JR.

THE UNIVERSITY OF GEORGIA PRESS
ATHENS

Paperback edition, 2021
© 2020 by the University of Georgia Press
Athens, Georgia 30602
www.ugapress.org
All rights reserved
Designed by Kaelin Chappell Broaddus
Set in 10/13 Minion 3 by Kaelin Chappell Broaddus

Most University of Georgia Press titles are
available from popular e-book vendors.

Printed digitally

The Library of Congress has cataloged the
hardcover edition of this book as follows:

Names: Franklin, Sekou M., author. | Block, Ray, Jr., author.
Title: Losing power : African Americans and racial polarization in
  Tennessee politics / Sekou M. Franklin and Ray Block Jr.
Description: Athens : The University of Georgia Press, 2020. |
  Includes bibliographical references and index.
Identifiers: LCCN 2019030000 | ISBN 9780820356051 (hardcover) |
  ISBN 9780820356068 (ebook)
Subjects: LCSH: African Americans—Tennessee—Politics and
  government. | Race relations—Political aspects—Tennessee. |
  Voting—Tennessee. | Tennessee—Politics and government—21st
  century.
Classification: LCC E185.93.T3 F73 2020 | DDC 305.8009768—dc23
LC record available at https://lccn.loc.gov/2019030000

Paperback ISBN 978-0-8203-6173-4

CONTENTS

LIST OF ILLUSTRATIONS vii
ACKNOWLEDGMENTS xi

INTRODUCTION 1

PART 1. THE DEEP ROOTS OF POLARIZATION IN TENNESSEE

CHAPTER 1. Race and Polarization 15
CHAPTER 2. Black Politics in Tennessee from the Antebellum Period to the Twenty-First Century 32

PART 2. REALIGNMENT OF PARTISAN POLITICS IN TENNESSEE

CHAPTER 3. Race, Electoral Realignment, and Polarization 65
CHAPTER 4. The Legislative Behavior of Tennessee's Black Lawmakers 80

PART 3. RACE AND POLARIZATION IN RECENT TENNESSEE POLITICS: THE ISSUES

CHAPTER 5. The Racial Politics of Tax and Spending Policies 105
CHAPTER 6. The Rise and Fall of TennCare 124
CHAPTER 7. Immigration and the New Tennesseans 163
CHAPTER 8. Controversies and Conflicts over Sentencing Policies and the Death Penalty 180

CONCLUSION 195

NOTES 201
INDEX 243

ILLUSTRATIONS

FIGURES

3.1. Democratic presidential vote for ten counties with the worst voter registration rates 71

3.2. Democratic presidential vote for ten counties with the best voter registration rates 71

5.1. Racial differences in the opposition to a state income tax 113

5.2. Racial differences in preference for flat versus graduated tax 114

5.3. Racial differences in opposition to an income tax, sorted by question order 116

5.4. Racial differences in opposition to various forms of state-level government spending 120

5.5. Racial differences in opposition to various forms of federal-level government spending 121

5.6. Racial differences in opposition to state- and federal-level government spending 122

6.1. Race of participants and assumptions about how many disenrolled TennCare clients would be able to find alternative sources of health care 151

6.2. Degree of economic disadvantage by average level of approval of cuts to TennCare, by racial group 152

6.3. Racial differences in approval of TennCare reform by economic disadvantage and perceptions of proportion of disenrolled TennCare clients who would find alternative health care in the purported safety net 153

7.1. Latino population trends for Tennessee, 2000–2010, as projected in 2004 170

7.2. Perceived importance of immigration in U.S. Senate race 171

7.3. Trends in Tennesseans' viewpoints regarding guest-worker programs, the impact of Latino immigrants on U.S. society, and immigrants' threat to jobs   172

7.4. Summary of the conditions in the MTSU survey experiment on issue framing and immigration attitudes   173

7.5. Average levels of the Anti-Immigration Attitudes Index across experimental conditions, sorted by respondents' race   176

7.6. Post-estimation results: How the effect of race on respondents' immigration attitudes differed across the framing conditions   178

TABLES

3.1. Party turnover in elections for the Tennessee House of Representatives   71

3.2. Select characteristics and network measures of Tennessee counties   74

3.3. Network-level and MRQAP measures of vote choice   76

4.1. Characteristics of sponsorship networks   93

4.2. Characteristics of the House of Representatives   93

4.3. Capability (network scores): Adopted legislation   94

4.4. Political and sociodemographic profile of TBCSL members, 103rd General Assembly   96

4.5. Capability network scores for subnetworks in the 103rd General Assembly   97

5.1. Predicting racial differences in the influence of question order on Tennesseans' opposition to a general income tax   118

6.1. Residents' assessment of the biggest problems in Tennessee   144

6.2. Relationship between assumptions about the existence of a health-care safety net and approval of cuts to TennCare   146

6.3. Relationship between assumptions about the existence of a health-care safety net, income level, and approval of cuts to TennCare   147

6.4. Race of respondents and approval of cuts to TennCare   148

A6.1. Summary of the experimental conditions in the 2008 TennCare study   160

7.1. Social and political background of participants in the fall 2006 MTSU poll   174

7.2. Summary of the theoretically central variables in the immigration framing experiment 175
7.3. OLS regression models of the influence of issue framing on Tennesseans' opposition toward immigration 176
8.1. Exploring attitudes about the death penalty (regression tables), 1999 191
8.2. Exploring attitudes about the death penalty (regression tables), 2007 192

ACKNOWLEDGMENTS

We owe a great debt to many people. *Losing Power* would not have been published but for the generosity of our loved ones, colleagues, and benefactors, who helped us travel the long and often arduous journey of writing this book. We give special thanks to those who are nearest and dearest to us. Sekou Franklin's wife, Tené Hamilton Franklin, and two daughters, Sojourner and Langston, have been indispensable to this book project and his academic career. Ray Block's wife, Christina S. Haynes, and their daughter, Reece Justice Haynes-Block, deserve special thanks for their unwavering support. We can say without exaggeration that *Losing Power* would not have been possible without the unconditional love and emotional support of our families.

We give additional thanks to a network of colleagues and students spanning several universities, including Middle Tennessee State University (MTSU), the University of Wisconsin at La Crosse, the University of Kentucky, and Pennsylvania State University. Marian V. Wilson, Barbara Patton, and Forrestine White Williams in MTSU's Office of Institutional Equity and Compliance, as well as Stephen Morris, Moses Tesi, Clyde Willis, Pam Davis, Chanera Pierce, and Nejib Adem in MTSU's Department of Political Science provided institutional and research support for the book project. For granting us access to survey data, we thank the principal investigators of the MTSU poll, Ken Blake and Jason Reineke, along with the faculty members and students in MTSU's School of Journalism and Strategic Media.

We are grateful to Jeremy Arney, Jo Arney, Tim Dale, Grace Deason, Regina Goodnow, Brittney Greeno, Chandra Hawkins, Jacob Holt, John Kovari, Cecilia Manrique, Charles Martin-Stanley Sr., Stephen McDougal, Melissa Neilsen, Sam Scinta, Laurie Cooper Stoll, and Adam Van Liere at the University of Wisconsin at La Crosse for their comments on early chapter drafts and, more generally, for their advice about navigating the book-writing process. Horace Bartilow, Anastasia Curwood, Mark Peffley, Melynda Price, Ellen Riggle, Rick Waterman, Justin Wedeking, and Ernie Yanarella at the University of Kentucky provided valuable advice and mentorship. We also give special thanks to Pennsylvania

State University's Lee Ann Banaszak, Errol Henderson, and Candis Watts Smith for their feedback and encouragement.

Overall, we are grateful for the professional development resources from MTSU's Non-Instructional Assignment Grant, as well as the Departments of Political Science at MTSU, the University of Wisconsin at La Crosse, the University of Kentucky, and Pennsylvania State University. The American Political Science Association's Small Research Grant Program provided valuable assistance toward the completion of this project as well.

We would be remiss if we did not recognize Harwood McClerking, Ray Block's dissertation advisor, dear friend, and research collaborator. We value Harwood's candor, work ethic, and intellectual curiosity, and he was very encouraging as we grappled with the ideas that ultimately became the bedrock of this book. We further acknowledge the past and current members of the Gender and Political Psychology Writing Group (Nicole Bauer, Colleen Carpinella, Erin Casesse, Rosalyn Cooperman, Sarah Allen Gershon, Mirya Holman, Anna Mahoney, Heather Silber Mohamed, Heather Ondercin, Monica Schneider, Jane Lawrence Sumner, and Jennie Sweet-Cushman) who provided feedback on the book.

The following colleagues at the National Conference of Black Political Scientists offered valuable comments when we presented early drafts of this research at conference panels: Valeria Sinclair Chapman, Brandon Davis, Pearl Ford Dowe, Andra Gillespie, Tyson King-Meadows, and D'Andre Orey. We also shared the results of our research informally with helpful colleagues Lakeyta Bonnette, Randolph Burnside, Christopher J. Clark, Jonathan Collins, Christopher Sebastian Parker, and Alvin B. Tillery. In addition, a network of less visible but nonetheless important people assisted us on this journey. Darla Brock, an archivist at the Tennessee State Library and Archives, helped us navigate gubernatorial papers, old cases adjudicated by the Tennessee Supreme Court, and records documenting the slave trade in Tennessee. Archivists at the Albert Gore Research Center gave additional assistance. Jackie Sims, the co-coordinator of Democracy Nashville–Democratic Communities, also offered support for this project as did Leslie Collins at Fisk University, who assisted with interviews of state and local advocates.

We also thank our editorial team at the University of Georgia Press. Jon Davies deserves a heartfelt thank you for taking a chance on this project. It would have been impossible to complete the book without his diligence and perseverance. Bethany Snead, Merryl A. Sloane, and Denise Carlson assisted with the editing and indexing.

We give a special shout-out to Kate Babbit, the founder of https://writersfriend.org. Kate reviewed and fact-checked drafts of the chapters. She was the master of all trades: editorial assistant, writing counselor, constructive critic, translator, and coach. Throughout the entire project, she pushed us to resist our training as social scientists and speak boldly about issues of racial discrimination in Tennessee. The result is a manuscript that contains both careful analyses and unapologetic truth-telling.

Finally, we thank the people of the great state of Tennessee. The state has a rich and colorful tradition of politicians, activists, and narratives, which has much to teach the country about racial politics, African Americans, and the politics of the U.S. South.

LOSING POWER

INTRODUCTION

> Black politics [are] a function of the brand of segregation found in different environments in which black people found themselves.
>
> —HANES WALTON (1972)

This book originated from a series of conversations in the mid-2000s when we both were faculty members in the Department of Political Science at Middle Tennessee State University (MTSU). This was a contentious period in Tennessee politics that included a nationally covered U.S. Senate race that matched Congressman Harold Ford Jr., an African American Democrat from Memphis, against Bob Corker, the Republican mayor of Chattanooga. Progressives and fiscally conservative Democrats were further embroiled in a battle over the Medicaid program in Tennessee (officially called TennCare) that invited protests from health care, disability rights, and other grassroots advocates. Another controversy, the Operation Tennessee Waltz bribery scandal, ensnared a number of Democratic Party lawmakers, including several high-ranking black officials from Memphis. The first signs of party realignment also emerged during this period as Republicans were steadily making inroads in state politics and would soon become the majority party in the state legislature.

Several years later, we both participated in the Southern Coalition for Social Justice's Community Census and Redistricting Institute in Durham, North Carolina. The institute trained social scientists to provide expert analyses for voting-rights and minority-redistricting court cases for the 2010–2012 round of legislative redistricting. It provided yet another venue for us to discuss racial politics in Tennessee, especially the political status of African Americans.

This book builds on the extant research of racial politics in the South by documenting the political experiences of African Americans in Tennessee. We give specific attention to assessing how political and racial polarization has shaped African American politics in the state during the twenty-first century. This includes investigating the impact of polarization on black political influence and multiracial coalitions that advance what political scientist Robert C. Smith refers to as "racial equalitarian" policies.[1] With the terms "racial equalitarianism" or "racial equity," we imply a political agenda that promotes racial justice and civil rights initiatives, but also seeks to ameliorate poverty or other regressive measures that affect economically vulnerable blacks and nonblacks. By examining polarization, we also underscore the difficulties confronting African American and civil rights activists who seek to advance racial equalitarian policies.

Tennesseans in general and African Americans have made tremendous strides since the end of de jure segregation. Blacks are routinely elected and appointed to state and local offices, the black vote has tremendous sway in statewide elections, and legally explicit forms of racial segregation have been outlawed. Yet the transformation of Tennessee into a racial equalitarian state—a notion that was central to the black freedom movement during the antebellum and Jim Crow periods—remains elusive for many blacks, especially those living in the most underresourced and economically distressed communities.

Throughout this book, we show that race and especially the political and social status of African Americans have shaped executive and legislative decision-making, elections, and redistricting and have influenced taxes, health care, immigration, capital punishment, and other social and public policies. In some respects, these debates still raise the important question of whether a racial hierarchy will continue to structure the life circumstances of blacks and other disadvantaged groups just as much as they did in the antebellum and Jim Crow eras. Hence, although Tennessee blacks no longer live under legal segregation, the struggle for racial equalitarianism still very much rests on whether they wear the badge of second-class citizenship.

The period under study (2000–2012) marked a rupture in the status quo politics in Tennessee. The most significant phenomenon was party turnover with Democrats losing control of both the House and Senate in the Tennessee General Assembly. Democrats had solid majorities in both chambers at the beginning of the decade. The Senate was led by Lieutenant Governor John S. Wilder, the longest-serving elected official in a state legislature in the country's history. Leading the House was Jimmy Naifeh, and his second-in-command was Memphis representative Lois DeBerry, the highest-ranking black elected official in the state's history. Democrats also had control of the state's executive branch throughout much of the decade. Yet they were pushed out of power by the end of 2010, experiencing a net loss of two dozen seats in the Tennessee House of Representatives.

Meanwhile, Republicans gained supermajority control of both chambers in the Tennessee General Assembly for the first time since the nineteenth century.

Party realignment contributed to the loss of black political power in the state legislature. In the 105th General Assembly (2007–2008), the last session controlled by Democrats, blacks chaired four of the fifteen full committees and seven of the twenty-five subcommittees in the House. Four years later, after Republicans gained control of the House, no committees or subcommittees were chaired by black lawmakers. A similar decline of black political power occurred in the Senate. The loss of power meant the retrenchment of social policies, civil rights, and other measures championed by African American politicians and progressive interest groups. These included voting protections, social welfare and reproductive rights, and economic safety-net initiatives, such as a living wage, anti–wage theft measures, and prevailing wage policies.

THESIS OF THE BOOK

Throughout this book, we reject the normative assumption that political polarization is a new phenomenon in American politics or has been exacerbated by the ideological dogmatism of contemporary party politics. Instead, polarization and its different manifestations (racial, electoral, partisan, political, and issue polarization) are an enduring characteristic of Tennessee and the foundation of American politics. Polarization has been constitutive of American political culture since before the Revolutionary War and the King Caucus coalition in Congress during the 1790s; in the pre–Civil War debates over state sovereignty, slavery, and territorial expansion; and during the post–Civil War disputes over Reconstruction, civil service reform, and industrial regulation.

Our work seeks to explain how polarization has contributed to anti-minority rhetoric, racially regressive policies, the increasing difficulty African American voters experience in electing politicians of their own race, and a growing number of barriers faced by blacks who are fortunate enough to win political office. We contend that two factors reproduce patterns of polarization: political realignment and the failed attempts of political elites to resolve racial conflict.[2]

Polarization in Tennessee is the most toxic around hot-button issues, such as health care, immigration, voting rights, and government spending. These high-profile issues ignite the passions of voters and can decide the outcomes of elections. The hot-button issues we examine in this book provoked contentious debates at both the federal and state levels during the period of study. Because local events reflect and determine the national political picture, civic activism in Tennessee—for example, voting, interactions with lawmakers, and membership in social movement groups—is a good indicator of unfolding national trends. This is especially true because before 2010 Tennessee was considered more ideologically centrist than the other Deep South states. In this sense, Tennessee politics are a representation of American politics on a smaller scale, and by exploring Tennessee's transition from a centrist to a right-leaning political culture, we can gain insights into what is happening in other regions of the country.

TENNESSEE AND STATE POLITICS

This book situates the study of African American and racial politics within the broad spectrum of state politics and southern politics. We give acute attention to how polarization influenced racial politics and the status of blacks in Tennessee during the early twenty-first century. Research on state politics sits at the nexus of federalism and regionalism, and it serves as a critical site for investigating how racial polarization is affixed to geographic and class-based formations.[3] Despite the importance of state politics, it is still an understudied area in the political science discipline. The bias toward national political institutions and public opinion, as well as low voter turnout in state and local elections, has devalued the importance of state politics in the field of political science.[4]

Research investigations of state politics have typically fallen into three methodological categories: covariation, single case study, and comparative case study.[5] The covariation method, which tends to rely on survey or aggregate data to measure political and election behavior across several states, is considered superior to the case study approaches.[6] This method allows for an examination of regional variations of racial politics, as exhibited in Rodney Hero's groundbreaking work on social diversity.[7] It demonstrates that the racial composition of states provides some predictive lens for assessing what kinds of public policies they will adopt. Covariation approaches can even uncover intragroup (or intraracial) variations based on region, such as political distinctions between southern and northern whites or between southern blacks and midwestern blacks.

Despite the popularity of the covariation method, it suffers from several shortcomings regarding the study of state politics. Though the approach allows social scientists to develop unifying themes for interpreting political behavior, it regularly utilizes crude indicators or indices to categorize complex phenomena, such as ideology, racial resentment, and party loyalty. Jeffrey Stonecash, one of the leading critics of the covariation method, points to the example of how social scientists assess legislative professionalism in state politics. Indices are constructed using ranking: low to high scores that evaluate the competence of staff working in state governments. Southern states may score low on the professionalism scale, thus prompting social scientists to conclude that professional lobbyists who are prone to support conservative policies will overly influence public officials in the South.[8] The problem is that these indices can present problems of validity. There may be selection bias in how they are created, or social scientists may rely on outmoded or older constructs of indices.

Another example that amplifies Stonecash's concerns can be found in a 2014 report on political polarization sponsored by the Pew Research Center for the People and the Press. The study, which sampled ten thousand people, constructed a "political typology" index that ranked partisan leanings and ideology.[9] The indices revealed that polarization is entrenched in American politics and will continue to shape partisan politics in the twenty-first century. Yet the cluster analyses used to define ideologically based groups in the survey (e.g., steadfast conservatives, business conservatives, solid liberals, young outsiders, hard-pressed skeptics, next generation left, faith and family left, and bystanders) still fall prey to the validity problems identified by Stonecash. Some of the questions measuring political ideology were first asked in the 1990s. The survey also included generic questions evaluating racial resentment that are found in other surveys. And there was little reference to the impact of regional identity and federalism on polarization.

Also problematic is that the covariation method treats the "South" as a homogeneous geographic region. Southern states are clustered together because of their shared histories of slavery, racial segregation, the Civil War, and enthusiasm for states' rights. Yet this approach ignores subregional variations, such as differences between the Deep South and the Mid-South, as well as intrastate or cross-state variations that are difficult to interrogate in national surveys. And, as referenced by noted political scientist Hanes Walton, it is important to account for the distinct histories, especially racial histories, even within the same region.[10] For example, the Florida panhandle and southern Alabama may have more in common in terms of their political cultures than the panhandle has in common with Miami-Dade County, Florida. The Appalachian region of East Tennessee has more of a shared identity with the Appalachian regions of Kentucky and North Carolina than with rural towns in West Tennessee.

Interestingly, studies of the civil rights movement present a more complex portrait of subregional politics than covariation studies do. Civil rights historiographies describe the different responses by southern public officials to the civil rights movement based on locality and political culture. In Tennessee, after the *Brown v. Board* decision and the Montgomery bus boycott in the 1950s, Governor Frank Clement rejected attempts by hardline segregationists to repress civil rights activists involved in school desegregation campaigns.[11] Clement's gradual approach to desegregation mirrored that of Tennessean Albert Gore Sr., who served in the U.S. Senate from 1953 to 1970.[12] Both rejected rigid segregation and endorsed civil rights measures that were opposed by most southern lawmakers.

The Albany, Georgia, civil rights movement in 1961–1962 provides another example of the different responses of southern officials to civil rights demonstrations. Albany sheriff Laurie Pritchett was intent on "maintaining segregation in a fashion that eschewed [the kind of] public violence and brutality" that occurred during the Montgomery, Alabama, protests and would soon take place in the Birmingham, Alabama, movement of 1963.[13] Pritchett studied nonviolent tactics in anticipation of the civil rights protests. He concluded that an overtly violent counterresponse to civil rights demonstrators—similar to how public officials responded to civil rights demands in other parts of the South—would backfire and encourage support for the Albany movement. Instead, he arrested protestors while using little violence in order to avoid media scrutiny. He then sent civil rights activists to jails in neighboring counties where many were brutalized by segregationists, including law enforcement officials. Yet because the media were concentrated in Albany and not in the other counties, there were no major news stories of these actions.[14]

In point of fact, Albany had a shared history with Montgomery, Birmingham, and other southern localities where violent responses to protestors were captured by the media. Racism, racial segregation, and state-centered federalism were forces that united the white power structures of these jurisdictions. These phenomena allow for generalizable conclusions to be made about the racial politics in the South during the 1950s and 1960s. Yet they fail to explain interstate differences or subregional distinctions within different states. Each state (Georgia, Alabama, Tennessee), despite having shared histories of de jure segregation, has a distinct history of how blacks have been disenfranchised and how public officials have maintained the dominant racial order. These distinctions have not been fully appreciated by covariation approaches because the South is treated as a singularity instead of addressing its complexity.

Our book uses the single case study method to assess racial politics in Tennessee. The approach accounts for Tennessee's shared history with other southern states, but it also allows us to disentangle the state from crude measurements of southern politics. It is worth mentioning that covariation techniques can be incorporated within case studies; they are utilized to examine the internal operations of state politics, racial attitudes inside a single state, and interjurisdictional (regional or county) variations in a state.[15] Fortunately, the availability of state-level surveys and other sophisticated tools, such as social network analysis, allow us to apply the covariation approach to a case study in Tennessee.

In addition, the case study method allows us to probe the micro-contexts or background underlying policy debates. In her edited volume on racial politics in Georgia, Pearl Ford Dowe found that the contemporary manifestations of institutional racism have impeded racial progress in the state despite its growing diversity and burgeoning black middle class.[16] In policy areas such as education, health, and criminal justice, African Americans have yet to experience the fruits of racial democracy in Georgia. Sharon D. Wright Austin's investigation of black politics in the Mississippi Delta came to similar conclusions despite the growth in the number of black elected officials in the state.[17] The deep-rooted patterns of racial segregation, intergenerational poverty, and concentrated wealth have dampened economic opportunities for Delta blacks.

An underappreciated characteristic of the case study approach is that it challenges common assumptions about race, partisanship, and politics. Typically, it is assumed not only that political contests are polarized along party lines, but that race and partisanship are interrelated with blacks and whites aligning with the Democratic and Republican parties, respectively. Although this is true in many cases, microscopic investigations into southern politics occasionally refute this assumption. In the 2003 governor's race in Louisiana, Republican Bobby Jindal, who at the time was a senior administrator in President George W. Bush's Health and Human Services agency, courted blacks and even received the endorsement of the mayor of New Orleans. Yet Republicans opposed this outreach effort, and it may have cost him the election.[18] Four years later, Jindal sharpened his conservative bona fides by aggressively seeking the white vote and ignoring black interests.

Later in this book, we provide examples of how race and partisanship diverged from the conventional portraits of party politics in Tennessee. At times, polarization exposes intraparty divisions. Before the 2002 gubernatorial election, Republican governor Don Sundquist introduced a proposal to establish a state income tax. Tennessee is one of the few states in which no such tax exists. Liberal Democrats, including black lawmakers, supported versions of the measure, yet Republicans and conservative activists opposed it.[19] The antitax coalition eventually defeated the measure. Several years later, Democratic governor Phil Bredesen proposed downsizing the state's workers compensation and TennCare/Medicaid programs.[20] Both measures were contested by liberal activists: labor groups criticized the workers compensation plan, and the Medicaid reforms were opposed by health-care advocates and civil rights groups. The income tax, workers compensation, and Medicaid debates underscore that polarization has been endemic to Tennessee politics. These issues were shaped by interparty and intraparty divisions as well as a broad array of interest groups. Though none of the proposals were explicitly driven by racial animus, they conflicted with the racial equalitarian agenda that has been central to black politics in the state.

It is also worth noting that much of what we know about polarization revolves around certain policy debates instead of the hundreds of policies where there is general agreement among Americans. These high-profile debates, or "take-off" issues, to use Delia Baldassari and Peter Bearman's term, ignite intense passions among the American public. Party elites and activists discuss these issues selectively in their own political networks and in ideological or partisan-based media channels that filter out dissenting viewpoints.[21] Climate change policy, for example, was one of the key issues during President Barack Obama's first presidential term.[22] But there was actually a significant decline in Americans' belief in the existence of global warming from 2008 to 2010.[23] The polarization around the issue paralleled congressional and conservative media attacks on Environmental Protection Agency regulations aimed at curtailing climate change. Similar divisions emerged over the Patient Protection and Affordable Care Act (also known as Obamacare or the Affordable Care Act) during Obama's presidency. Racial divisions were more starkly present over this measure than over most others.[24] Racial polarization was more evident, by a wide margin, in the debate over Obamacare than during the health-care debate that engulfed President Bill Clinton's first presidential term in 1993 and 1994.

The last part of this book examines polarization around take-off issues involving health-care policy, immigration politics, taxes, and public expenditures. These topics swallowed up the legislative debates in Tennessee during the period of study.

METHODOLOGICAL APPROACH

A large portion of this book utilizes data from the Middle Tennessee State University (MTSU) poll, a statewide survey delivered twice a year by the MTSU Survey Group. The Survey Group is a nonpartisan research organization administered by MTSU's Office of Communication Research, College of Mass Communication, and School of Journalism.[25] Since the poll was first administered in 1998, it has become a reliable source of public political opinion in Tennessee.

In addition to evaluating attitudes about national and state politics, the MTSU poll asks questions regarding take-off issues that are particularly contentious at the time. By doing this, the poll functions as a litmus test for assessing attitudes about salient topics that are at the forefront of statewide legislative or political debates. We draw from several MTSU polls that measured Tennesseans' attitudes and an original survey experiment we administered in 2008 and 2009. We also utilize primary and secondary data, such as interviews, government records, election returns, and archival materials.

Finally, we created two original data sets for the purposes of this book. The County Vote Choice Profile (CVCP) examines countywide voting patterns in Tennessee's presidential elections from 2000 to 2012. The CVCP was developed with a two-stage process using ecological inference (EI) analysis of racially polarized voting and dynamic network analysis (DNA) that measured county-level voting patterns in presidential elections. DNA and the companion software called ORA were developed by Carnegie Mellon University's Center for Computational Analysis of Social and Organizational Systems (CASOS). The network technique integrates traditional social network and link analyses, as well as multimodal and time-series approaches not commonly associated with traditional network procedures.[26] DNA permits researchers to integrate social network tools that involve interdependent entities or variables with traditional statistical measures, such as regression analyses.

The second data set, the Legislative Political Network Profile (LPNP), uses network analysis to investigate coalition building and the political support networks of black lawmakers in Tennessee. The LPNP compiles the sponsorship and cosponsorship networks of bills sponsored by African American lawmakers in the Tennessee General Assembly from 2003 to 2012.

PLAN OF THE BOOK

The book is divided into three parts.[27] Part 1 consists of a theory chapter and a historical overview of racial polarization in Tennessee. In the first chapter, we elucidate our theory of polarization and its relationship to realignment (i.e., the shift from a one-party region controlled by the Democratic Party to a region dominated by Republicans), the devolution of federal power to state governments (which paved the way for Tennessee politicians to implement divisive policies), and the politics of "capture" (a term we borrow from Paul Frymer),[28] which in the case of Tennessee represents the work of political elites to manage intraparty racial conflict. We focus specifically on how polarization impedes racial progress and cultivates a political climate that is hostile to black interests. By merging the academic literature on southern politics with news coverage of the controversial senatorial race between Harold Ford Jr. (an African American Democrat) and Bob Corker Jr. (a white Republican), we contend that recent developments in realignment, devolution, and capture contributed to the circumstances we are currently observing in Tennessee: voters are becoming increasingly more Republican, and this party shift in the electorate has altered the political landscape and, ultimately, adversely affected black elected officials, voters, and residents.

Chapter 2 provides a historical overview of black politics in Tennessee. Drawing from primary sources (e.g., memoirs of prominent residents, governors' archives, and Tennessee Supreme Court case briefs from the Tennessee State Library and Archives) and secondary sources, we discuss the shifting political alliances that have reinforced polarization since the mid-nineteenth century. We assess the internal debates among black leaders about which strategies could best reduce polarization. The first part of the chapter is a historical overview of black political development from the early nineteenth century to the 1940s. This is followed by a discussion of black politics during the 1950s and 1960s, the peak of the civil rights movement, with a brief look at several civil rights initiatives, including the Highlander Folk School, the Nashville students' sit-in campaign, the Memphis sanitation workers strike, and the rural West Tennessee voting rights movement. Finally, we examine the institutionalization of black politics in Tennessee and the growth in the number of black elected officials from the 1970s to the 2000s.

Part 2 of this book focuses on partisan realignment in Tennessee. Chapter 3 highlights the disintegration of the Democratic Party's electoral coalition, a process closely tied to racially polarized voting. We focus specifically on the impact of party realignment on polarization, especially concerning race, geography, and party. Tennessee was historically considered more politically moderate and less racially conservative than the states of the Deep South. Yet particularly since the mid-2000s, Republicans have cemented their influence in the state. We use a combination of ecological inference analysis and network analysis to investigate partisan realignment, a key factor shaping racial divisions in Tennessee politics in the twenty-first century. We look at voting patterns and at other sociodemographic and political factors from the 1996 presidential election to the 2012 general election. We argue that partisan realignment best characterizes Tennessee politics and that this realignment has created a surplus of right-leaning voters who have been critical to the Republican Party's resurgence in the twenty-first century. We use the term "surplus politics" to describe what happens when a political party has a large supply of constituents and structural advantages that enable it to build a winning political coalition. Surplus politics allow this coalition to extend its influence across multiple election cycles.

In chapter 4, we turn our attention to the Tennessee General Assembly and assess the influence of the Tennessee Black Caucus of State Legislators (TBCSL) and the evolving networks these politicians cultivated with other members of the legislature to advance their legislative agendas. Specifically, we explore whether the agenda of the TBCSL was shaped by advocacy groups outside the legislature and whether pressure from those advocacy groups helped the caucus build alliances with white and Republican lawmakers. To examine the challenges associated with building bipartisan and cross-racial coalitions during the period of realignment in the state legislature, we use evidence from a computer-assisted network analysis of more than two thousand bills that black lawmakers sponsored or cosponsored in the period 2003–2012. We also use qualitative analyses, including interviews with members of the TBCSL, to augment the chapter.

Part 3 is composed of four chapters that highlight race and polarization regarding take-off issues in Tennessee. Chapter 5 evaluates polarization and the state economy in the context of contentious debates over a state income tax in 2001–2002 and the federal budget in 2012. Using the 2002 and 2007 waves of the MTSU poll, we uncovered a racial divide in opinions about government spending. Respondents in the 2002 survey tended to reject the idea of raising the state's income tax. The strength of this opposition changed, however, depending on whether Tennesseans believed that the increase in income tax would lower sales taxes or would provide resources to public education. If the state must charge its residents income taxes, white participants in the MTSU poll preferred that it be implemented using a flat tax structure (in which all residents pay equally, regardless of their income), while residents of color tended to favor a graduated system in which the affluent would pay more in tax than the poor would. Our analysis of the 2007 poll revealed that Tennesseans are generally less antagonistic toward government spending when they are asked about spending at the federal level. There are also fascinating racial gaps in attitudes toward spending: whites are more suspicious than nonwhites of spending at the state level, but there are no racial differences in opinions about spending at the federal level.

The sixth chapter assesses polarization around the state's TennCare/Medicaid program from 1995 to 2006. Much of this chapter relies on public opinion data from a 2006 poll conducted by the MTSU Survey Group and a survey-based experiment of 604 respondents administered in the fall of 2008 and the spring of 2009. We supplement these results with qualitative data, such as government records regarding the TennCare reforms in 2005 and 2006. For example, during the TennCare debate, Sekou Franklin worked closely with several organizations, including the TennCare Saves Lives Coalition, which tried to rescue the program. In his capacity as a health-care advocate, Franklin obtained TennCare records after a federal court ordered the governor to submit them to health-care advocates and the *Tennessean*, Nashville's daily newspaper, during the legal battles over TennCare.

Immigration is another controversial issue among Tennesseans. Debates have intensified in recent years because of the growing number of Latinos migrating to the Volunteer State. In the seventh chapter, we explore how political elites have framed the issue, which has affected attitudes about Latino immigrants, and how changes in attitudes about immigration have contributed to polarization. We use survey responses from the fall 2000, spring 2004, fall 2006, spring 2006, spring 2007, and fall 2008 waves of the MTSU poll to examine the extent to which race influences how Tennesseans view the topic of immigration. We took advantage of a question-wording experiment embedded in the fall 2006 wave of the MTSU survey to show that anti-immigration attitudes are most strong when immigrants are characterized as being "illegal" rather than "undocumented."

The focus of chapter 8 is racial and political polarization around criminal justice reform in Tennessee. We pay special attention to the politics of sentencing for criminal convictions and the death penalty. We draw from two state surveys (1999, 2007) by the MTSU Survey Group. We argue that polarization, specifically along the lines of race, shifted in the twenty-first century. As the state legislature and advocates gave renewed attention to the death penalty, whites and nonwhites diverged in their attitudes toward this policy. Nonwhites, and blacks in particular, were more acutely concerned that the death penalty lacked procedural due process.

The concluding chapter explores how our theory of polarization has been illustrated in recent Tennessee politics. For example, the state's increasingly hostile racial environment has paved the way for Tea Party members of Congress, such as Scott DesJarlais and Diane Black, whose anti-Islamic rhetoric emboldened bigoted residents in the state and contributed to the vandalizing of a mosque in Murfreesboro. We argue that polarization in Tennessee can be attributed to factors related to changes in party alignment, devolution, and capture and that these factors combine in unique ways to foment racial divisions in Tennessee. *Losing Power* is a story about how the confluence of these polarizing factors helped reverse the political gains African American legislators, social movements, and activists had made before 2003.

PART ONE
THE DEEP ROOTS OF POLARIZATION IN TENNESSEE

CHAPTER ONE

RACE AND POLARIZATION

> The eyes of the nation are on Tennessee.
>
> —POPULAR STATEMENT IN TENNESSEE
> DURING THE 2006 SENATE RACE

The campaign for the U.S. Senate in Tennessee was one of the most closely watched contests of the 2006 congressional elections. The race matched Harold Ford Jr., a five-term member of Congress from Memphis and a rising star in the Democratic Party, against Chattanooga mayor Bob Corker, a businessman. For many political observers, the election was a case study for assessing racial progress in the South. A victory by Ford would have made him the first African American to represent Tennessee in the U.S. Senate, a remarkable feat considering that blacks make up only 17 percent of the state's population.

Like other states below the Mason-Dixon Line, antebellum slavery, racial segregation, and antifederal attitudes have shaped Tennessee's political culture. The state also has a rich tradition of political moderation, mainly center-right pragmatism, when compared with other southern states, such as Mississippi, Alabama, and South Carolina. From the passage of the Voting Rights Act of 1965 to the election of Bill Haslam in 2010, an equal number of Democrats and Republicans had been elected governor of the state. Though Democrats had historically controlled the state legislature until the realignment wave of the 2000s, there was a recent history of bipartisan coalitions and conflicts in Tennessee. What journalist Dan Balz called a "consensus building politics," or a pragmatic conservatism sewn together by conservative Democrats and traditional Republicans, had characterized Tennessee politics since the 1950s and 1960s.[1]

Despite the tradition of consensus building, the prospects of electing an African American to the U.S. Senate seemed unlikely until the 2006 election. Ford's youth, ambition, and mastery of "retail politics" (a campaign style that focuses on local events and personal interactions with voters) made him the ideal candidate to break the state's political color barrier. More important, his moderate political ideology made him attractive across the racial divide.[2] Throughout his ten-year career in Congress, he had willingly crossed the aisle to ally with Republicans on issues such as fiscal austerity, immigration, and Social Security reform.

To some extent, Ford's pathway to victory had been outlined by the incumbent governor, Phil Bredesen, a fiscally conservative Democrat who had served as mayor of Nashville from 1991 to 1999. Bredesen was elected governor in 2002, eight years after losing a close gubernatorial race to Representative Don Sundquist. He was backed by liberal and moderate Democrats and won votes in predominantly white East Tennessee counties that were Republican Party strongholds.[3] His 2002 campaign provided a valuable lesson for Democrats seeking to win statewide elections. To win that election, Bredesen increased voter turnout in established Democratic jurisdictions and made inroads in rural Tennessee counties that Republicans had historically dominated. He also won Knox County, the largest urban county in eastern Tennessee, even though Republicans had more recently controlled it.

As governor, Bredesen was not particularly skilled at party-building activities or helping other Democratic candidates get elected. He maintained his governing coalition by extending patronage to his party base, endorsing some social and civil rights policies, and expanding comprehensive education for preschool children. However, he angered progressive activists because of his reforms to TennCare (the state's Medicaid program) and workers compensation. Nonetheless, the 2006 Senate race was a test to determine if Ford could repeat the success of Bredesen's 2002 campaign. Political observers were keenly interested in seeing if Ford could build a statewide electoral coalition, a task that entailed winning support from moderate and conservative whites.

Neither Ford nor Corker had a considerable lead throughout most of the campaign, although the Federal Bureau of Investigation and Tennessee Bureau of Investigation (TBI)'s public corruption case (known as the Operation Tennessee Waltz scandal), which occurred a year before the election, dealt a major blow to the Ford camp. This sting operation led to the convictions or guilty pleas of a dozen state and local lawmakers, including Harold's uncle John Ford, who had served for three decades in the Tennessee Senate.[4] Because half of the lawmakers targeted by the FBI/TBI were from Ford's hometown of Memphis, a majority-black city that has known its share of corruption, the scandal exposed racial stereotypes about the ethical conduct of black elected officials.[5] (A decade earlier,

Ford's father, Congressman Harold Ford Sr., had nearly been indicted on bank fraud charges.) The scandal and subsequent court proceedings, which extended into the 2006 election season, provided cannon fodder for Ford's opponents, who claimed that he was prone to corruption because of his family connections and Memphis origins.

Another controversy engulfed the Senate race three weeks before the general election. The Republican National Committee released an attack advertisement that implied that Ford had engaged in a sexual encounter with a white woman at a Super Bowl party hosted by Playboy Enterprises. Critics charged Republicans and the Corker campaign with injecting old racial taboos regarding miscegenation into the campaign. They believed that the advertisement fueled racial animus and convinced white voters that Ford had crossed the color line and violated the state's racial mores. Corker, in response, claimed that the advertisement was not racially motivated but was intended to expose Ford's soft commitment to Christian values.[6]

Although Ford lost the Senate race, the close margin of defeat (51–48 percent) was celebrated as an example of racial moderation in the South, especially since he garnered 42 percent of the white vote.[7] Some political observers believed that Ford's performance symbolized the reemergence or reincarnation of the New South—a region where black Democrats could garner support among white moderates in statewide elections despite the long history of racism.

However, the Ford-Corker race of 2006 may have been an aberration in contemporary politics in Tennessee. Racial polarization trumped racial moderation in statewide elections throughout the first years of the new millennium. Much of the animus was exacerbated by racial-priming strategies that triggered whites' deep-seated anxieties about blacks gaining political power. "Racial priming" is the use of negative messages or coding, racial imagery (e.g., pamphlets, direct mail, television advertisements), and subtle appeals by politicians to the racial fears of white voters, often without the direct awareness of those voters or constituents.[8]

Examples of racial priming during the Ford-Corker race included a racially coded pamphlet distributed in East Tennessee that urged whites to "vote early to preserve your way of life," a radio commercial that criticized Ford with African-sounding drums beating in the background, and an Internet advertisement that altered Ford's skin color to make his complexion appear darker.[9] In 1994, racial priming was used in a pamphlet that was distributed throughout rural Tennessee linking Senator Jim Sasser, the Democratic Party incumbent, to former Washington, D.C., mayor Marion Barry and President Bill Clinton's black surgeon general, Joycelyn Elders. In 2008, a controversial mailer was distributed throughout the Second District of the Tennessee General Assembly that targeted Representative Nathan Vaughn, an African American. Many believed that the "blackbird" mailer (an ad with the heads of Vaughn, President Barack Obama, and Speaker of the House Nancy Pelosi superimposed on the bodies of blackbirds) was used to stimulate white racial resentment during the race.[10] Vaughn, whose district was more than 90 percent white, lost the general election by fewer than 350 votes.

This chapter lays out a theoretical framework for understanding racial politics in twenty-first-century Tennessee. We focus specifically on how polarization impedes racial progress and cultivates a political climate hostile to black interests. The legal definition of "racial polarization" focuses on voting outcomes. As characterized in *United States v. Charleston County*, racial polarization implies "a consistent relationship between [the] race of the voter and the way in which the voter votes, or to put it differently, where black voters and white voters vote differently."[11] We expand this definition to include more than just vote choice. At its most general level, "polarization" refers to the entrenched divisions among Tennesseans produced by policies that are antagonistic to a racially equalitarian agenda. Examples include the proposed flat state tax discussed in chapter 5, the severe cutbacks to the state Medicaid plan described in chapter 6, and the legislation designed to limit the influx of Latino migrants into Tennessee analyzed in chapter 7. Our definition works just as well for Tennesseans in the electorate as it does for those in elected office, for it can also pertain to racial divisions (between whites and nonwhites) that are cultivated by coalitions of political leaders who seek to either maintain or undermine such policies. Polarization, simply put, is about the concentration of racial groups' political viewpoints. When a significant portion of white voters have diametrically opposed views to those of a significant portion of black voters—such that few voters will cross over into the other camp—there is polarization.

As we show in this book, such polarization is evident when it comes to the topics of government spending, health care, and immigration. Using this definition of polarization, we seek to explain what is happening in Tennessee politics, particularly why recent political decisions have been injurious to African American residents. We contend that realignment (i.e., the South's shift from a one-party region controlled by the Democrats to a region dominated by Republicans), the devolution of federal power to state governments (which paved the way for Tennessee politicians to implement divisive policies), and the failed attempts of political elites to manage racial conflict have contributed to patterns of polarization that are disadvantageous to African Americans and to policies that seek racial equality in Tennessee. We say "have contributed to" rather than "have caused" because we concede that the arrow of causality can go in both directions: it is possible that the loss of black political power created this division among voters. And it is equally plausible that polarization led to the loss of black power, and not vice versa. The political divisions between whites and blacks can be especially wide—and the road to racial civility excessively winding—during contests that include controversial issues.[12] Thousands of legislative measures are introduced into the Tennessee General Assembly each session, but only a handful resonate broadly with the public and qualify as hot-button issues. Four topics in particular—health care, immigration, taxes and government spending, and criminal justice reform—are the subject of this book because they stirred contentious debates both in Tennessee and across the nation during the period under study.

THEORIES OF RACIAL POLARIZATION

Theories that attempt to explain polarization fall into three main categories: those that look at the entire electorate, those that look at subsets of politically active voters, and those that look at the behavior of political elites, or those who govern. Theorists who focus on the entire voting population believe that cleavages in the electorate produce partisan or political polarization among lawmakers.[13] As Anthony Downs noted in his seminal book *An Economic Theory of Democracy*, and as numerous other scholars confirm in their studies, elected representatives often weigh the decisions they make while in office against their prospects of reelection.[14] Divisions in the electorate, according to these theories, motivate vote-seeking public officials to take ideologically dogmatic positions on key issues in order to win over some constituents (often at the expense of others).

On the subject of prized constituents, another theory suggests that the voters who are most politically active drive polarization. Alan Abramowitz refers to these constituents as "polarized publics," a small, active citizenry who shape the orientations of elected officials because of their political fervor.[15] In this theory, the most politically active members of the electorate have a tremendous amount of influence on politicians.[16]

The third group of theorists, those who focus on elite political actors, contend that polarization is related to the posturing and preferences of those in charge. Because political elites (i.e., politicians and prominent opinion makers in the media) serve as information brokers, educating their loyal constituents about the unexpected or complex policy issues that come to the public's attention, they are mostly responsible for polarizing the public.[17] Another version of the elite theory claims that candidates who run for office are more polarized than the electorate. This is partly because elections in the United States are open:

anyone can run for office, and this allows the most polarizing figures to enter political races.[18]

Two elected officials exemplify how political elites can influence the public. Huey Long, who served as governor of and senator from Louisiana in the 1920s and 1930s, and Joseph McCarthy, a senator from Wisconsin in the 1950s, are examples of leaders on the left (Long) and right (McCarthy) who successfully mobilized the public around salient issues. More recently, Republican presidential candidate John McCain's selection of Alaska governor Sarah Palin as his running mate in 2008 demonstrates how leaders can polarize the public. Political scientist Jonathan Knuckey found that positive evaluations of Palin resonated more strongly among conservatives. In contrast, moderates and swing voters were turned off by the McCain campaign once she was added to his ticket.[19] Palin's ideological dogmatism divided the electorate and exacerbated tensions within the Republican Party.

Scholars John Evans and Lilliana Mason claim that the zero-sum game of two-party politics (the idea that a win for one party constitutes a loss for the other party) encourages polarization through a "sorting effect."[20] Voters must often sort out, or choose between, Democrats and Republicans amid polarized debates. There may be unanimity or little disagreement among the electorate over most issues, but because political elites are driving the debate and polarizing the public, voters must align themselves with the positions of their parties. According to this theory, the sorting effect may not represent divisions in the electorate (electoral polarization) as much as it reflects party polarization or divisions between party elites.

A convincing case can be made that these three camps of theories about what causes polarization are mutually reinforcing in the context of governing. All three sets of actors—the entire electorate, the subset of the electorate that is very active politically, and political elites—are essential to determining both election outcomes and how lawmakers govern and sustain party unity. While we acknowledge the value of the various theories about why polarization happens, we look at race as a key explanatory variable. Specifically, we argue that political realignment in the South, a trend toward the devolution of certain functions from the federal government to the states, and a political style that values racial compromise all contribute to racial polarization in Tennessee. We are not so concerned with making proclamations about how entrenched patterns of polarization underscore the failings of American democracy or how such patterns work against bipartisan consensus. Our analysis derives from the evidence we have collected about how racial polarization has had harmful consequences for African Americans and other disadvantaged groups in Tennessee.

RACE AND REALIGNMENT POLITICS

Party realignment and party politics are central features of southern politics. Realignment began in the South in the 1960s and continued into the 1980s. It culminated with the 1994 congressional elections, when Republicans took over Congress for the first time in fifty years.[21] The most common interpretations of this shift draw from V. O. Key Jr.'s seminal work on southern politics. Key and his intellectual progeny argued that race and class divisions are at the center of southern political culture.[22] He believed that racial hostilities are both more prevalent and most intense in places where blacks have a population advantage and can seriously threaten the white power structure if they can vote.[23] Because their political position is threatened by black political power, white southerners (particularly the white men who benefit most from the status quo) dominate southern politics through rigid patterns of racial segregation.

Although some social scientists feel that Key's analysis privileged race over class as the major factor that has shaped party politics and partisan realignment in the South, this is a misinterpretation of his work.[24] Key believed that wide disparities in land and wealth make poor whites susceptible to social and political control by segregationist elites in the South. This control stems from the fact that segregationists are often large property owners and the employers of poor whites. The realignment can also be attributed to a sense of shared racial animus: even though poor whites have fared considerably worse than the affluent members of their racial group, they resent the idea of blacks making social and political gains and they want to maintain the current racial order, even if it means taking measures that ultimately hurt the economic progress of themselves and fellow whites.

Before the passage of civil rights legislation in the 1960s, many students of southern politics focused on the relationships among de jure (legally mandated) segregation, economic underdevelopment, and party politics. Since the 1960s, much of the research has examined party realignment and its impact on political polarization. The race-class-geography nexus that Key and others discussed is also relevant to understanding post-1960s realignment politics. Nicholas Valentino and David Sears offered a modern interpretation of Key's framework, arguing that partisan realignment (the ascent of the Republican Party) in the South is attributable to racial resentment and ultimately to white flight from the Democratic Party that stems from national Democrats' support for civil rights.[25]

Another theory about party realignment in the South suggests that the electoral coalitions that propelled the Republican Party into power were formed because of economic growth in underdeveloped and predominantly white legislative districts. These coalitions, which are composed of middle-class and mostly white voters, shifted their allegiance to the Republican Party because of its positions on taxes and fiscal austerity.[26] Instead of being motivated by racial animus, southern whites, according to this theory, migrated to the Republican Party to protect their class interests. This line of argument concludes that most working-class whites still look to the Democratic Party as the place to air their political grievances.[27]

A different analysis of class and party realignment in the South contends that racial segregation and economic inequality reinforce ideologically based polarization. In southern counties where hypersegregation exists, whether the black populations are small or large, whites tend to be less supportive of redistributive policies.[28] Geographic segregation limits contact between blacks and whites and prevents the exchange of ideas and policy debates between the two groups.

While we recognize the importance of class and geography in shaping realignment politics, our theory pays specific attention to the roles played by the politics of race and its consequences (institutional racism, race-based resentment, racial priming, and racially polarized voting) in shaping political polarization. Throughout much of southern political history, race, specifically anti-black animus, has been at the forefront of contentious debates.[29] Racial animus can be overt and operate through de jure instruments, or it can be covert and operate through less visible forms of communication and political channels. Racial animus is also articulated through insidious or covert tactics, such as racial coding and racial priming. Tali Mendelberg contended that subtle racial messaging may be more effective than de jure discriminatory tactics in contemporary politics.[30] Prioritizing race as the critical ingredient of realignment allows us to pay attention to discursive forms of racial animus.

From our perspective, the desire of whites to maintain their advantage in the racial hierarchy as an explanation for realignment does not conflict with explanations based on class or geography. The latter factors merely complicate the politics of race. Students of polarization and realignment politics emphasize that the political orientations of most politically engaged actors are influenced simultaneously by their race, class, ideology, and gender. These simultaneous influences (sometimes called "cross-pressures") may motivate voters to analyze candidates or issues through multiple lenses or frameworks in a way that affects ideological dogmatism.[31]

To summarize, realignment politics are an important element of racial polarization. Racial animus increases the likelihood that partisan realignment will produce uneven and adverse patterns of polarization that are harmful to the political status of blacks and to policies that seek racial equality. These realignment-intensifying factors are then reinforced by cross-pressures, such as class and geographic divisions.

THE AGE OF DEVOLUTION

At its most basic level, federalism in the United States is the relationship between the national government and state and local governments. By design, the federal government has the upper hand in this relationship: article 6, section 2, of the U.S. Constitution established the federal government as the "supreme law of the land." But there are instances when the national government transfers some of its power to the states. Scholars use the term "devolution" to characterize periods when the federal government is voluntarily "devolving" (passing on) some of its powers and functions to lower-level governments. The devolution of U.S. federalism is another factor that has complicated analyses of polarization. Since President Richard Nixon's New Federalism program, state-centered federalists and anti-(federal) interventionist conservatives have circumscribed nationally anchored public initiatives. Nixon, President Ronald Reagan, and conservative Supreme Courts invested tremendous energy in reviving the platform of state-centered federalism. Their outlooks were augmented by a conservative movement that rolled back civil rights and social welfare policies. Examples of these rollbacks include the 1980s crusade against affirmative action (arguably one of the most important policy initiatives of the post–civil rights era) and the rhetoric against Aid to Families with Dependent Children, which was used to both subvert policy reform and racialize voters' perceptions of aid recipients using the image of the "welfare queen."[32]

Reagan's approach to federalism, which he termed "devolution," was most damaging to disadvantaged populations. In addition to curtailing antipoverty initiatives, he cemented in the political culture the belief that the federal government should have limited input in the affairs of the states. When Democrats gained control of the presidency in the 1992 and 2008 elections, even some of that party's leaders had embraced devolution as a governing principle.

Antipoverty initiatives are thus weakened by a bipartisan consensus that privileges state-centered approaches to administering federal programs. This was no more evident than in the responses to the heavily criticized American Recovery and Reinvestment Act (ARRA) of 2009, the stimulus package Congress passed at the height of the Great Recession of 2008–2009. The law was one of the first domestic policy initiatives the Obama administration approved. Although Republicans condemned it, the ARRA was crafted as an intergovernmental program that gave states the power to shape welfare, employment, housing, and environmental initiatives.³³ Despite the fact that the ARRA did not preclude state-level decision-making (in fact, Obama envisioned this legislation as *encouraging* decision-making at that level), conservatives campaigned vehemently against the so-called wasteful government spending, sometimes doing so while secretly accepting stimulus money. For example, even though Piyush "Bobby" Jindal, the governor of Louisiana at the time, was a vocal critic of the stimulus plan, local officials throughout the state (many of whom were Republican) not only requested federal money but also praised the federal government for helping improve the state's economy after the devastating blow dealt by Hurricane Katrina.³⁴

It is more challenging to analyze the devolution of state power to local governments. A "second-order" devolution gives state officials the power to allocate federal and state funds and allows for the transfer of power from states to localities.³⁵ To put it differently, state governments may be responsible for controlling the flow of federal expenditures and planning (e.g., for housing or transportation) to municipalities within the state.

Policy domains, such as welfare, crime, and health care, are shaped by how lawmakers view their relationships to racial minorities. Devolution of power often produces results that are not neutral. In some cases, the transfer of federal authority to state and local governments can organize communities into contentious hierarchies based on racial, class, gender, and geographic factors. Jill Vickers argued that states structure gender relations through "policies, laws, practices, spending patterns, and discourses [that determine] how men and women should act."³⁶ Joe Soss, Richard Fording, and Sanford Schram built on this argument with their "racial classification model" for assessing policymaking at the state level. They interpreted race as more than shared phenotypic and cultural characteristics; they defined it as a social classification also. They claimed that race will "become more salient as guides for policy choice in periods, locales, and policy domains where racial minorities are more central to policy discourse and/or are prevalent targets."³⁷

Soss, Fording, and Schram argue that state officials rely on social classifications "to identify the 'kinds' of people being addressed and *group reputations* to intuit how such people are likely to respond to a particular intervention."³⁸ According to this theory, the race or geographical distribution of constituents will bias the public officials in charge of allocating goods and services. State lawmakers may be reluctant to support policies that are perceived to benefit large cities or majority-black cities, or they may favor allocating a disproportionate share of federal and state funds to counties where large numbers of their voters are likely to reside. Second-order devolution essentially gives state officials the power to polarize the public by determining who are winners and who are losers, and the losers are often communities of color or municipalities with sizable black populations.

African American politicians and many of the black voters they represent are typically skeptical of state-centered federalism and its different manifestations (e.g., states' rights, dual federalism, New Federalism, devolution). Nixon's and Reagan's orientations were bolstered by the "southern strategy," which encouraged whites to think about the implications for their own lives of civil rights, crime, taxes, and progressive social policies.[39] Devolution has usually led to attacks on civil rights or the rollback of initiatives designed to ameliorate inequalities.

RACE AND THE POLITICS OF ELECTORAL CAPTURE

The politics of realignment and devolution are integral to our understanding of southern politics. The shift from a one-party region controlled by the Democrats to a region dominated by Republicans has caused much concern among liberal activists and Democrats. Social scientists note that Republicans have enjoyed built-in advantages in southern politics since the 1960s that have increased their chances for winning elections in the South. That is the decade when a generational shift in support for the Republican Party took place, a product of growing concerns about taxes, fiscal austerity, and cultural issues.[40] The fact that the Republican Party candidates consistently outnumbered Democratic candidates also increased the prospects for Republican dominance in the South: the increasing pool of right-wing candidates ultimately altered the landscape of state and regional governments as they started winning elections. There was also an influx of blacks into local Democratic Party machines that had long been controlled by conservative whites.[41] In response, many whites left the party.

Although there has been an abundance of research on the roots of partisan realignment in the South, we need to pay more attention to how realignment politics have affected racial equalitarian policies, African Americans, and other historically disadvantaged groups wedded to the New Deal wing of the Democratic Party. The general assumption is that the Democratic Party in the South moved to the right to survive. To stave off the defection of whites, party elites created the Democratic Leadership Council and the Blue Dog Coalition in the 1980s. These groups promoted low taxes, fiscal austerity, and culturally conservative policies, which appealed to moderate and conservative whites, while still maintaining support for civil rights and other social reform measures championed by progressives.[42] The sacrificial lambs in the new Democratic agenda were social welfare and antipoverty policies that helped mitigate racialized poverty. This is what we mean by "capture": as the Democratic Party in the South made concessions to the Republican Party, the political position that African Americans occupied became more precarious. Republicans were antagonistic to them and their politics, and the Democratic Party was moving away from their interests. As a result, black politicians and community leaders were in a position where they had to make sometimes unappealing agreements with political power-holders to advance parts of their agenda.

Paul Frymer said that the zero-sum game of party politics limits the policy options available to African Americans who seek to advance racial equalitarian policies within the Democratic Party. As a result, African Americans are faced with what he called "electoral capture." On one side, the Republican Party attacks their interests. On the other side, the Democratic Party leadership may take positions that are harmful to racial equalitarianism (as President Clinton demonstrated with his attack on welfare) or completely avoid racial justice policies that are perceived as wedge issues.[43] Yet because of the racial and party contexts of the post-realignment South, many African Americans are unwilling to leave the Democratic Party or penalize officials for taking positions that are against their interests. Thus, black voters are trapped between a reluctant Democratic Party and a Republican Party that is ambivalent about (if not hostile to) their interests. Frymer made this point strongly when he noted that "even when black leaders and voters have expressed interest in defecting to the opposition party or to a third party, the opposition's party leaders have generally been reluctant to make even the most general of political appeals to blacks."[44]

Thus, the politics of capture can simultaneously explain the decrease in party polarization in Tennessee and the increase of race-based polarization: as blacks become a captured electorate, the political parties should move closer to one another on numerous racially tinged issues, like taxes and government spending, TennCare, immigration, and the death penalty. However, the tensions arising from a context in which Republicans and Democrats both have incentives to ignore blacks' political interests will entrench more firmly the racial divisions and disparities within the state.

Another theory argues against the notion that electoral capture has made blacks politically acquiescent. Some scholars believe that after the civil rights legislation of the 1960s, black politicians and moderate white Democrats entered a phase of political compromise that entailed quiet negotiations between the two groups or political accommodations that deemphasized racial antagonisms. Glen Browder and Artemesia Stanberry's "stealth reconstruction" model of southern politics argued that black and white politicians cooperated in a period "wrought with racial tensions" by "purposely and positively address[ing] black issues, without antagonizing the white majority."[45] They contended that by engaging in quiet cooperation or negotiations, southern Democrats reduced racial discord even while successfully passing legislation that benefited African Americans. These negotiations produced both symbolic and substantive rewards for blacks and protected white moderates, who hoped to build biracial electoral coalitions in their jurisdictions.

Despite its value, the theory that stealth reconstruction explains the southern political landscape in the period of Browder and Stanberry's study (1970s–1990s) needs more empirical testing in institutional contexts, such as different local and state legislative bodies and executive administrations. The theory also needs testing in states that have racially heterogeneous populations.[46] The period was still plagued by racial discord. A white backlash against voting rights engulfed much of the South after the passage of the Voting Rights Act, which continued into the 1970s. This was followed by the Reagan revolution, whose proponents used white racial resentment as a mobilizing force and recruiting tool. The strongest support for Reagan's political realignment came from the South.[47] In addition, during the 1980s and 1990s, the federal government and many states passed laws that attacked social welfare and racial justice programs.

In general, we are sympathetic to the underlying concerns of social scientists and lawmakers who believe that attempts to foster political compromise are the appropriate responses to polarization. Their main belief is that because progressives and African Americans in the South are consistently the focus of political and racial animus, attempts to cultivate comity between African American and white Tennesseans are the best way to reduce tensions and maintain unity in the Democratic Party. They argue that without such political coalitions, it will be difficult for Democrats to sustain cross-racial voting blocs, and whites may continue to defect from the party.

However, it is debatable whether political comity can develop in the absence of public scrutiny of the process by which blacks make political concessions to whites or in the absence of visible changes in the existing political system. During the 1980s and 1990s, a period of bipartisan cooperation and quiet negotiations between moderate white Democrats and black Democrats, the Democratic National Committee (DNC) made changes to its internal apparatus as a way of attracting southern whites. Frymer described how the DNC worked with congressional and state leaders to implement election strategies to appeal to whites. Two examples of such strategies are the use of front-loading (i.e., pushing primaries and caucuses to the beginning of the nomination calendar) and Super Tuesday (a day in March when most southern states hold presidential primaries).[48] These momentum-building strategies raised the profiles of southern states, which gave them and, by extension, moderate whites more influence over the outcomes of national elections. In other words, attempts to build bridges with moderate whites became part of structural changes to the Democratic Party. A rightward policy shift complemented these structural changes as centrist Democrats moved the party away from its traditional support of social welfare programs.

The Democratic Party's practice of making structural changes to appeal to white voters may also augment a strategy of elite collaboration in which a select group of black and white political elites privately negotiates policies that should be debated in a public process. Adolph Reed Jr. referred to this strategy as "race management" politics. It enables African American leaders to suppress grassroots dissent or to manage race relations instead of promoting racial justice policies.[49] In such negotiations black elites present themselves as representative voices ("trustees") for their communities.

Lawmakers may further negotiate a series of trade-offs that privilege some policies over others. Dara Strolovitch's study of progressive advocacy groups found that the policies that most poor and disadvantaged groups support receive less attention than those middle-class interests support.[50] Women's groups, for example, supported affirmative action policies much more actively than they supported welfare or AIDS/HIV initiatives. Black interest groups and lawmakers may advocate for minority business contracts or local employment opportunities in police and fire departments instead of supporting antipoverty initiatives that organizations working in low-income communities endorse. Even progressive interest groups or lawmakers prioritize issues that are supported by wealthy organizations and policies that lawmakers believe will not polarize the public.

Interestingly, even when political comity is present, political discourse sometimes remains polarized. Mendelberg found that racially vitriolic political campaigns and overt forms of racism in the mode of Bull Connor or George Wallace are rare in contemporary politics. This is because the civil rights movement produced a "norm of racial equality" such that overt racism is socially prohibited in electoral campaigns and in the practice of governance.[51] However, racial hostility is expressed through discursive policy instruments or implicit racial appeals that activate adverse racial predispositions "without the awareness of those who hold them."[52] Haney-Lopez referred to this as "dog whistle politics": racial coding that provokes white racial resentment even as the people practicing this type of politics divorce their message from the overt and more offensive racial attacks associated with the Jim Crow era.[53] The advertisement used in the Ford-Corker race (in which a blonde woman winked and asked Ford to "call her") is an example of an implicit racial appeal.

The impact of implicit racial messaging has been disputed, most notably by Gregory Huber and John Lapinski, who argued that racial priming has a limited effect and that when it is used in elections, it only influences the attitudes of the least educated or most uninformed voters.[54] However, Mendelberg found overwhelming evidence of the effectiveness of racial priming in her review of seventeen studies from 1993 to 2007.[55] Racial priming has the same effect as explicit racial appeals commonly associated with Jim Crow, but it is "less likely to be perceived as having violated the norm of racial equality."[56] In contemporary politics, implicit racial appeals are more effective at mobilizing white racial resentment than are explicit appeals. Implicit appeals are difficult for voters to recognize, and politicians or policy advocates on the receiving end of priming tactics have difficulty responding to them.

Because they are difficult to recognize and respond to, racial primings are a particularly troublesome by-product of the politics of comity. Attempts to depolarize the public through building political biracial coalitions may fail in part because the way racism is used in elections and governance has changed. Instead of reducing polarization, comity can allow racial stereotypes and resentments to proliferate without being challenged by counternarratives. Mendelberg argued that racial priming needs to be exposed, not managed through comity or quiet cooperation, regardless of the potential backlash. Her point is that bringing attention to racial priming may force voters who are its unwitting targets to recognize these tactics and be more critical of them.[57] However, many Democrats and progressive activists believe that calling attention to the racial dimension of implicit appeals or advancing racial equalitarian policies will distance white voters from the Democratic Party.

We recognize that because of racial polarization in Tennessee, African Americans sometimes need to use compromise strategies to advance their political agendas. That said, we argue throughout this book that racial advocacy is a better antidote to polarization than is political acquiescence. By "advocacy," we are referring to the long tradition of resistance, both outside and inside political institutions, to public agendas that promote racial inequality. Those who use advocacy strategies often assume that political and racial divisions are an inevitable and permanent feature of American politics. Electoral tactics used by African Americans to combat racial divisions include, but are not limited to, voter registration and get-out-the-vote drives. Higher turnout typically reflects increased minority-group mobilization, which ultimately helps Democratic candidates.[58] Protests (sit-ins, marches, boycotts, etc.) are common "outsider" strategies used by blacks to promote ameliorative or equitable policies. Regardless of whether the mode of advocacy works "with" or "against" the political system, these types of strategies help expand the boundaries of democracy, and they serve as a counterweight to the politics of polarization.

Advocacy is a strategy that social movement members sometimes choose when they calculate that it will have the intended effect of educating voters, garnering media attention, or pressuring legislators.[59] Doug McAdam and Karina

Kloos argued that both the civil rights movement and the white resistance movement have been more dynamic forces in shaping southern politics than political parties have been.[60] Significant cleavages developed among both the electorate and political elites in the wake of the successes of the civil rights movement, which produced a racial environment in which whites (particularly those in the South) felt as if their way of life was threatened. White resistance to civil rights, as articulated through the activism of the Ku Klux Klan, "exacerbated deep divisions among community members in local settings."[61] Southern counties where visible forms of KKK activism took place were much more polarized and more likely to realign into the Republican Party. The KKK's ability to recruit whites to the GOP stems, in part, from the fact that the Republican Party began employing its "southern strategy" in response to black political gains in the 1960s. This strategy, made (in)famous by Barry Goldwater and later employed by Richard Nixon, used anti-black messages to mobilize white voters.

Politically active groups of citizens have also used both autonomous political structures (organizations and groups outside the system) and independent political structures to push for ameliorative policies. Two good examples are the Mississippi Freedom Democratic Party (MFDP) in the 1960s and Jesse Jackson's Rainbow Coalition in the 1980s. The MFDP provided an alternative and racially integrated political outlet for blacks, who were at the time blocked by segregationists and discriminatory state laws (such as literacy tests) from joining the Democratic Party. The Rainbow Coalition, an organization that grew out of Jackson's 1984 presidential bid, sought to advance a policy agenda that was, its leaders argued, more racially inclusive than that of the Reagan administration. The late political scientist Ronald Walters believed that this strategy can increase the bargaining power of blacks (and other racial justice activists) even when they are "electoral captives."[62] However, the strategy must be anchored by strong organizations and by substantial voting power. In the next chapter, we describe how both autonomous strategies and independent party structures that push for racially redistributive policies have been part of the black political tradition in Tennessee and how they expanded the boundaries of democracy even though they polarized the public.

CONCLUSION

In this chapter we have outlined a theoretical framework for assessing racial politics in Tennessee at the turn of the twenty-first century. We suggest that racial politics are shaped by a form of polarization in which political forces fuel racial and political divisions while cultivating a political climate that is hostile to African Americans. However, we do not see African Americans, multiracial coalitions, and racial justice activists as mere political bystanders. Through social movements and independent leverage politics, they have expanded the boundaries of democratic politics and advanced racial equalitarian policies, even though these actions may also have increased racial tensions.

We argue that political polarization in Tennessee is shaped by three interrelated factors. First, partisan realignment, or whites' defection from the Democratic Party, has dramatically reshaped Tennessee politics. This process has also been influenced by class and by the geographic distribution of voters. Second-order devolution is another factor that has affected racial polarization in Tennessee. It has allowed state officials to prioritize some jurisdictions over others based on their voting potential and racial predispositions. Finally, seeking political acquiescence has shaped polarization. Because African Americans represent an electorally captured group (the Democratic Party takes their votes for granted, but most blacks are not likely to defect because the Republican Party has been even less responsive to African American interests since the realignment), blacks in Tennessee face the dilemma of pushing for race-friendly policies in an unwelcoming political environment. The attempts of political elites to suppress dialogue about racial equalitarian policies and to privately negotiate racial equity policies among themselves have often failed, requiring African American organizations and politicians to engage in comity to protect previous political gains, mitigate the scale and scope of rollbacks, and move forward in small increments.

In the next chapter, we examine black politics from the early nineteenth century to the end of the twentieth century through the lens of polarization and how it has shaped the political status of blacks. We also give considerable attention to black political agency, even during the Redemptionist period of the nineteenth century and when Jim Crow dominated Tennessee politics in the twentieth century.

CHAPTER TWO

BLACK POLITICS IN TENNESSEE FROM THE ANTEBELLUM PERIOD TO THE TWENTY-FIRST CENTURY

I am not here, Mr. Speaker, asking any special legislation in the interest of the negroes, but in behalf of a race of outraged human beings. I stand here today and enter my solemn protest to mob violence in Tennessee. Hundreds of negroes, yes thousands, from all parts of this south's land, are to-day numbered with the silent majority, gone to eternity without a tomb to mark their last resting-place, as the result of mob violence for crimes which they never committed.

—REPRESENTATIVE SAMUEL MCELWEE (1887)

In 1866, in the aftermath of a race riot in Memphis, Tennessee, John Marshall, a black resident of the city, testified to congressional investigators that he had seen two white men brutally kill his neighbor. The men broke into his neighbor's house, dragged the man outside, shot him twice, and then shouted over his dead body, "God damn, you will never be free."[1] The riot, which one Union general called a massacre, resulted in the brazen murders and rapes of dozens of black adults and children and the murders of several whites who sympathized with black emancipation. It exemplifies the resilience of anti-black sentiment at the end of the Civil War and is indicative of the larger pattern of racial terrorism that plagued Tennessee well into the twentieth century. After the war and during Reconstruction, former Confederates and white supremacists continued their violent campaigns to discourage blacks from voting and to minimize the political power of blacks.[2]

The Memphis riot was fueled by the political environment that took shape near the end of the Civil War. Two years before the end of the war, former slaves turned contraband camps into informal political sites where they discussed the prospects of black suffrage. In October 1864, black men from Memphis and Nashville seeking the right to vote traveled to Syracuse, New York, to attend the National Convention of Colored Men.[3] Months later, after Union soldiers captured control of Tennessee, several black leaders formed the first southern chapter of the National Equal Rights League so they could petition for citizenship.[4] In August 1865, black leaders organized the Tennessee State Convention of Colored Citizens, which also pushed for black suffrage and citizenship.[5] Within a decade of the Memphis riot, blacks were elected to the state legislature and campaigned for the governor's office and the U.S. House of Representatives. Later, they stood defiantly against the wave of lynchings that occurred in the 1880s, as indicated in the quote from Samuel McElwee in the epigraph to this chapter. McElwee, who had attended Oberlin College and Fisk University, was the first African American to serve three terms in the Tennessee legislature.

Racial terrorism and the black suffrage movement highlight two political traditions that have shaped racial politics in Tennessee. Racial terrorism was a product of the state's (and the region's) historic and systemic racial hierarchy, which was characterized by white supremacy, institutional racism, and white opposition to civil rights for blacks and to social welfare policies. This hierarchy impeded black political advancement and still serves today as a formidable barrier to black political participation.

The second tradition consists of black political agency and resistance to racial hierarchy. Black leaders and multiracial coalitions have worked persistently to shape the racial composition of the electorate and influence the issues that come to the attention of voters during campaigns. Blacks and allied coalitions have been active agents in efforts to ameliorate or address the racial inequities embedded in the social, economic, and political framework of the state. They have displayed considerable fortitude, even during the Redemptionist and Jim Crow eras of the nineteenth and twentieth centuries.

Both traditions have shaped black political development and political polarization in Tennessee. The dynamic interplay between anti-black terrorism and the movement for black suffrage helps explain the trajectory of black politics in the state, both historically and in recent decades. An understanding of the interactions between these two traditions is useful for interpreting intraracial/intracommunity disagreements and debates among black leaders about the strategies and tactics that can best leverage black political influence.

Rogers Smith's seminal study *Civic Ideals* outlined how different and contradictory traditions operate simultaneously in American politics. He wrote that it is erroneous to conclude (as many political theorists do) that American political culture has been shaped solely by liberalism and republicanism, two ideological perspectives that are said to have commitments to liberty, equality, and self-governance.[6] Smith argued that the notion that these two perspectives promote an untarnished democracy is a parochial and incomplete interpretation of U.S. politics. For example, it ignores the fact that American political culture has been shaped by *multiple* traditions and was (and is) dynamically structured by unequal principles and laws. White supremacy, racism, sexism, class inequalities, and other forms of discrimination were present at the nation's founding. These forms of inequality have rendered blacks and other groups as "unequals" in the body politic.[7] Smith believed that it is essential to view such hierarchies as being just as constitutive of American political culture as liberalism and republicanism have been.

This intellectual framework is useful for assessing the political status of African Americans in Tennessee. An examination of black politics in Tennessee must account for how multiple traditions have operated simultaneously. The perception of racial politics in Tennessee is that, apart from the Reconstruction period and the 1950s–1960s, blacks have been absent from the state's politics or were minor actors in developing policies pertaining to their political livelihoods. However, blacks have been protagonists—in some cases, the chief protagonists—who actively shaped Tennessee's political landscape. Despite the adverse impacts of white supremacy and its accompanying racial hierarchies, blacks have worked to democratize the state and expand the boundaries of inclusion.

BLACKS IN ANTEBELLUM TENNESSEE

The early nineteenth century serves as a useful starting point for assessing racial hierarchies and the status of blacks in Tennessee. As was the case in other southern states, slavery was the foundation of Tennessee's early economic and political development. Lawmakers began debating a series of "slave laws" as far back as 1741, when much of the land comprising what is now called Tennessee was subject to the laws of North Carolina, and the great Negro Law of North Carolina was the dominant slave code of the land.[8] Several factors propelled the issue of slavery to the forefront of political debates in Tennessee, the first of which was territorial expansion in the early 1800s. In 1801, the state's twenty-two counties covered less than 40 percent of the geographic area of what is now contemporary Tennessee. The surrounding land was Native American territory. In 1834, the year Tennessee held its first constitutional convention, almost all of what is contemporary Tennessee had been removed from Native American hands.

Territorial expansion in Tennessee in those thirty-three years came at the expense of Cherokees, Choctaws, and Chickasaws, who experienced losses of their land and their numbers because of encroachments. Whites in Tennessee needed a labor force to harvest the major cash crops of cotton and tobacco, and Native Americans could not be relied on to fuel such a labor force, forcing lawmakers to address the complexities of slavery and to legitimate it as an institution in the body politic. Although lawmakers who represented plantation owners from western Tennessee, where slavery was most prevalent in the state, had the strongest interest in supporting the institution, most politicians and Tennesseans were proslavery because they understood that it was the underpinning of the state's economy.[9] The prices to buy enslaved blacks varied depending on the people's age, gender, and earning potential. For example, an adolescent boy or a girl under ten years old could be sold for as much as $275–$300 ($7,630–$8,330 in 2015 dollars) in the 1830s.[10] The earning potential of those children, as measured by the accumulated hours of labor over years or decades, was much more than the price of their purchase.

Although most Tennesseans supported slavery, a small and influential segment of the state's residents opposed it. Opposition to slavery in the early nineteenth century often came from Quaker groups, and in 1809 Tennessee Quakers began to form antislavery groups. As historian James W. Patton noted, by the mid-1820s there were more than twenty manumission and antislavery groups in Tennessee, and these organizations contained roughly one thousand members.[11]

The most vocal antislavery advocates in Tennessee supported a colonization scheme for emancipated blacks or a gradual end to slavery that would result in their emigration to Africa. The Tennessee Colonization Society (TCS), which was formed in 1829, was a state chapter of the American Colonization Society. Its members attempted to reshape slave laws, especially in the early 1830s, when the state legislature developed a set of uneven policies regarding slavery. Though the TCS had little influence during its first decade, it experienced a revival of sorts after Liberia gained sovereignty in the late 1840s.[12]

Leading up to Tennessee's constitutional convention in 1834, both slaveholders and non-slaveholders feared that free blacks would encourage slave revolts in the state. Though free blacks constituted a small part of the state's population, the proportion had grown by 68 percent in the 1820s. Nat Turner's Rebellion in Virginia in 1831 further convinced lawmakers that free blacks would incite enslaved blacks in Tennessee to revolt.[13] Thus, the state legislature passed laws that prohibited free blacks from moving into the state and required "emancipated slaves to leave the state upon gaining their freedom."[14] It is clear that slavery was an issue in Tennessee political culture from the earliest decades of statehood.

Although some abolitionists supported the colonization schemes of the antebellum decades, these plans were fueled by political elites who were either perplexed by the slavery question or wanted to rid Tennessee of blacks. In 1833 and 1834, at least a dozen county delegations wrote petitions asking the Tennessee constitutional convention to either endorse their gradual emancipation plan or make Tennessee a free state by 1866.[15] The petitioners proposed freeing blacks who were born after 1835 when they turned twenty-one. After that, they would be either sent to Liberia with "subsistence for twelve months" or sent to a nonslave state or territory.[16] These proposals failed to convince the delegates to the convention to use the state constitution to end slavery in Tennessee. On the contrary, they enshrined slavery in the new constitution in article 2, section 31, which prevented the state legislature from passing any emancipation laws without the consent of individual slaveholders.

The emigration/colonization scheme focused on emancipated and free blacks. By the 1850s, free blacks made up 1 percent of the population of East Tennessee and more than 5 percent of the population of Nashville.[17] Many lawmakers and slaveholders saw them as a growing problem. Thus, when the colonization movement was reinvigorated after Liberia became a sovereign state, several prominent slaveholders in Tennessee supported it. One example is the iron ore tycoon Montgomery Bell, who in 1853, two years before he died, sent approximately a hundred of the slaves he had emancipated to Liberia in two groups.[18] The emancipated blacks were known as the "iron men of Tennessee" and had been the principal workers for Bell. Some of these black men had helped build the weapon machinery used in the Battle of New Orleans during the War of 1812.[19] Bell commissioned his nephew George C. Bain to locate a region of West Africa that was rich in iron ore so the people he emancipated would have a livelihood in their new home. By several accounts, Bell's arrangement was mutually beneficial: Bell helped his former slaves become landowners and independent operators of iron works, and the emigrants continued to sustain Bell's enterprise by trading with him in iron ore from a new international source.

Many Tennesseans felt that sending emancipated blacks to Liberia was the best option for resolving the slave problem. As Richard Blakett wrote, both antislavery and proslavery advocates saw it as the "best hope of minimizing tensions on both sides of the slavery divide" and addressing the social and political status of free blacks.[20] However, many free blacks opposed colonization schemes. There were reports of high mortality rates among those who traveled to Liberia.[21] This may partially explain why so few blacks emigrated. Two years before the start of the Civil War, the Tennessee legislature attempted to address the status of free blacks by introducing the punitive Free Negro Bill, which sought to expel free blacks from the state. Although the bill was championed by proslavery Democrats who feared that free blacks would incite slave rebellions, it was derailed by intraparty divisions.[22]

Interestingly, from the 1820s to the 1850s, the one institution that was sympathetic to the rights of emancipated blacks (or blacks who disputed their enslavement) was the Tennessee Supreme Court. According to Arthur Howington, the court "articulated a much less erratic policy [than the legislature] toward emancipation and one that consistently favored the slave" during this period.[23] Theodore Brown Jr. noted that the state's supreme court provided an "analytic framework that facilitated rather than obstructed the slave's path to freedom," especially in the 1820s and 1830s.[24] Even though most of the jurists on the court owned slaves, they levied strong criticisms against the institution of slavery.

One example of the court's sensitivity is found in *Fisher's Negroes v. Dabbs* (1834). Prior to this case, enslaved people who had been freed by their owner still had to submit a bill to the legislature for final confirmation of emancipation. To reduce the legal barrier, the state legislature shifted the responsibility for final confirmation to the county courts. Despite this improvement in the process, the confirmation provision set up a procedural hurdle for blacks. Even after people were freed, if they failed to obtain their owner's confirmation through the state legislature or a county court or if the slave owner died before this could be accomplished, the formerly enslaved person was left in "an intermediate state between slavery and freedom."[25] The ruling in *Dabbs* addressed this legal loophole by looking at the intent of the owner. Even if the owner did not complete the confirmation process, if the decision to emancipate a slave had been made and could be proven, the enslaved person was set free. The *Dabbs* case is one of several that was decided in favor of former slaves and is the reason that the Tennessee Supreme Court (TSC) was considered more progressive on emancipation issues than other supreme courts in the South.

Ford v. Ford (1846) is perhaps the most famous case deliberated before the TSC in the antebellum decades because of the remarkable majority opinion written by Judge Nathan Green. The case adjudicated the status of African Americans who had been emancipated after the death of their owner, Lloyd Ford Sr. The court had to determine whether the slave owner was legally able to leave his estate to enslaved black people with whom he felt a closer kinship than he did with his biological children. Ford had requested in his last will and testament that his "black children" receive his property. The resolution of the dispute, which arose when his white offspring challenged the will, rested on the legal status of the blacks who were transitioning from slavery to emancipation. At this moment in Tennessee, the individuals to whom Ford had left his property were caught on the horns of a dilemma. Tennessee law required emancipated blacks to leave the state after obtaining freedom; however, doing so would have forced Ford's former slaves to relinquish any property left to them as part of a testamentary trust once they were emancipated.[26]

In pronouncing that African Americans had both the moral and the legal right to acquire freedom, Judge Green claimed that slaves were "not in the condition of a horse or an ox"—that is, their status as "property" (resulting from what Green called the "accidental position [of slavery] in which fortune has placed [them]") should never undermine their humanity. Green's characterization was evidence of a stance that was favorable toward slaves in the sense that it viewed African Americans more as people than as property. This was an important legal distinction: people could motivate the judicial system to act on their behalf, but property could not.[27] Of course, this emphasis on slaves' humanity did not offset white Tennesseans' reluctance to manumit slaves, nor did it diminish whites' general mistrust of free blacks. But the Tennessee court's position was more progressive than the proslavery postures taken in the court systems of other southern states and was more slave-friendly than the stance of Tennessee's legislative and executive branches.[28]

THE POLITICS OF RECONSTRUCTION, REDEMPTION, AND JIM CROW

The Reconstruction era is another important period for investigating the political status of blacks in Tennessee. During this period and continuing into the twentieth century, black leaders made symbolic attempts to win important political offices and spent considerable amounts of energy mobilizing and educating their constituents. Black political activism increased during Reconstruction not only because black leaders worked to mobilize black men to vote,[29] but also because Republicans depended on new black voters to withstand the attempts of former Confederates to take control of southern state governments. Most African Americans during this period identified with the Republican Party, the party of Abraham Lincoln. In Tennessee, the black vote was critical to determining the outcome of the Reconstruction-era power struggle that united Lincoln loyalists and southern Republicans, chiefly incumbent Republican governor William Brownlow, against Redeemers (or ultraconservative Democrats) and even racial conservatives in his own party.[30] Brownlow sponsored several civil rights reforms that attacked black codes, racial segregation, and the disenfranchisement of black voters. Under his leadership, Tennessee was one of the first southern states to ratify the Fourteenth Amendment. Black men voted in Tennessee as early as 1867, three years before the Fifteenth Amendment was ratified.[31] The forty thousand black men who voted in the 1867 gubernatorial campaign contributed to Brownlow's reelection victory.[32]

The black vote had a substantive impact on the state's political landscape. Competing factions within the Republican Party openly recruited blacks for political organizations throughout the last decades of the nineteenth century. The Lewis/Eaton political machine in Memphis, organized by Barbour Lewis and John Eaton and Lucien Eaton, was one of the first political organizations to actively seek the support of African Americans. It endorsed several blacks for political office, including Edward Shaw, a renowned Memphis activist who later became the state's first black congressional candidate. A few conservative groups also attempted to recruit blacks, although they remained committed to the radical wing of the Republican Party.[33]

Former Confederates and white supremacists responded to the growing presence of black men in state politics with hostile attacks. They organized a violent campaign of racial terrorism that targeted black voters and the Freedmen's Bureau, the federal agency that assisted emancipated blacks with the franchise and with education and social services.[34] The Ku Klux Klan, which was formed in 1865 in Pulaski, Tennessee, recruited Nathan Bedford Forrest, Tennessee's celebrated Confederate general, as its grand wizard.[35] Forrest's involvement in the Klan symbolizes the response of many southern whites to black enfranchisement. Although the legislature responded by directing the state militia to control the Klan and other white supremacist groups, this did little to quell the attacks against blacks.[36] By the time Brownlow left the governor's office to run for the U.S. Senate in 1869, conservatives and ex-Confederates had organized through the Democratic Party and had gained control of the state's most important political offices.

Black political development in Tennessee did not follow the typical pattern of racial politics in the South in the Reconstruction and post-Reconstruction decades. Although the Fifteenth Amendment gave black men the right to hold office in 1870, most blacks were not elected to the Tennessee General Assembly until the 1880s, as Reconstruction was coming to an end. One of them, Samuel McElwee (who served in the Tennessee General Assembly from 1883 to 1889), was nominated for Speaker of the House. Though most Republicans in the lower chamber supported him, he failed to obtain the majority required to gain the nomination.

Blacks ran for state and local offices from the 1870s through the 1890s: in Chattanooga, George Sewall, Robert Marsha, David Medlow, and W. B. Kennedy were elected to local offices; in Knoxville, J. B. Young made a failed attempt at the mayor's office in 1872; William Yardley served on the Knoxville City Council in the 1870s and ran for governor in 1876. From 1871 to 1890, nine blacks were elected to the Knoxville City Council, and several blacks served on the Knox County court, including Yardley, Melvin Gentry, William Brooks Sr., and Sam Maples.[37] In 1875, Randall Brown served on Nashville's city commission, and blacks comprised almost one-third of the municipal government personnel.[38]

Because of the political success of these individuals, Tennessee has often been labeled as a racially moderate state compared to the rest of the South. However, these achievements occurred against the backdrop of militant white resistance. Although black men voted in Tennessee earlier than they did in the rest of the South and won local offices, the first black state legislator, Sampson Keeble, was not elected until 1872, five years before the Compromise of 1877, which turned control of the South back into the hands of the racial conservatives and ex-Confederates. In addition, blacks entered the state legislature in a somewhat weak position: the Republicans, especially the moderate and radical wings of the party, lost ground to conservative unionists and Democrats by 1876.[39] Black leaders were disappointed that Republicans refused to support the candidacies of Edward Shaw and William Henderson Young for Congress in 1872 and 1888, respectively.[40]

Despite its reputation for taking a moderate stance on racial matters compared to Deep South states, Tennessee was one of the first states to launch a legal attack on civil rights. For example, the Tennessee General Assembly implemented some of the South's first disenfranchisement laws.[41] In addition, members of the General Assembly debated several anti–civil rights measures in 1875 and 1881. These bills ultimately passed, reinforcing the segregation that already existed in public accommodations like railroad cars and schools.[42] They further expanded vagrancy laws that criminalized unemployed blacks (or those who worked in occupations not recognized by whites) and promoted prison-leasing practices that created incentives to arrest blacks and offer up convicts as laborers to plantation owners and corporations.[43] Tennessee blacks were also the targets of an extensive lynching campaign in the 1880s. After the brutal lynching of a black woman named Eliza Wood in the summer of 1886 in Jackson, Tennessee, Representative Samuel McElwee introduced an anti-lynching bill in the state legislature, but it was narrowly defeated in the House.[44]

In 1889 and 1890, southern white resistance and the shifting political attitudes of moderate whites led to franchise restrictions that created new barriers for black voters. These laws included raising the poll tax and the use of confusing ballot and voter registration procedures that turned voter registration into a quasi-interview process and placed registration in the hands of a select group of election commissioners.[45] The Democratic Party, which at the time was run by ex-Confederates, gained control of all but one of the majority-black counties by using voter fraud and intimidating black voters.[46] The Tennessee legislature also added a white primary option for localities. Localities were not required to hold a white primary—a provision in many southern states that limited voting in Democratic Party primaries to whites—but the new law gave them the option of experimenting with it.[47]

The resurgence of conservatism that emerged during Reconstruction and continued into the twentieth century adversely affected the black vote and black political power, particularly outside the capital city of Nashville. From 1887 to 1964, few blacks served in the Memphis city government.[48] From 1885 to 1900, fewer than twenty blacks were elected to any county office in Tennessee, and from 1887 to 1964, no blacks were elected to the state legislature.[49]

The Progressive Era of the early twentieth century did not offer opportunities for electoral participation for blacks nor did it slow down the pace of black repression. At the outset, it appeared that Progressive Era reforms would assist blacks, yet many of the reforms stifled black political participation. New electoral procedures, such as appointed (rather than elected) commissions and city councils and at-large elections, were designed to eliminate corruption by preventing political machines from controlling electioneering. Interestingly, it was members of political organizations and business leaders who championed these procedures, primarily so they could replace the political machines with a power structure that was friendlier toward reform. An unfortunate consequence of these changes was that they forced some black politicians out of office and prevented other black candidates from participating in competitive elections. For example, the at-large election system meant that blacks no longer had the opportunity to elect representatives from racially homogeneous, politically cohesive districts. Instead, it forced black candidates to conduct costly citywide or countywide campaigns that required them to win support from voters who lived outside black jurisdictions.[50] One of Chattanooga's most influential black public officials, Hiram Tyree, was forced out of office in 1928 because of these changes.[51]

The combination of retrenchment of civil rights and white backlash in the early decades of the twentieth century disrupted the amicable relationship between black leaders and the Republican Party, which was increasingly influenced by the lily-white movement. This isolated black Republicans and caused a subtle but noticeable shift in black political behavior. Some urban black leaders seriously considered leaving the Republican Party to join the Democrats. Some, including black politicians in Nashville, went so far as to support Democratic candidates even though the party was still controlled by segregationists. For instance, many Nashville blacks voted for Democrat Hilary Ewing Howse, a white businessman, when he ran for reelection as Nashville's mayor in 1911. In turn, Howse assisted with the election of Solomon Parker Harris, the city's first black council member since the 1880s.[52]

The shifting political winds fueled disagreements among black leaders over how to best leverage their influence. Black leaders were torn between three strategies: carving out an independent political base, balancing their votes between Republicans and Democrats, or using their clientele relationship with Republicans to secure some political rewards for blacks. Many blacks were distrustful of the Democratic Party because of its alliance with segregationists, but others believed that the Republican Party took them for granted. Both assessments were correct. White leaders in both the Republican and Democratic parties attempted to selectively incorporate blacks into their machines and political organizations while at the same time rejecting broader reforms, working to moderate black demands, and controlling the vote in jurisdictions where black suffrage rights had not been eliminated.

Blacks who were not completely discouraged from political participation stayed in the Republican Party until the 1930s and 1940s. James Carroll Napier, Nashville's most influential black leader in the early twentieth century and a proponent of Booker T. Washington's accommodationist philosophy, was a resolute supporter of the Republican-black alliance. He served on the city council, was appointed to the executive committee of the Republican Party, and served as the register of the U.S. Treasury under President William H. Taft.[53] However, Napier's experience was the exception, and independent-minded blacks accused the Republicans of overlooking blacks for federal patronage and appointments and criticized them for refusing to support black congressional and gubernatorial candidates. Even Napier criticized the Republican Party's "lily-whitism."[54]

Despite the political realities of the Progressive Era, blacks vigorously protested segregation laws. Despite Tennessee's environment of institutional racism, blacks organized social movements to advance racial equalitarian policies. These movements influenced Tennessee politics even during the nadir of black influence in the early twentieth century. For example, Nashville blacks organized a boycott in 1905 to protest their unequal treatment in public transportation and the recent passage of segregation laws. Blacks across the political spectrum—progressive leaders who believed in a more militant approach to combating white supremacy, moderates, and accommodationists—supported this boycott. In that same year, organizers created the black-owned Union Transportation Company, which provided public transportation during the boycott. James Carroll Napier endorsed the boycott because he viewed the transportation company as congruent with Booker T. Washington's support of black business initiatives. During the boycott, black intellectuals established the *Nashville Globe* to publicize the demands. Though this social movement was short-lived—it collapsed within a few months after the transportation company suffered financial problems—the boycott spread from Nashville to some jurisdictions in East Tennessee.[55]

Booker T. Washington's influence on black leaders and intellectuals is an interesting element of black politics during this period. Because of the strong support of Napier and others for Washington's philosophy, the black community in Nashville was aware of his accommodationist program for racial advancement. However, Washington's supporters generally disagreed with him about the extent to which blacks should work to expand their political and civil rights.[56] Washington's loyal supporters in Tennessee were moderates, and to some degree they were the black elite. But because of their active involvement in politics, they resisted the push by other Washingtonites—many of whom were members of the city's chapter of the National Negro Business League—for political withdrawal.[57] These Washingtonites espoused the belief expressed most eloquently in Washington's famous Atlanta Compromise Speech, in which he encouraged blacks to "dignify and glorify common labour" by becoming agricultural workers, mechanics, and domestic servants.[58] Anti-Washingtonites, who took exception to the idea of placating whites with industriousness and docility, chose to take a more radical (if not militant) approach to advocating for racial inclusion.

Black women in Tennessee were excluded from full political participation and were unable to vote during the Reconstruction era. Even though the Nineteenth Amendment gave black and white women the right to vote in 1920, few black women were elected to office until the 1970s and 1980s. This is not to suggest that black women were passive participants or were politically disengaged. On the contrary, they were politically active and, probably more than any other group, helped launch the anti-lynching campaign that lasted for more than four decades. Ida B. Wells-Barnett, a Memphis schoolteacher, was a prominent civil rights activist. Before leaving the state in the early 1890s, and despite her young age, she earned a reputation as a fierce anti-lynching crusader. She also made a widely publicized legal challenge to the Chesapeake, Ohio and Southwestern Railroad's segregationist policies.[59] Mary Church Terrell, another educator and Memphis resident, was a civil rights activist and worked tirelessly on behalf of the women's suffrage movement. In 1896, she was the first president of the National Association of Colored Women, an organization whose motto was "Lifting as We Climb." In 1909, she became one of the founding members of the National Association for the Advancement of Colored People (NAACP).[60]

A class hierarchy existed in the African American community. Though most blacks were poor, the leadership consisted of educators, business leaders, and others who were able to carve out some measure of economic independence. This group was much more apt to privately negotiate concessions than to encourage black popular resistance to Jim Crow. Although this strategy tempered racial discord, it did so at the expense of substantive deliberations of public policy among a broad group of political actors and voters.

In general, black elite leaders vigorously challenged racism and white supremacy, but they were also adamant that they should be the beneficiaries of federal patronage jobs and appointments from the Republican Party. Although they wanted to democratize Tennessee, at times their politics were parochial and narrowly construed. Some black leaders even considered endorsing education qualifications for voting in order to appease their racially conservative white colleagues. However, most black leaders, many of whom insisted that federal supervision was the best safeguard of the black vote, rejected this proposal.[61]

PARTY POLITICS AND BLACK POLITICAL REALIGNMENT

Black voting in Tennessee declined at the turn of the twentieth century after whites began to limit black participation in the political process. Although black voter registration rates in the state remained higher than in many of the Deep South states, whites engaged in voter intimidation, fraud, and manipulation, especially in the state's rural counties. Despite these attacks on black suffrage, some blacks continued to exercise influence in party politics and never abandoned political organizing.

Most politically active blacks were members of the Republican Party from the Reconstruction era to the 1930s. Blacks celebrated the election of white politician Ben Hooper as governor in 1911, the first Republican elected since 1883. Hooper had a black advisor, Benjamin Carr, and he appointed John Henry Hale, an African American physician, as a delegate to the National Education Congress.[62] Robert Reed Church Jr. of Memphis (the son of an African American entrepreneur and the brother of well-known civil rights activist Mary Church Terrell) was a prominent black Republican who helped finance a political organization called the Lincoln League in 1916. Church was also a leading advisor to national Republican leaders in the 1920s.[63] As Linda Wynn and Bobby Lovett note, the Lincoln League "was established to organize the masses of black citizens to register and vote.... Within a few months, the League had registered 10,000 voters."[64] In 1927, Church and other political leaders created the West Tennessee Civic and Political League, which sought alternative candidates to those the white political machine put forward.[65] Church had a rocky relationship with Edward Hull Crump, a powerful political boss from Memphis. Initially Church worked with him to secure black support for Crump's political machine, but their relationship became tense in the 1920s and 1930s as Democrats began to recruit more black voters in the state.[66]

Both the Lincoln League and the West Tennessee Civic and Political League are examples of what political scientist Ronald Walters called an "independent leveraging strategy." Walters argued that it is important for black politics to be anchored by autonomous formations that allow African Americans or progressive multiracial coalitions to become the balance of power within or in relation to political parties. By consolidating the black vote or organizing a multiracial voting coalition, these formations can "establish a bargaining environment for the exchange of commitments."[67]

As Tennessee blacks began leaving the Republican Party in the 1930s, Church encouraged Republican leaders to endorse progressive policies. According to Wynn and Lovett, he organized as many as 200 black Republicans to "pressure Republican senators and congressmen to enact fair employment and other civil rights legislation."[68] He also partnered with A. Philip Randolph, one of the most influential labor and civil rights activists of the 1940s, to influence Republicans. Church's pressure politics had some success: although he was unable to stop the exodus of African Americans from his beloved party, his efforts contributed to the Republican Party's adoption of a more ideologically progressive platform.[69]

The 1928 presidential election between Republican Herbert Hoover and Democrat Al Smith was a watershed event for party politics in Tennessee. White Democratic and Republican campaigners for both candidates accused each other of endorsing civil rights measures. Democrats assumed that Hoover supported civil rights because Congressman Leonidas Dyer, a Republican from Missouri, had sponsored several anti-lynching bills beginning in 1918 and into the early 1920s.[70] In order to placate segregationists, Hoover distanced himself from the Dyer bills. Hoover's Tennessee supporters accused Smith of sympathizing with civil rights causes. This response helped erode black support for the Republican Party in the state.

Franklin D. Roosevelt's New Deal programs in the 1930s helped facilitate the transition of blacks into the Democratic Party. Clarence Robinson of Chattanooga, who served in the legislature in the 1970s, recalled the party shift among blacks during that time. He felt that much of this swing was generational: younger blacks who had been shaped by Roosevelt's New Deal were attracted to the Democratic Party while older blacks were not. Robinson stated, "Around 1936, we organized the Young Black Democratic Club, and that's when we shifted the politics from Republicans to Democrats."[71] In East Tennessee, blacks gave an increasing amount of attention to the Democratic Party because of their desire to be included in some of the New Deal programs, especially opportunities like jobs with the Tennessee Valley Authority, the Works Progress Administration, the Civilian Conservation Corps, and the Federal Emergency Relief Administration.[72] Memphis and Shelby County blacks, under the aegis of the Crump machine, also worked in Roosevelt's presidential campaigns.[73] Thus, despite the decline in black voting after the Reconstruction era and the segregationists' stronghold in the Democratic Party, blacks were able to exert some influence over both parties during the early part of the twentieth century because both parties were realistically competing for black votes.

BLACK POLITICS AND THE MODERN CIVIL RIGHTS ERA IN TENNESSEE

In the late nineteenth and twentieth centuries, as Tennessee segregationists launched a concerted attack on black suffrage rights and overturned many of the Reconstruction era reforms, many blacks left the state. Blacks made up one-fourth of the residents in Tennessee in 1870, but by 1930 the black population had declined to about 18 percent.[74] By the 1960s, most black Tennesseans were concentrated in the urban and suburban communities of Chattanooga, Nashville, Knoxville, and Memphis. During this period, the locus of black power was situated in Memphis and in Shelby County, which had the highest concentration of blacks in the state. Even though these areas were controlled by segregationists, they tended to be more racially moderate than rural counties in Tennessee in the 1950s and 1960s.[75] This geographic distribution and the competing political factions in the state created some political opportunities for blacks.

From the 1940s to the 1960s, the black electorate was subjected to varied access to voting. Although blacks could register to vote in urban jurisdictions, their votes were manipulated by local and state political machines. For example, there are numerous stories about the vote totals in predominantly black voting districts being purposefully miscounted, voters being falsely accused of "spoiling" their ballots by marking them incorrectly, elections being called prematurely before all votes had been counted, and blacks being discouraged because they were unable or unwilling to pay the poll taxes required for voter registration.[76]

The black vote provides a window for assessing racial hierarchy in the state in the 1940s for several reasons. Whites wanted to restrict blacks' voting power. Within black communities, mobilization for the war raised concerns about mandatory registration with the Selective Service at a time when many African Americans were denied the right to vote. These interrelated concerns were particularly burdensome to Governor Prentice Cooper, who served from 1939 to 1945. In a closed-door meeting with NAACP representatives and other black leaders in October 1940, Cooper purportedly made disparaging remarks about the contributions of blacks to American history and political development. (The media reports at the time relied on first-person accounts from black leaders at the meeting.)[77]

In the months leading up to that meeting, blacks had faced stiff resistance at the voting booth. There was even a reported lynching of a black man who tried to register to vote in the West Tennessee town of Brownsville. The delegation met with the governor about a range of issues that included establishing more

African American parks in Nashville, hiring or appointing blacks to local federal agencies, the treatment of African Americans in hospitals, youth employment opportunities, and internship opportunities for Meharry Medical College students.[78] When the NAACP committee brought up the issue of black representation on Selective Service boards, Cooper's reaction was negative. In response to the request, the governor told the group that "this is a white man's country" and that "Negroes had nothing to do with the settling of America," unlike white men, who "cut down the trees, plowed the fields and developed America."[79] Finally, he said that if blacks refused to register for the draft, they could face imprisonment or a large fine.[80] Cooper's comments enraged blacks and their white allies from all over the country. His office and local newspapers were inundated with letters scolding the governor about his inaccurate version of U.S. history. The NAACP, black fraternity and sorority groups, the Universal Negro Improvement Association, and Congressman Arthur Mitchell of Chicago all publicly challenged the governor's assertions.[81]

A second debate that involved Governor Cooper centered on the poll tax, which voters had to pay when they registered. Civil rights groups were determined to pressure the governor to abolish the poll tax because it placed an undue burden on poor people. In 1941, Cooper's allies in the legislature introduced a measure to repeal the poll tax, but it was decisively defeated. Two years later, they introduced a similar bill. Before the first vote, the City Federation of Colored Women's Clubs of Nashville had pressured Cooper to repeal the poll tax because it would lead to "leaner and purer ballots."[82] They urged him to call a special legislative session to discuss the bill. The Nashville chapter of the NAACP and the Tennessee League of Women Voters urged the governor to do the same.

Other civic groups also pressured the governor to repeal the poll tax. Predominantly white groups wanted to repeal the tax because of the economic burden it placed on working-class and poor white voters. The Young Democratic Clubs of Tennessee explained to Cooper that households in the "rural sections of our state" were faced with the choice of whether the husband or wife would pay the poll tax. Invariably, the poll tax for men was paid, which meant that "thousands of our women have never enjoyed the privilege of voting."[83] Opposition to the poll tax also came from labor unions and workers rights associations, such as the Amalgamated Clothing Workers of America, the Industrial Union Council of Nashville, the Nashville Trades and Labor Union, the Workers Progressive League of North Nashville, the National Maritime Union's Inland Boatsmen Division in Memphis, the Textile Workers Union, and the American Federation of Hosiery Workers based in Chattanooga.[84]

Civil rights groups believed that the poll tax was a morally and politically reprehensible relic of the political battles of the late nineteenth century, when ex-Confederates made various attempts to seize power in the state. Labor and civic groups saw the poll tax as a political offense, and they also felt that it was too expensive to sustain and too inextricably linked to the corrupt machine politics that plagued all regions of the state. Although some classes of voters were exempt (those over the age of fifty, disabled and indigent people, veterans, and Works Progress Administration workers), the poll tax was a major source of revenue for the state. In 1939, it raised revenue of nearly $500,000 (approximately $8 million in 2014 dollars) from the more than one million Tennesseans who registered to vote.[85]

In a victory for civil rights activists, the state legislature repealed the poll tax in 1943. However, the TSC overruled the law in a 3–2 decision that confused many political observers. The court ruled that the state poll tax could be eliminated only by repealing the 1870 constitutional amendment that initially enshrined the tax in the state's political framework.[86] Poll taxes, while part of the state's constitution, only had the force of law when they were backed by legislation, and this backing had come in the early 1890s when segregationist politicians assumed power in the state and the politics of the Redeemers invaded the Tennessee General Assembly.

Some political observers believed that Cooper did not aggressively push for repeal because of his close associations with machine boss E. H. Crump, especially since Crump's ally on the state supreme court, Justice Frank Gailor, cast the deciding vote in the ruling that overturned the repeal of the poll tax.[87] Crump's political power in Memphis was tied to his ability to manipulate the poll tax to control which blacks could vote. Yet despite his relationship with Crump, Cooper sought to do away with the poll tax. In the 1940–1941 debate over the tax, he contacted the governors of Florida, Louisiana, and Kentucky for advice on how to repeal the law.[88] Legislatures in these states had recently passed laws that eliminated the poll tax, and the governors sent Cooper copies of successful legislation.

Crump is a seminal figure for understanding both the scope and the limitations of black political participation in Tennessee, particularly between the two world wars. He was one of the most powerful political bosses in the South in the first half of the twentieth century. He served as the mayor of Memphis from 1909 to 1915, when the state legislature ousted him for refusing "to enforce the Tennessee prohibition law."[89] Despite this setback, he remained a dominant force in Tennessee politics into the 1940s.

Crump's problematic relationship with blacks underscores the instability of black politics in Tennessee during this period. He was a segregationist, yet he needed the black vote to maintain power in Memphis. Thus, he protected blacks from violent attacks from other segregationists but controlled the black vote through intimidation, corruption, and minor patronage.[90] He used the poll tax to control and manipulate the black vote, paying the poll taxes of many black voters who, in turn, voted for the Crump candidates. It was also common for members of his machine to pay the poll taxes of black voters and then mark their ballots without their consent.[91] These shenanigans distorted the number of black registered voters in the state who had control over their own votes.

After World War II, Tennessee politics underwent major changes that had an impact on black political activity. In the late 1940s, Crump began to lose power after his candidates failed to win key offices. This political development and Crump's death in 1954 created an opening for black leaders to carve out a political agenda. One example of such activity is the formation of an independent political organization in Memphis called the Volunteer Party, which ran a slate of black candidates that included William C. Wathers, Theodore Spencer, Russell Sugarman, Archie "A. W." Willis, and Benjamin Hooks, who would later become the longest-tenured president of the NAACP.[92] Although none of these candidates won, the initiative demonstrated their willingness to challenge Crump loyalists.

The emergence of a new group of racially moderate white leaders in the 1950s and 1960s also signaled a shift in the state's political landscape. Tennessee senators Estes Kefauver and Albert Gore Sr. were two of three southern senators (the other was Lyndon Johnson) who rejected the Southern Manifesto, a nonbinding resolution from southern members of Congress that protested the *Brown v. Board of Education* decision.[93] Kefauver and Gore supported much of the civil rights legislation of this period, although Gore voted against the 1964 Civil Rights Act.

No politician epitomized the shifting political winds of Tennessee in the 1950s and 1960s better than Governor Frank Clement. Clement, who was elected in 1952 while still in his early thirties, became the state's longest-serving governor of the twentieth century. Like Kefauver and Gore, he was considered a New South politician who welcomed urbanization, industrialization, and a gradual movement toward biracial cooperation.[94] Speaking before the Atlanta Chamber of Commerce in the spring of 1953, Clement said the South's history of slavery had "tortured the subsequent course of our national history and swung like an albatross about our necks—a problem that even today is far from resolution."[95]

Clement stood out among southern governors throughout much of his career. He refused to oppose school desegregation, and under his watch Oak Ridge, Tennessee, was one of the first cities to desegregate public schools, a year after the *Brown* decision.[96] In 1956 he used the state's National Guard to integrate schools in Clinton, Tennessee, and he appointed several blacks to positions in his administration. His major policy initiatives focused on prison and mental health reforms. African Americans constituted a disproportionately high percentage of prison inmates and were also likely to benefit from policies that increased access to mental health care. During his last term in office, Clement tried (unsuccessfully) to convince the state legislature to repeal the death penalty. Clement also created the Governor's Commission on Human Relations to investigate discrimination complaints.

These leaders' sympathies with civil rights led to a white backlash in the state that was mostly directed toward blacks and white racial moderates in the Democratic Party. Segregationists, who had once made up the bulk of the Democratic Party, began shifting their allegiance to the Republican Party, and this transition continued into the 1990s. In 1966, one year after the passage of the Voting Rights Act, Republicans gained seats in the state's House of Representatives.[97] Both Gore and Clement were stigmatized as allies of the civil rights movement and failed to win election after the passage of the Voting Rights Act. Clement lost a senatorial bid, his second in four years, and Gore was defeated in his 1970 reelection campaign.[98] These losses were largely attributed to the changing political landscape in the country and the ascent of racial conservatives in the state.

BLACK FACTIONALISM AND CIVIL RIGHTS

One of the most contentious political debates in the 1960s occurred over the 1964 Civil Rights Act, which desegregated public accommodations, established civil rights monitoring departments in each of the federal agencies, and provided a formal grievance process in cases of employment discrimination against blacks and other protected classes.[99] Southern whites were especially opposed to Title VI of this law, which banned discrimination in federally funded programs, and Title VII, which attempted to remedy employment discrimination.

The Civil Rights Act debate had a direct impact on Tennessee politics. Al Gore Sr., the state's senior senator, was facing a tough reelection campaign and voted against the bill. Although he later regretted his decision—he called it "one of [my] most colossal blunders as a legislator"—it left a bad imprint on his political career. After that vote, some black leaders started an "Ignore Gore in 64" campaign. Interestingly, despite Gore's opposition to the Civil Rights Act, his civil rights record may have been the best among southern senators during this period. He voted for the Civil Rights Act of 1957, the Civil Rights Act of 1960, and the Voting Rights Act of 1965. His vote for the latter act may have contributed to his reelection defeat in 1970. He also advocated for Medicare and Medicaid, which civil rights leaders supported, and later spoke against the Vietnam War.[100]

Many black activists in Tennessee drew on the federal Civil Rights Act to propose state legislation to fight racial discrimination in state agencies. The newly created biracial Governor's Commission on Human Relations used the Civil

Rights Act debate to pressure Governor Clement to back a state Fair Practices Code. This code, which had been proposed in 1963, mirrored the Civil Rights Act; it focused on nondiscrimination against state personnel, pressuring state contractors to comply with nondiscriminatory measures, and giving blacks access to government jobs.[101] For many black leaders, the Fair Practices Code was a litmus test that gauged whether the state's leading politicians were willing to support employment desegregation efforts and that measured their broader commitment to the Civil Rights Act. Although Clement supported funding for education and public health and proclaimed his opposition to segregation, in 1964 he refused to sign the Fair Practices Code.[102]

The debates about the Civil Rights Act and the Fair Practices Code took place during the special election campaign to fill the seat vacated by Senator Estes Kefauver, who had died unexpectedly in 1963. Clement and former senator Ross Bass both waged campaigns for the Senate seat in the Democratic Party primary. Both candidates actively sought endorsements from black organizations. The debate was troublesome for Clement, despite his cordial relationship with black leaders, because he was not committed to the Civil Rights Act. He objected to a provision in the early drafts of the bill that authorized jury trials for violators of the proposed law. Several black leaders and organizations expressed concern about Clement's stance, especially after Bass indicated his support.[103] Clement's aides advised him not to explicitly endorse the Civil Rights Act based on the argument that civil rights protections were already guaranteed in the Fourteenth Amendment. Clement also said that he could not weigh in on the proposed law because he was not yet a member of the U.S. Senate. Some black leaders, angered by his position, interpreted these explanations as disingenuous.

There was additional concern that the Civil Rights Act and the Fair Practices Code would divide African Americans in the special election. Willis was critical of Clement's reluctance to aggressively challenge the state's hiring practices. J. Willard Bowden, executive secretary of the Tennessee Federation of Democratic Leagues (an African American organization), warned the governor that his position on the Fair Practices Code could divide the members of the federation.[104] The Tennessee Voters' Council, which supported Bass, used its influence on his behalf, and blacks overwhelmingly voted for Bass in the Democratic Party primary.[105]

CIVIL RIGHTS AND POPULAR MOBILIZATION

In the 1950s and 1960s, numerous popular mobilization campaigns attempted to tear down the edifices of Jim Crow segregation in the South. Tennessee was a hotbed of civil rights activities during this period, and those activities entailed a mix of strategies and tactics: protests, sit-ins, grassroots activism, education, litigation, and legal advocacy.

An important institution in the civil rights movement (and the labor movement) was the Highlander Folk School, an interracial adult school that trained civil rights and labor activists in movement politics.[106] For three decades (1932–1961) Highlander was an incubator for local activists and organizations at its campus near Monteagle, Tennessee. Its original focus was on popular education, leadership development, and organizing workers, but as the civil rights movement gained momentum in the 1950s, Highlander incorporated civil rights activism into its training initiatives. Highlander temporarily closed its doors in 1961 before quickly reopening under a new name, the Highlander Research and Education Center. Previously, Highlander had earned a reputation as one of the most important social movement schools of the civil rights era. Virtually every civil rights leader, including Rosa Parks, Dr. Martin Luther King Jr., and members of the Student Nonviolent Coordinating Committee, received training in Highlander's leadership development seminars and workshops in the 1950s and early 1960s. In its last year in operation, Highlander also conducted several workshops on electoral politics.[107]

One of the widely publicized initiatives of the civil rights movement was the Nashville sit-in movement of 1960, which desegregated the city's downtown business community. The movement was part of a broad campaign that attacked segregated public accommodations throughout the South and the Midwest. It was propelled by the Nashville Christian Leadership Conference, college students mainly from historically black colleges and universities, and community activists.[108] These activists believed that nonviolence and a radical Christianity could be used to advance social and racial justice claims in Nashville.[109] Bernard Lafayette, a prominent young participant in the movement, later stated that the activists were adamant that the gospel "was practical and could be applied" within the context of the movement.[110] However, the movement's distinct contribution was its demonstration of nonviolent resistance as a strategy for social and political change. The nonviolence philosophy and tactics that guided the movement were taught in leadership development workshops organized by James Lawson, a divinity graduate student at Vanderbilt University and an organizer with the Fellowship of Reconciliation. Lawson also played a leading role in the Memphis sanitation workers strike in the late 1960s.

The Memphis strike of 1967–1968 was another movement that garnered national attention. The strike occurred after T. O. Jones of the Independent Workers Association, a black sanitation workers organization, requested that the city recognize the union and authorize higher wages for union members.[111] After the city rebuffed union representatives, more than a thousand black sanitation workers went on strike. Mayor Henry Loeb was strongly opposed to the new union, and the Tennessee General Assembly attempted to pass legislation that would have punished the striking workers.[112]

The Memphis sanitation workers campaign is primarily known for its connection to the assassination of Dr. Martin Luther King Jr., who was killed in Memphis when he traveled to the city to lend his support to the striking workers. But it should also be remembered for the successful efforts of Memphis activists to draw attention to employment discrimination and because it emphasized the need for both economic justice and political inclusion: conventional civil rights movement approaches tended to prioritize the latter over the former. Historian Michael Honey wrote that the strike "engaged the concern of black trade unionists, who saw it as a merging of labor and civil rights battles they had fought for years."[113] Despite the fact that it drew support from labor and civil rights leaders, such as Dr. King and the Southern Christian Leadership Conference, the strike was an indigenous movement spearheaded by local black trade unionists with the assistance of a cadre of ministers and community activists.

Finally, it is important to discuss the voting rights struggle in Haywood and Fayette counties in West Tennessee from 1959 to 1962. Similar to the Memphis strike, this movement was led by a group of local activists that included war veterans, sharecroppers, and middle-class activists who belonged to civic welfare and civil rights organizations.[114] James Forman, a prominent civil rights leader who traveled to these counties, recorded his observations of the movement in his memoir *The Making of Black Revolutionaries*.[115] He celebrated the leadership role of local activists in rural West Tennessee, especially since earlier movement campaigns in the 1950s had often received too much direction from national civil rights groups.

The rural activists in these counties were first concerned with the lack of black representation on juries after an elderly black man was arrested for a two-decade-old shooting.[116] Blacks could not serve on juries because jury duty was limited to registered voters. Because of voter suppression and intimidation, black voter registration in these rural communities was much lower than in Memphis and Nashville. Thus, the movement wanted to remove barriers to black political participation, and it also sought to liberalize racially discriminatory jury pools.

The voting rights movement led to brutal reprisals, many of which targeted black sharecropping families. These families were blacklisted and therefore unable to get work; they were prevented from buying groceries, gasoline, and medical supplies; and many were evicted from their homes and forced to live in makeshift tents.[117] Voter intimidation in rural West Tennessee towns sparked an investigation by the Highlander Folk School.[118] The repression also caught the attention of John Doar, an attorney in the Justice Department's Civil Rights Division, who investigated the retaliations against the activists.[119] The Tent City movement, so called because the evicted sharecroppers lived in tents, became a major test case for the 1957 Civil Rights Act. This legislation had created the U.S. Commission on Civil Rights and the Civil Rights Division in the Justice Department and authorized the Justice Department to investigate complaints about voter discrimination and intimidation. Although the bill gave the Civil Rights Division weak investigative powers, to the surprise of many, Doar aggressively examined complaints and assisted the West Tennessee activists.

The Tent City movement was a signature victory for the civil rights movement. It galvanized the mainline civil rights organizations, forced the Justice Department to put some enforcement powers into the Civil Rights Division, and eventually opened the door to black voter registration in Fayette and Haywood counties. Moreover, it laid a foundation for grassroots organizing in West Tennessee for future decades.

Yet the victory was tempered by the repeated attempts of whites to violently intimidate black voters and civil rights activists in Fayette and Haywood counties and in neighboring counties in the years following Tent City. James Smith, a civil rights activist who represented the West Tennessee Voters' Project and the Tipton County Congress of Racial Equality, wrote to the governor on June 25, 1965, requesting protection from white vigilantes who were targeting black voters.[120] Fred L. Shuttlesworth, a veteran of the Birmingham civil rights movement who was active with several national civil rights groups, investigated the stabbing of a black seventeen-year-old civil rights activist in the area.[121] The Waterproof Garment Workers and the president of the American Federation of Teachers also raised concerns about racial attacks.

The problems in the small towns of West Tennessee continued to persist long after the end of the Tent City movement. As late as 1970, black residents still faced political exclusion. For instance, even though Fayette was a majority-black county at that time, there were no blacks on the county election commission. The Tennessee State Advisory Committee found evidence that "black citizens ha[d] been systematically discriminated against" and were "victims of unequal protection of the law."[122]

The rural West Tennessee voting rights movement highlighted a larger concern about how the original version of the Voting Rights Act would be applied in Tennessee. The Voting Rights Act was the most important civil rights legislation of the twentieth century. It attacked racial discrimination and intimidation in the voting booth and brought millions of blacks into the electoral process. The act's major shortcoming was that its preclearance provision (section 5) only applied to states and counties that met certain criteria, as outlined in section 4 of the legislation.[123] Sections 4 and 5 said that the supervisory component of the act would apply to states and jurisdictions that had the most restrictive voting patterns or jurisdictions with voter registration or turnout rates below 50 percent in the previous presidential election. These jurisdictions were subject to preclearance, which meant that changes to their electoral laws and procedures had to be approved by the Justice Department or the U.S. District Court of Appeals.[124] Because Tennessee's overall and black voter registration rates before 1965 were above 50 percent, it was excluded from the Voting Rights Act's preclearance provision.[125] Voting rights suits in Tennessee were thus adjudicated through section 2 of the law. Black voter registration was 59.1 percent in 1960. One decade later, in 1970, it was estimated that 240,000 blacks, or 71.6 percent of the black voting-age population, were registered to vote.[126] Thus, the state had considerably less federal oversight over its elections than other southern states did during the first five years of the Voting Rights Act.

Furthermore, sections 4 and 5 of the Voting Rights Act did not account for differential registration rates for black voters in rural and urban jurisdictions throughout the state. Nor did the act account for racially repressive procedures not covered under section 5's preclearance provision, which focused on black voters *during* elections. In the first half of the century, a sizable number of black votes in Memphis/Shelby County had been controlled and manipulated by E. H. Crump through corruption and often without the input of black leaders.[127] Although it was common for blacks to register to vote, blacks had little input into whom they could vote for or what candidates they could support.

In the late 1960s and early 1970s, several cities experienced civil unrest, and new calls came from black leaders for redistributive economic measures. For example, in the early 1970s, Edwin Mitchell and other black leaders in Nashville formed the Black Community Conference, which organized a series of mass meetings and initiated a boycott after the city refused to meet the group's demands regarding school busing, improvements in the city's education system, economic development, and service provision.[128]

Despite these activities and others across the state, black political resources and energy have been channeled into institutions rather than into social movements since the 1970s. The remainder of this chapter looks at the transition of black politics from protest and movement activism to institutional politics.

THE INSTITUTIONALIZATION OF BLACK POLITICS IN TENNESSEE

The early 1970s marked a significant shift in black politics in Tennessee. Although several cities experienced boycotts or civil disturbances during these years, instances of black militancy and civil disobedience were in decline. Institutional approaches to racial uplift replaced the protest strategies that had characterized much of black politics since the end of Reconstruction. Political scientist Robert C. Smith described institutionalization as occurring when "a group previously excluded from systemic institutions and processes [is] ... brought into those institutions and processes, either because [continuing to exclude this group] poses a threat to system stability or maintenance or because it is part of the normal, evolutionary adjustments of a democratic society to the claims of new groups for inclusion, incorporation or integration."[129] Institutionalization has been a product of the changing political environment since the mid-1960s. Social movement scholars highlight the Civil Rights Act of 1964 and the Voting Rights Act of 1965 as signature developments in this strategic shift. These two legislative acts opened the doors for many blacks to exercise their influence inside the political system. By the 1970s, blacks were far more willing to use conventional political channels to challenge racial hierarchy and regressive policies than to use nonmainstream social movements to create pressure for change.

Black politics in Tennessee had partially shifted toward institutional politics a decade before the Civil Rights Act and the Voting Rights Act. For example, several African American Memphis residents ran for the state legislature in the mid-1950s, including William C. Wathers, T. L. Spencer, and Benjamin Hooks.[130] In the 1960s, blacks in Memphis campaigned for the city's major political offices, including seats on the juvenile court, the public works commission, and the board of education.[131] Z. Alexander Looby and Harold Love were elected to the Nashville City Council in the 1950s and early 1960s, and five African Americans served on the city council in 1964. Thirty miles outside Nashville in the city of Murfreesboro, Robert Scales, a prominent civil rights activist and funeral home owner, was elected to the city council in 1963, the first black elected official in the city since Reconstruction. African Americans in Knoxville benefited from a change in the city's election system from at-large to single-member districts. As a result, J. Michael Broke and Maye Guyer Banner were elected in 1969.[132] J. Willard Bowden was the first black person appointed as secretary of the state's Board of Pardons and Paroles in 1964.[133]

The abolition of de jure segregation provided more political opportunities for black residents in electoral and institutional politics from the 1970s to the early twenty-first century. John Washington Butler Jr. of East Tennessee ran for governor in 1974, the second black candidate to run since William F. Yardley's campaign in 1876. Previously, Butler was on the Oak Ridge City Council, and after losing the gubernatorial campaign he was appointed to a state-level position as a commissioner of the Office of Urban and Federal Affairs in 1975. Eva Malone became vice mayor of Gallatin, a small city located outside Nashville.[134] By 1980, Tennessee had ninety-nine black elected officials in nonlegislative seats at the county, school board, city council, and magistrate levels.[135]

In 1991, Willie Herenton was elected as Memphis's first black mayor. He served four consecutive terms. A veritable who's who of black politicians and leaders had run for mayor of Memphis from the 1960s through the 1980s: attorney Otis Higgs, state representative Archie "A. W." Willis, state senator John Ford, state representative Dedrick "Teddy" Withers, and state senator James "J. O." Patterson, who won a plurality of the vote in 1982 but lost in a runoff election to Dick Hackett.[136] In 2002, A. C. Wharton became the first black mayor of Shelby County, and Howard Gentry was elected the first black vice mayor of Nashville/Davidson County's metropolitan government. Within a few years, Shelbyville in Middle Tennessee and Hardeman County in West Tennessee elected their first black chief executives.[137]

THE RISE OF BLACK LEGISLATIVE INFLUENCE

The institutionalization of black politics must be considered against the backdrop of urbanization and industrialization in the state. By the 1960s, most Tennesseans had migrated to cities, which tended to be less conservative and less isolated than rural communities. As a result, the locus of power shifted from rural areas to the four major metropolitan areas of Chattanooga, Knoxville, Memphis, and Nashville. The 1962 Supreme Court decision in *Baker v. Carr*, which originated in Tennessee, acknowledged the political impact of these population shifts. The court's decision required the state to redistrict and reapportion its legislative seats to account for these demographic changes as a central component of the "one person, one vote" principle.[138] The case had a profound impact on Tennessee's legislative districts and political makeup because it diminished the influence of rural legislators in the General Assembly. Before the *Baker* decision, Tennessee's state legislature had not undergone a process of redistricting for sixty years, despite ample evidence that most Tennesseans lived in metropolitan areas. This case forced rural legislators, who tended to be conservative and racially homogeneous, to relinquish their control over the state legislature, which then gave urban jurisdictions greater representation in state government.

Redistricting and reapportionment have generally been central fronts in the struggle for voting rights. The *Baker* decision and the subsequent redrawing of legislative districts helped increase black political representation in the state legislature. The first black lawmaker, A. W. Willis, entered the legislature in January 1965, two and a half years after *Baker* and in the same year that the General Assembly convened a special session to finalize the new legislative districts. During Willis's short two-year tenure in the House of Representatives, he pushed for a minimum-wage bill that challenged the right-to-work, pro-business atmosphere of Tennessee's employers. Although this bill failed, his legislative advocacy indicated that future black legislators would be concerned about this policy.

Like Willis, many legislators in the first wave of blacks who were elected to the General Assembly in the period 1965–1975 were from the civil rights community. Willis was a prominent Memphis attorney and one of the leaders of the city's school desegregation fight.[139] Russell Sugarman, who was elected to the Tennessee House of Representatives in 1966, and J. O. Patterson, the first black senator in the state's history, were well-known activists from Memphis. Robert Booker was elected in 1966 as the first black legislator from Knoxville. He played an active role in helping desegregate the city's downtown movie theaters and lunch counters, having joined forces with prominent ministers W. T. Crutcher and Robert E. James.[140] Avon Williams, a civil rights activist who was instrumental in the creation of the Davidson County Independent Political Council and the Tennessee Voters' Council in the 1960s, was elected in 1968.[141] Clarence Robinson, a well-known civil rights activist and community leader, was elected in 1975, the first black legislator from Chattanooga since Reconstruction.

Black legislators garnered a substantial amount of political capital shortly after the first wave of them entered the Tennessee General Assembly because they formed a significant voting bloc in the House of Representatives, where Democrats held a slim majority. After the 1972 elections, black legislators lobbied Democratic Party leaders for appointments to one of the three constitutional offices (secretary of state, comptroller, and secretary of the treasury). Those who hold these offices are not elected but are appointed through a series of negotiations among the House, the Senate, and the governor. At the time, Democrats controlled the legislature by a margin of 70–61, and a cohesive group of black legislators was critical to the Democrats' governing coalition.[142] After some negotiations, black legislators were given several leadership posts: one was appointed the chair of a standing committee, one was appointed the vice chair of a standing committee, three were appointed as the secretaries of standing committees, and five were given positions on the influential House Calendar and Rules Committee.[143] This is an example of African American leaders shaping politics directly through their increased numbers in political office.[144]

In 1975, the eleven blacks in the legislature created the Tennessee Black Caucus of State Legislators (TBCSL). Its objective was to lobby for policies that would be beneficial to African Americans and other marginalized groups in Tennessee.[145] The group attempted to organize the votes of black legislators into a solid coalition to maximize their influence. The Office of Minority Affairs at the legislature, which was created in 1974, assisted in the formation and logistics of the TBCSL.

The first black woman legislator in the history of the state was Dorothy

Brown, a Nashville physician who was elected in 1966 to the House of Representatives but was defeated two years later. Thelma Harper of Nashville was the first black woman elected to the Senate in the state's history; she won after Avon Williams's departure in 1991. The most influential black woman in the history of the General Assembly was Lois DeBerry, the second black woman elected to the legislature and the first black woman from Memphis/Shelby County. Elected in 1972 at the age of twenty-seven, DeBerry was a direct beneficiary of the *Baker* decision and the new round of redistricting that occurred after the 1970 Census. She further benefited from the ratification of the Twenty-Sixth Amendment in 1971, which enfranchised eighteen- to twenty-one-year-olds. A number of people in this age group worked on DeBerry's first campaign.[146]

DeBerry was the first black woman elected as the speaker pro tempore, the second-ranking position in the House of Representatives; she was in that position longer than anyone in the state's history. In addition, she was the majority whip in the ninety-second and ninety-third legislative sessions and served as president of the National Black Caucus of State Legislators. She died in 2013.[147] Perhaps more than any other leader, she was responsible for the formation of the TBCSL's annual legislative retreats, which bring together intellectuals, policymakers, and professionals to discuss policy issues.

THE FORD POLITICAL DYNASTY

An assessment of black politics in Tennessee would be incomplete without some discussion of the political dynasty of the Ford family of Memphis, arguably the most influential African American political family in Tennessee from the 1970s to the mid-2000s. Historically, the political character of Tennessee (and the rest of the South) has been defined by strong political families that use professional connections and financial resources to win or hand over political offices to family members and friends. Political scientist Daniel Elazar's seminal study on federalism and American political culture emphasized this point. He called it the South's "traditionalistic" culture, which privileges hierarchy and powerful families.[148] Hence, the Ford family's ascent is not unusual in the South.

Before entering the political arena, the Ford family catapulted to prominence as the proprietors of a South Memphis funeral home. Initially the business was a modest undertaking, but it allowed the Fords to build a loyal following among many black residents, who requested their assistance with finances, transportation to hospitals, and burial costs.[149] At least nine members of the Ford family have been elected to public office since the 1970s, including two to the U.S. Congress.

Harold Ford Sr., Tennessee's first black congressional representative, is probably the most well-known of the Fords. He was only twenty-nine when he defeated four-term incumbent Dan Kuykendall in 1974 by fewer than 600 votes. At the time, his congressional district was about 45 percent African American, but currently it is majority black.[150]

Ford was not the first black politician to seek this congressional seat. Two years before his election, state senator J. O. Patterson made a failed attempt to unseat Kuykendall.[151] As Sharon Wright Austin pointed out, 1974 was more opportune than 1972 "because of the slumping economy and continuing anti-Republican mood in the country in the aftermath of Watergate."[152] The congressional district had also been redrawn to include more black voters by 1974.

Harold Ford Sr. and his brother John Ford were liberals. Harold Ford Sr. championed civil rights and social welfare causes during his twenty years in Congress. John Ford, one of the state's longest-tenured senators, sponsored numerous progressive measures. In 2005, his last year in public office, he sponsored a bill that would have paid overtime to executive, administrative, outside sales, computer, and professional employees; a bill that prevented employers from extracting money from employees when they cashed their payroll checks; and a workers protection bill for employees at temporary employment agencies.[153]

Yet the Fords' progressivism has been overshadowed by legal problems related to their alleged involvement in unethical activities and political bribery. Both lawmakers have been charged with abusing their powers, and their departures from public office were expedited by scandals. Harold Ford Sr. left office in 1995, and John Ford departed in 2005.

Since the 1990s the most prominent figure in the Ford family has been Harold Ford Jr., who took over his father's congressional seat when he was twenty-six and fresh out of law school. After entering Congress, Ford Jr. distinguished himself as more conservative than his father and uncle. He fashioned himself as a "new" black politician who was not beholden to the policy agenda of the civil rights movement and traditional black leaders; he thus had greater appeal to moderate and conservative whites. During his congressional tenure, he was a member of the Blue Dog Coalition, a group of centrist and conservative lawmakers. He was also a prominent figure in the Democratic Leadership Council, a coalition of centrist Democrats who criticized the Democratic Party's attachment to social welfare policies.[154]

Some of the controversial measures supported by Ford invited criticisms from progressive activists, such as his endorsement of military action against Iraqi dictator Saddam Hussein. He offered early support for a variation of President George W. Bush's Social Security privatization plan but backed away from this position after Democrats and senior citizens organizations expressed opposition to it. In 2002, he challenged Nancy Pelosi for the highest-ranking position among Democrats in the House of Representatives, but only after most members of the Congressional Black Caucus had already endorsed her for the position. He was soundly defeated by almost 150 votes.[155] Despite his ideological predispositions, his policy positions on social and racial policies were more liberal than those of most conservative lawmakers.

In 2000, Ford was a keynote speaker at the Democratic National Convention, and in 2004 he was the national chair of John Kerry's presidential campaign. In 2006, he campaigned for the U.S. Senate, running against Republican Bob Corker in the general election. Despite his underdog status, Ford lost the race by only fifty thousand votes. Had he won, he would have been the first black senator to represent the South since Reconstruction.

CONCLUSION

In this chapter, we put Tennessee's story of racial polarization into historical context. We examined the implications of such polarization to our understanding of Tennessee politics. And we paid particular attention to the dynamics of race, class, and geography and how these factors contribute to electoral and partisan divisions in the state. We have highlighted the many ways in which polarization impedes racial progress and black interests. Rather than presuming that recent changes in the state's racial politics took place in a vacuum, this historical account is a reminder that the changes in the 2000s exposed the racial polarization that has existed in the state for many decades.

While we have examined black politics from the Reconstruction era to the twenty-first century, it is important to remember that African Americans have been actively involved in shaping the state's political landscape since the Civil War ended. This is so even though the racial hierarchy in Tennessee politics has contributed to long-standing political polarization. Black leaders and racial justice coalitions have taken advantage of small and large political opportunities to maximize their power and influence. They have drawn on many strategies and tactics, including protests, lobbying, and institutional politics, to advance their claims, and they have contributed to the broader democratization of the state. Their movement activism and leveraging strategies have expanded the boundaries of inclusion and democratic participation in Tennessee.

We have also acknowledged that, despite a long history of racial repression in the state, some black activists took a more aggressive stance in their fight for black rights.[156] This is highlighted in the anti-lynching activities of Samuel McElwee and Ida B. Wells-Barnett, the Nashville boycott of 1905, and Robert Church's political organizing in the first half of the twentieth century. The civil rights campaigns in the 1950s and 1960s and the lobbying activities surrounding the 1964 Civil Rights Act and the 1964 Fair Practices Code also exemplify black political agency in Tennessee. Moreover, members of large-scale organizations like the Tennessee Voters' Council worked tirelessly to create an infrastructure through which black interests could be articulated by voters and heeded by politicians. By exploring the institutionalization of black politics in Tennessee and the growth in the numbers of black elected officials from the 1970s to the 2000s, we gain an appreciation for the strategies black leaders developed to address racial polarization.

In the next chapter we give attention to electoral realignment and racially polarized voting in Tennessee from 2000 to 2012. During these years, Tennessee shifted from a centrist state that was typically led by conservative Democrats or by traditional/pragmatic Republicans to a state that has fundamentally shifted to the right. In 1992 and 1996, Tennessee voted for Bill Clinton in the presidential elections. However, Republicans now have a supermajority in the state legislature, and most Tennessee voters supported the Republican candidate in the presidential elections of 2000, 2004, 2008, and 2012. We seek to explain this electoral and partisan realignment by focusing specifically on how the combination of racially polarized voting, geographic distribution, and class-based politics produced a majority of Republican voters in Tennessee.

PART TWO
REALIGNMENT OF PARTISAN POLITICS IN TENNESSEE

CHAPTER THREE

RACE, ELECTORAL REALIGNMENT, AND POLARIZATION

> When our voters go into the booth, we want them to start at the top and stay in the column as they go down. If they don't like the people at the top, that's not going to happen.... In this area, they are not going to elect an African-American to be president of the United States. It's just the way people have been brought up.
>
> —DON FARMER, MEMBER OF THE EXECUTIVE COMMITTEE, TENNESSEE DEMOCRATIC PARTY (2008)

When the polls closed on November 7, 2012, few observers of Tennessee politics were surprised that the state had voted overwhelmingly for Republican Party presidential nominee Mitt Romney. Republicans had been gaining ground in the state since 2000 when native son and Democrat Al Gore Jr. lost Tennessee by more than eighty thousand votes to George W. Bush. Gore's defeat in Tennessee, perhaps even more than the heavily contested and controversial outcome in Florida, cost his party the presidential election.

The Republican Party's growing strength in Tennessee was evident during the first years of the twenty-first century. The Democratic Party lost considerable ground in the 2004, 2008, and 2012 presidential contests despite Tennessee's previous status as a swing state. For example, Barack Obama won only four out of ninety-five counties in 2012 and five in the 2008 presidential election. This was in stark contrast to the eighteen counties that voted for John Kerry in 2004 and the thirty-five won by Gore in 2000. Obama in the 2012 election garnered fewer votes in Tennessee than in Mississippi, Texas, Louisiana, Georgia, North and South Carolina, Florida, or Virginia—all states that were historically considered to be more racially conservative than Tennessee. Some longtime activists,

65

such as the Democratic Party official Don Farmer (quoted in the epigraph), believed that the racial animus toward Obama's candidacy even spilled over into state and local elections.

In addition, the Republican Party captured control of the Tennessee General Assembly in 2010 for the first time since Reconstruction. Two years later, Republicans gained a supermajority in both chambers of the Tennessee legislature for the first time since the nineteenth century. Yet unlike the Reconstruction era, when twelve black Republicans were elected to the legislature, the state's modern-day party is undeniably conservative and overwhelmingly white.

In this chapter we examine partisan realignment in the twenty-first century, which is a key factor shaping polarization (or embedded divisions) in Tennessee politics. Partisan realignment in Tennessee has created a surplus of voters, who have been critical to the Republican Party's resurgence. We use the term "surplus politics" to describe what happens when a political party has an unending supply of constituents as well as structural advantages to building a winning political coalition. Surplus politics allows this coalition to extend its influence across multiple election cycles.

In examining partisan realignment, we focus specifically on how the politics of race and the status of African Americans have affected electoral politics in Tennessee. Yet racial animus by itself does not adequately explain partisan realignment in the state, even though black and white voting behavior is more sharply polarized than a decade ago. For example, racially polarized politics are also shaped by overlapping phenomena, such as geography and the decomposition of the Democratic Party.

We use a combination of approaches (ecological inference analysis, network analysis, and multiple regression quadratic assignment procedures) to investigate partisan realignment in Tennessee. We look at voting patterns along with other sociodemographic and political factors, dating back to the 1996 presidential election and continuing to the 2012 general election. The first part of this chapter is a brief overview of partisan realignment, polarization, and surplus politics. This is followed by a discussion of our research design, data, and findings. We conclude the chapter by relating our results back to our theory of racial polarization in Tennessee.

PARTISAN REALIGNMENT IN THE SOUTH

For much of the latter half of the twentieth century, southern politics were largely interpreted through two frameworks. V. O. Key Jr.'s seminal work *Southern Politics* underscored the significance of racial divisions in the South. He maintained that white resistance to political and racial reform was the most stubborn in jurisdictions where high concentrations of blacks appeared to threaten white political power.[1] These jurisdictions were plagued by troubling patterns of racial hostility, presumably because whites feared that civil rights reform would create a surplus of black voters, who would undermine the southern political order. The transformation of the U.S. South from a region dominated by a pro-segregation Democratic Party to one dominated by a racially conservative Republican Party is often explained by the politics of race.

However, racial segregation and its appendages (racial polarization, racial resentment, racial conservatism) are not the only phenomena that contributed to partisan realignment. Some critics have contended that race is not the principal explanation for why southern whites shifted from being Democrats to being Republicans. They believe class divisions and the political ascent of affluent whites inside the Republican Party have also fueled realignment politics.[2] As we discussed in the first chapter, Shafer and Johnston claimed that most enthusiasts of Key's work have misinterpreted his central arguments, which were that racial segregation *and* economic underdevelopment defined the character of southern society. The erosion of both the segregationist racial order *and* the plantation economy laid the groundwork for undermining Democratic Party rule in the South. The authors further contended that class is a major reason that the South has realigned itself into the Republican Party.[3] The economic development that emerged out of the post-agricultural economy in the South expanded the middle class and created a surplus of middle-class and affluent constituents who voted for Republican Party candidates due to class-based grievances.

Despite the utility of these arguments, the race-class dichotomy is problematic for several reasons. First, there were jurisdictional differences across the South and even within the same state. Even during the Jim Crow era, southern jurisdictions were shaped by their own unique histories of racial segregation.[4] Some states and localities actually produced cross-racial alliances between white moderates and black voters.[5] Because blacks migrated to Nashville and Memphis, two cities controlled by political machines, during the first half of the twentieth century, they had more voting power than rural blacks in Tennessee and blacks from other parts of the South did.[6] Although these machines placed some restrictions on black voting rights, they attempted to politically absorb rural blacks migrating to the cities.

The urban political machines in Memphis (Shelby County) in West Tennessee, Nashville (Davidson County) in Middle Tennessee, and to a lesser extent, Chattanooga (Hamilton County) in the southeastern part of the state, allowed racial moderates in Tennessee to build political coalitions. For example, Tennessee senators Albert Gore Sr. and Estes Kefauver cultivated cross-racial coalitions and advocated for New Deal–style redistributive policies.[7] On the other hand, rural counties adjacent to Shelby County that had large numbers of prospective black voters experienced limited or no voting rights. These counties were controlled by landowner elites who were threatened by civil rights activists. Consequently, within the same region, adjacent counties experienced uneven and complex patterns of racial exclusion.

Another challenge with the race-class dichotomy, especially regarding class, is that socioeconomic status can be an ambiguous category. Rodney Hero expressed reservations about the "socioeconomic school of state politics."[8] Evaluating the impact of socioeconomic class can often produce contradictory results in which educated and higher-income constituents may disagree among themselves on some policy prescriptions. He found that racial diversity has greater significance in predicting support for social policies than socioeconomic status does.

It is also worth mentioning that partisan realignment has occurred in both poor and affluent predominantly white counties in Tennessee. It has occurred in counties that experienced economic growth and in those with rising unemployment due to industry closures. By some accounts, Williamson County, which is adjacent to Nashville, is one of the most conservative and wealthiest counties in the country.[9] Tennessee's five poorest counties (Perry, Hancock, Scott, Marshall, and Lauderdale) in 2009 and 2010 were rural jurisdictions that experienced Depression-level unemployment.[10] Yet these counties voted for the Republican Party presidential candidate during the 2000–2012 election cycles.[11] For example, Perry County had one of the highest unemployment rates in the country in 2009 due to industry closures.[12] It was traditionally a Democratic-leaning county, but the share of the Democratic Party's vote decreased by more than 15 percent from 2000 to 2012.

POLARIZATION AND SURPLUS POLITICS

In surplus politics, the surplus of constituents is so bountiful that a winning coalition can cement its influence across election cycles. Surplus politics shape the internal deliberations of the governing coalition as well as relations between the governing and opposition parties. They lead to an ideological shift in the winning coalition: for example, surplus politics can move the Democratic Party to the left in jurisdictions dominated by Democrats and to the right in locales dominated by Republicans. They can also discourage the opposition party that is losing support from extending the requisite resources in swing electoral districts.

We add to the discussion of realignment politics by emphasizing several overlapping factors that explain the partisan shift in Tennessee. Not surprisingly, this shift is related to the politics of race and the departure of whites from the Democratic Party. As Badger states, the "Southern Republican Party is a crucial element in the racial polarization of Southern politics. It is almost exclusively a white party: its voter registration drives are conducted in white communities only. Its agenda is racially defined."[13] Many southern whites left the Democratic Party after the passage of the Voting Rights Act. However, Tennessee's partisan shift, especially what appears to be the long-term departure of whites, is a more recent phenomenon of the post-1980s. It reflects structural impediments in the state's body politic that may disadvantage African Americans and the Democratic Party.

Even before the debates over *Baker v. Carr*, which altered the makeup of Tennessee's state legislature in the 1960s, geography has been central to party politics in Tennessee.[14] Currently, most of Tennessee's counties are rural or small (under one hundred thousand residents) and overwhelmingly white, with black majorities only existing in two of the ninety-five counties. It is in the rural counties, many of which were once solidly Democratic, where Republicans have gained a surplus of voters.

In the decade following the Voting Rights Act, geographic uniformity helped white Democrats win elections and build biracial coalitions. White candidates ran what Glaser referred to as "segregated campaigns": one version was designed to specifically appeal to whites, and another was used for black jurisdictions.[15] These campaigns were similar to the situationally deracialized strategies utilized by black candidates, in which they make different appeals to segregated black and white audiences.[16] Yet segregated campaigns are increasingly difficult to operate with the aging out of older white and black Democrats and with the emergence of social media, which scrutinizes white Democrats who seek to run segregated campaigns.

Finally, we consider the long-term consequences of party fragmentation and the diminishing influence of the Democratic Party. Perhaps even more important was the reinvigoration of the Republicans' state parties from dormant to competitive organizations in the 1970s. The state GOPs in the South became aggressively activist after the passage of the Voting Rights Act and took advantage of the vacuum left by decaying state and local Democratic parties, some of which fractured after black voters flooded into the party.[17]

The democratizing impact of the civil rights movement altered the southern political order. It reduced institutional barriers to political participation that not only had prohibited blacks from voting but also were injurious to poor white voters. The civil rights movement also undermined the segregationist one-party system in the South, thus inviting a healthy two-party competition. According to Lublin, with the erosion of the one-party system, Republicans were then able to build a political apparatus that could mobilize a surplus of new voters and exploit the racial fragmentation in the Democratic Party.[18]

The Democratic Party gave little attention to a changing electorate and became increasingly fragmented after the 1970s. A. J. Starling, a seasoned lobbyist and labor union activist who also served as a senior campaign advisor to Harold Ford Jr.'s 2006 senatorial campaign, claimed that the Democratic Party failed to adjust to changing demographic trends in Tennessee:

> I think what happened [is] the Democrats didn't pay attention to changing attitudes. Our workforce got a little younger. We didn't adapt to that as well in presenting change. We didn't change as change was happen[ing]. I think that if you take a look at Republicans where they are as far as average age in the legislature, they are much younger than the Democrats. They have done a decent job in adding women. They have done a horrible job in adding minorities... but the Democratic Party didn't pay attention to change.[19]

The last successful statewide Democrat in Tennessee was Phil Bredesen, who after losing a competitive gubernatorial race in 1994 was elected in 2002 and reelected four years later. Yet Bredesen's governance coincided with the resurgence of the Republican Party in the state legislature, as referenced by Starling. As seen in table 3.1, Republicans in Tennessee's House of Representatives had a net gain of twenty-seven seats between his 2002 election and the last year of his administration. The Republicans who won seats in 2008 and 2010 came from counties whose average white voting-age populations exceeded 90 percent.

In addition, the percentage of Tennesseans registered with the Republican Party outpaced the percentage of those aligned with the Democrats. Figures 3.1 and 3.2 show the ten best- and worst-performing counties as measured by the declining percentage of registered voters. In the counties that experienced the worst average rate of change in registered voters, the Democratic Party vote in four presidential election cycles was 41.5 percent, with the average percentage of registered voters decreasing by 6.7 percent. Moreover, Democrats underperformed in the counties that experienced the highest rates of increase of registered voters (increasing by an average of 16.9 percent). They only garnered 36.5 percent of the vote in those counties during presidential elections. The results show that the Republicans won the counties that had the highest increases of registered Democratic Party voters.

In the remainder of this chapter we examine partisan realignment while accounting for race, geography, and electoral fragmentation. These factors have

TABLE 3.1 Party turnover in elections for the Tennessee House of Representatives

	2002	2004	2006	2008	2010	Total
Seats turnover	11	1	0	6	14	32
Democratic Party gain	4	0	0	1	0	5
Republican Party gain	7	1	0	5	14	27

Note: The results were calculated using ecological inference analysis.

FIGURE 3.1 Democratic presidential vote for ten counties with the worst voter registration rates

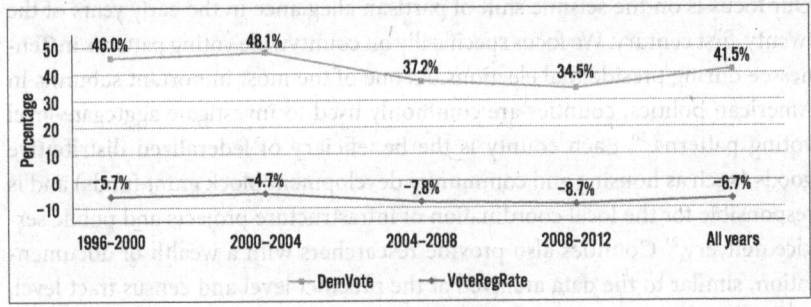

Sources: Tennessee Secretary of State, Division of Elections, https://sos.tn.gov/products/elections/election-statistics and https://sos.tn.gov/products/elections/election-results.
Note: Percentages represent the mean scores for Democratic Party vote and rate of change for voter registration.

FIGURE 3.2 Democratic presidential vote for ten counties with the best voter registration rates

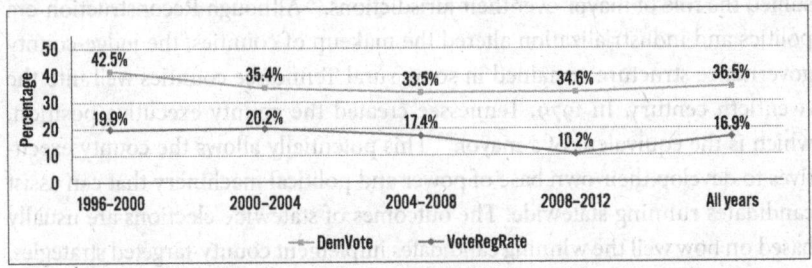

Source: Tennessee Secretary of State, Division of Elections, https://sos.tn.gov/products/elections/election-statistics and https://sos.tn.gov/products/elections/election-results.
Note: Percentages represent the mean scores for Democratic Party vote and rate of change for voter registration.

contributed to the trend of polarization that defines state politics in Tennessee. For example, we consider that there is a close relationship between party turnover and race. We further expect geographically uniform counties to express the most resistance to Democratic Party candidates. Finally, we suggest that electoral fragmentation has eroded the Democratic Party in the state.

METHODS

Our focus is on the seismic shift of partisan allegiance in the early years of the twenty-first century. We focus specifically on countywide voting patterns in Tennessee during presidential elections. As one of the most important subunits in American politics, counties are commonly used to investigate aggregate-level voting patterns.[20] Each county is the beneficiary of federalized distributive goods (such as housing and community development block grant funds) and is responsible for the local coordination of infrastructure projects and public service delivery.[21] Counties also provide researchers with a wealth of documentation, similar to the data archived at the precinct level and census tract level, while allowing for cross-jurisdictional comparisons between racially heterogeneous and homogeneous areas.

For the greater part of the nineteenth century, county governments played a special role in Tennessee politics. With legislative meetings occurring quarterly, the governance of the state was significantly shaped by county judges, who assumed the role of mayor over their jurisdictions.[22] Although Reconstruction-era politics and industrialization altered the makeup of counties, the judge-county governance structure remained in some rural Tennessee counties well into the twentieth century. In 1979, Tennessee created the county executive position, which is the equivalent of a mayor.[23] This potentially allows the county executives to develop their own base of power and political machinery that can assist candidates running statewide. The outcomes of statewide elections are usually based on how well the winning candidates implement county-targeted strategies.

We analyze general election results at the county level for the 2000, 2004, 2008, and 2012 presidential elections. Ecological inference (EI) analysis is used to estimate county-level black and white voting patterns.[24] The results from the EI analysis allow us to compute a race differential measure (conceived here as the difference between the Democratic vote choice of blacks and whites) by county. We then use dynamic network analysis (DNA), an expansive social network, as a second-stage process for assessing party realignment. We created four county-based networks that measured voting patterns for Al Gore Jr. in 2000, John Kerry in 2004, and Barack Obama in 2008 and 2012. These networks allow us to identify similarly situated counties in terms of vote choice.

We also incorporate a multiple regression quadratic assignment procedure (MRQAP) in our assessments of county-level voting patterns. MRQAP is a statistical procedure that measures the relationship between two interdependent variables (dyads) and is the preferred method for network analyses that suffer from autocorrelation—for example, when the relationships between members of a network influence the actions of those within the network.[25] The dependent variables are the networks of counties that favored the Democratic Party candidate in a presidential cycle. Rather than measuring partisanship using the national popular vote, we use a threshold measure based on the twelve-year average of Democratic Party votes in a county. (A detailed description of this threshold measure is in appendix 3.1.) For each presidential year, a county was assigned a threshold score ranging from 1 to 3. Counties voting below the threshold were assigned a score of 1; counties received a score of 2 if they were swing or toss-up counties; and counties were given a score of 3 if they voted at a higher rate than the twelve-year average.

For the purposes of this book, a unique data set (the County Vote Choice Profile) was created for the state's ninety-five counties that includes a host of independent variables or what network analyses refer to as "attributes." For example, a race differential score was derived from the EI analysis to measure racially polarized voting patterns. Another variable, the percentage of the white population, also measures race and geographic uniformity at the county level. Geographic uniformity is further evaluated by rural density, the presence of many military veterans, and decade-long population growth.

Table 3.2 summarizes the sociodemographic profile of the ninety-five counties and reports the average racial difference score for each county. Although there are counties with large black populations in Tennessee, no county has more than a 55 percent black voting-age population. In fact, no county has a white population lower than 40 percent, and only nineteen of the ninety-five counties have black populations over 10 percent. The county-level racial differential score between blacks and whites was 19.1 percent in the 2000 election cycle, yet by 2012, racially polarized voting grew to 46 percent.

The unemployment rate during the year of a presidential election, specifically if the unemployment rate for a county was higher than the national average, is one of the socioeconomic variables. We also include an economic development measure that identifies the average number of business openings and closures from 2005 to 2010. (This variable is only applicable to the 2008 and 2012 election cycles. See also table 3.3.)

Earlier in the book, we argued that Tennessee's Democratic Party became more fragmented from 2000 to 2012. As the Republican Party has captured homogeneous white jurisdictions, some of which were once one-party Democratic

TABLE 3.2 Select characteristics and network measures of Tennessee counties

Black-white vote differences (ecological inference analyses)	Mean (%)	Standard error
2000	19.1	1.0
2004	28.6	1.4
2008	38.9	0.63
2012	46.0	0.62
AVERAGE (2000–2012)	33.2	0.81
White population per county (2000)	90.4	1.1
White population per county (2010)	89.1	1.2
Black population per county (2000)	7.3	1.1
Black population per county (2010)	7.2	1.1
Democratic Party vote (president)		
2000	47.4	0.94
2004	41.2	0.85
2008	35.2	0.83
2012	31.2	0.86
AVERAGE (12 years)	40.0	0.82
Bill Clinton vote (1996)	48.9	0.01
Phil Bredesen vote (2002)	51.4	0.01
Harold Ford Jr. vote (2006)	46.7	0.88
Rural (2000)	68.8	0.03
Rural (2010)	66.5	2.8
Industry closures/start-ups per county	−2.5	0.87
Unemployment	7.3	9.5

Sources: U.S. Census, 2010 Census Summary File 2, https://www.census.gov/prod/cen2010/doc/sf2.pdf; Tennessee Secretary of State, Division of Elections, https://sos.tn.gov/products/elections/election-results; Tennessee Department of Labor and Workforce Development, Employment Security Division, Labor Market Information, https://www.jobs4tn.gov/vosnet/Default.aspx.

counties, the Tennessee Democratic Party has become less cohesive, especially outside the central cities. Assessing electoral fragmentation is difficult without engaging in on-the-ground data collection on a county-by-county basis. As a proxy for fragmentation and cohesion, we networked the association between party turnover in the Tennessee General Assembly and the drop-off in Democratic Party votes in a county. We identified counties that contained a legislative district where the incumbent party was defeated. The greatest partisan turnover occurred from 2002 to 2010, a period that saw twenty-seven jurisdictions change from Democratic to Republican.

In addition, the coattails effect may influence electoral realignment. There were only three competitive elections involving Democratic Party candidates between 1996 and 2012. President Bill Clinton followed his 1992 victory in Tennessee by winning more than 48 percent of the state's popular vote in 1996. Democrat Phil Bredesen defeated Republican Van Hilleary by a 52–48 percent margin in 2002. And senatorial candidate Harold Ford Jr., despite losing the 2006 campaign, surpassed expectations with a 48–51 percent margin, almost becoming Tennessee's first black senator.

The coattails variable assesses whether these high-profile campaigns positively improved the Democratic Party's chances of winning in the next election cycle. The presidential candidates are thus grouped with their predecessor candidates to determine if they shared similar voting profiles: Bill Clinton's 1996 election and Al Gore's 2000 campaign; Phil Bredesen's 2002 gubernatorial election and John Kerry's 2004 presidential campaign; and Harold Ford Jr.'s 2006 run and Barack Obama's 2008 election. If the coattail effect improves the successor candidate's chances of winning, then we consider this an indication of party strength. However, short coattails may provide evidence of party fragmentation.

FINDINGS AND DISCUSSION

Partisan realignment in Tennessee has been influenced by persistent patterns of racial polarization, geographic uniformity, and party fragmentation. Table 3.3 displays the network fragmentation measures that evaluate the cohesiveness of the Democratic Party vote networks. The results show that fragmentation among Democrats is particularly high. In all election cycles, Democrats experienced high levels of fragmentation (greater than .90 = 90 percent), indicating discontinuity among counties or voters backing the Democratic Party.

The clustering coefficient measures in table 3.3 offer further insights about the viability of the networks or geographic coalitions developed by the Democratic Party presidential campaigns in Tennessee. Higher scores for the clustering coefficient measures denote diffusion throughout the network of ninety-five counties.[26] They indicate that the campaigns were decentralized or influenced voters in various counties across the state. Although all coefficient measures are low, the Kerry campaign had a higher score than the Obama campaign and even the Gore campaign. This indicates that Kerry supporters were geographically diffuse and that Kerry made a more concerted effort to build relations in various counties throughout the state. It may also indicate that Gore took Tennessee for granted and assumed that his native son status would carry him to victory. Consequently, he may have spent less time and resources in developing a winning coalition in counties throughout the state.

Additional evidence underscoring the problems facing Democrats is revealed in the MRQAP analysis. Declining support for the Democratic Party candidate is associated with every variable in the analysis. Predominantly white counties were less likely to vote for the Democratic Party candidate as were counties with high racial difference scores. These trends preceded the Obama presidency and

TABLE 3.3 Network-level and MRQAP measures of vote choice

Network-level measures	Gore 2000	Kerry 2004	Obama 2008	Obama 2012
Network fragmentation	.97	.96	.94	.90
Clustering coefficients	.17	.46	.14	.14
MRQAP constant	.09***	.15***	.02***	.02***
Racial difference	−.09	−.15	−.02	−.02
	(−.003)***	(−.002)***	(−.002)*	(−.002)**
White population	−.09	−.15	−.02	−.02
	(−.003)***	(−.002)***	(−.002)**	(−.002)***
Rural jurisdiction	−.09	−.15	−.02	−.02
	(−.003)***	(−.004)***	(−.002)**	(−.002)***
Legislative turnover	−.07	−.12	−.01	−.01
	(−.002)	(−.01)	(−.002)	(−.002)**
Bill Clinton (1996)	−.09	—	—	—
	(−.003)***			
Phil Bredesen (2002)	—	−.15	—	—
		(−.001)***		
Harold Ford Jr. (2006)	—	—	−.02	—
			(−.002)**	
Veterans	−.09	−.15	−.02	−.02
	(−.003)	(−.01)***	(−.002)**	(−.002)***
Unemployment	−.07	−.12	−.01	−.01
	(−.002)*	(−.01)*	(−.002)	(−.002)**
Industry growth/loss (2005–2010)	—	—	−.02	−.02
			(−.002)*	(−.002)***
Population growth (10-year period)	—	—	—	−.02
				(−.002)**
R^2	7.3	.001	.0002	3.6

Notes: * = $p < 0.05$; ** = $p < 0.01$; *** = $p < 0.0001$. The ORA software was used to obtain the network fragmentation, clustering coefficient measures, and MRQAP results.

confirm the general perception that race is still a defining variable in southern politics.

Although the average racial difference scores per county increased in each election cycle, they only had a slight impact ($p < .10$) on vote choice in the 2008 election. In other words, racially polarized voting was more detrimental to the Democratic Party's outcomes in 2000, 2004, and 2012 than in 2008. This can probably be attributed to the initial optimism surrounding the Obama presidency. Nunnally pointed out that the 2008 election "likely renewed faith in the ability of blacks' sociopolitical mobility."[27] Yet shortly after arriving in office, the "glimmer of hope" for a racially tolerant society disappeared as Obama was forced to weather attacks from the Tea Party and other racial conservatives. This explains why the racial difference score increased to 46 percent in the 2012 election.

Counties with large veteran populations expressed less support for John Kerry and Barack Obama. Also, high unemployment and job losses due to business closures disadvantaged Democratic Party candidates. The rate of business closures (an average of 2.5 percent of the businesses per county collapsed by the first decade of the twenty-first century) was fueled by the economic recession of 2008–2009, yet Democrats were unable to convince Tennessee voters that they offered a better alternative to the Republican Party. However, unemployment trends produced uneven patterns in the four election cycles. High-unemployment counties were slightly associated with declining support for Democrats in the 2000 and 2004 election cycles,[28] but job loss had no significant impact on vote choice during the 2008 election. This was an indication that voters were unwilling to blame Obama for the economic crisis even if they chose not to support his presidency. On the other hand, by 2012 counties with high unemployment rates were more likely to vote against Obama.

Earlier in the chapter, we claimed that geographically uniform counties that were solidly Democratic for decades have shifted to the Republican Party. Geographic uniformity is understood as predominantly white, rural counties that do not have the social diversity of cities. We found some support for this argument as Democrats were routinely defeated in these counties during presidential elections.

We also expected party fragmentation to be more problematic for Democrats than Republicans. The network fragmentation measure described above provided an initial look at party fragmentation and indicated that Democrats were largely disconnected from each other. More problematic is that the state Democratic Party has a diffusion challenge—the challenge of extending its agenda beyond a few jurisdictions—that makes it difficult to win statewide elections. This dynamic worsened during Obama's first term as evidenced by the impact of partisan shifts in legislative races on declining support for him during the 2012 campaign.

We found no evidence that the coattails of successful Democratic Party candidates mitigated the Republican Party's resurgence. This may be a consequence of how these candidates were utilized in the successor elections. Gore rejected overtures from Clinton throughout most of the 2000 election. His campaign believed that Clinton's indiscretions, including the Monica Lewinsky scandal, would reduce support from cultural conservatives.[29] Ford's run was harmed by Republican-backed, racially charged campaign appeals, and he moved out of the state shortly after the 2006 election.[30] Bredesen, a center-right Democrat, also distanced himself from party-building activities and often advanced policy prescriptions opposed by the Democratic Party base. His rollback of workers compensation and the state's Medicaid program angered prominent health-care advocates and labor leaders.[31]

CONCLUSION

We set out to explain electoral and partisan realignment in Tennessee and how it affected racial polarization in the state. Tennessee has historically been shaped by a center-right, bipartisan pragmatism that masked party identification. For the greater part of the twentieth century, a coalition of moderate and conservative Democrats and traditional Republicans anchored the governing coalition in state politics. From 1971 to 2011, there were six governors (three Democrats and three Republicans).

Although Tennessee is a conservative state where slavery and Jim Crow have had an overwhelming influence on its political and economic development, it also has been historically governed by consensus builders or pragmatists instead of ideologues.[32] But the state has shifted considerably to the right, and Democrats lost control of both chambers in the state legislature. The 2012 election gave the Republican Party supermajority control of the General Assembly for the first time since the nineteenth century. That election and Republican Party victories in 2008 and 2010 have meant the loss of black political power in the state legislature.

We identified several factors that contributed to partisan realignment. Race remains a permanent feature of Tennessee politics. It appears that racial divisions worsened over the period of this study. This can be attributed to the responses by state lawmakers to Obama's presidency, the rise of the Tea Party in Tennessee, and the defection of whites from the Democratic Party. Further, race overlaps with other factors that have given the Republican Party a surplus of prospective voters. Geographic uniformity and the fact that Republicans have won victories in rural and overwhelmingly white jurisdictions, many of which were former Democratic Party strongholds, have also fueled partisan realignment. Taken together, racial polarization, geographic uniformity, and electoral fragmentation have shaped realignment politics in Tennessee. This realignment has forced the Democratic Party to reassess its electoral strategies in statewide races and its party machinery on a county-by-county basis.

Conventional wisdom suggests that electoral realignment was an outgrowth of an anti-Obama wave in the South and racial resentment among white voters. Without a doubt, Obama's presence on the national ticket made it more difficult for state and local Democratic candidates in Tennessee. As indicated in the epigraph by longtime Democratic Party activist Don Farmer, some Tennesseans were unwilling to vote for down-ticket candidates in 2008 (and probably in 2012) because of their opposition to Obama.

Still, our findings suggest that realignment preceded the Obama campaigns.

Democrats unexpectedly lost Tennessee in 2000 despite having a native son, Albert Gore Jr., as their candidate. The 2004 election may offer the best insight for assessing realignment politics—and may have been the last hope for Democratic Party control of the state. The Kerry campaign made a concerted effort to spread its wings across the state, perhaps more so than the Gore campaign, which may have taken Tennessee voters for granted. Accordingly, the Bush-Kerry contest is an important signpost for assessing whether the Democrats can regain their influence in presidential elections and probably in state politics.

In the next chapter we look more closely at how realignment affected racial politics in the state legislature. We investigate how polarization adversely affected black lawmakers in the Tennessee General Assembly during the early twenty-first century. Polarization also complicated bipartisan coalitions and biracial alliances in the state legislature and made it difficult for black lawmakers to successfully advance racially egalitarian policies.

APPENDIX 3.1

METHODOLOGY FOR MEASURING COUNTYWIDE VOTING PATTERNS

The four networks assess countywide voting patterns or the likelihood that a county will vote for the Democratic candidate. Our threshold for vote choice is not whether the county surpassed the percentage of the national popular vote by the candidate. This is because the percentage of the national popular vote can distort support for or opposition to a candidate, especially in non-battleground states that lack the resources and competition afforded to battleground states. Instead, we created a threshold measure that assesses whether a county surpassed the average Democratic Party vote for the county in the four election cycles. For example, Democrats won 47.1 percent of the Anderson County vote in 2000. They won 40.7, 36.1, and 34.1 percent in 2004, 2008, and 2012, respectively. The four-election average is 39.5 percent, which became the baseline threshold for determining whether Anderson County voted Democratic in each election cycle.

If a county surpassed the baseline threshold, it was interpreted as leaning Democratic and allocated a score of 3. Counties that were toss-up jurisdictions, meaning they came within 1.5 percent of surpassing the baseline threshold, were given a ranking of 2. Counties were given a score of 1 if they failed to surpass the average Democratic vote for the county during the twelve-year period. Generally, most counties that received a score of 1 were undergoing a realignment process or were solidly Republican. Once a baseline threshold was established, the counties were matched with similarly situated counties during the election cycle.

CHAPTER FOUR

THE LEGISLATIVE BEHAVIOR OF TENNESSEE'S BLACK LAWMAKERS

It seems to me that the bills that are passed are against the people who need it most, against the children who need it most.

—REPRESENTATIVE BARBARA COOPER (2012)

After receiving numerous complaints from child advocates in the late 1990s, Representative Tommie Brown, a well-respected legislator from Chattanooga, pressured the Tennessee comptroller of the treasury to investigate alleged abuses in the state's child welfare system. This response led to the landmark *Brian A. v. Sundquist* consent decree overseeing the Tennessee Department of Children's Services.[1] In 2002, Republican governor Donald Sundquist proposed a state income tax that was thwarted by grassroots conservative activists and lawmakers in his own party. Although his initial plan failed, members of the Tennessee Black Caucus of State Legislators (TBCSL) introduced several amendments that would have created a more favorable tax code for lower-income Tennesseans. A year later, the TBCSL sent a letter to the U.S. Food and Drug Administration urging it to collect racial/ethnic data evaluating how different groups responded to pharmaceutical products in clinical trials.[2] This position mirrored two resolutions authored by African American legislators from Memphis, Representative Kathryn Bowers and Senator Roscoe Dixon, which were ratified at the annual legislative conference of the National Black Caucus of State Legislators (NBCSL) in December 2002.[3]

The TBCSL was formed in 1975—four years after the founding of the Congressional Black Caucus—with assistance from the Tennessee General Assembly's Office of Minority Affairs.[4] Though black caucus members are involved in the routine operations of legislative decision-making, they are equally involved in their home districts via advocacy initiatives and constituent services. These initiatives overlap with the TBCSL's endogenous and intralegislative responsibilities and policy agendas.

The TBCSL has a long-standing commitment to racially egalitarian and poverty-mitigation policies. Many proposals by black lawmakers attempt to ameliorate inequities not only for black people, but for all poor Tennesseans, including whites, in economically distressed communities. Yet the partisan realignment of 2009–2012 diminished the influence of African American lawmakers. Representative Barbara Cooper (D-Memphis) lamented the adverse outcome of shifting partisan alliances, as seen in the epigraph of this chapter. She believed both black and poor white residents were harmed by the policies of the new Republican Party majority.

In examining the TBCSL's legislative agenda, we focus mostly on the sponsorship networks of the members; how these networks anchored the black caucus's agenda and helped the group build alliances with white (and even Republican) lawmakers; and how this agenda was informed by the TBCSL's linkages with extralegislative advocacy initiatives. Our analysis of sponsorship networks offers insight into the boundaries of black legislative politics and how lawmakers attempt to implement legislation in a highly polarized political environment. Legislative bodies are what Mary Hawkesworth called the "racially institutionalized environments" that often mitigate attempts to implement equitable policies.[5] Legislatures are naturally interactive institutions.[6] Therefore, because a legislator's ability to create laws successfully, engage in representation and oversight, and serve the needs of constituents all depend on the strength of that legislator's professional relationships, studying sponsorship networks can help us to explain how black lawmakers navigate the difficult boundaries and racial politics of the legislature.

James Fowler's study of Congress offered the most comprehensive analysis of how sponsorship networks influence legislative behavior. He highlighted two factors that shape these networks: personal connections and friendships between lawmakers, and ideological or policy-based agreements between lawmakers.[7] In this chapter, we examine the sponsorship networks in the Tennessee General Assembly and among TBCSL members. Specifically, we expand on Fowler's approach and examine how the development of sponsorship networks in the state legislature is contingent on political and sociodemographic variables that both positively and adversely influence legislative decision-making among the black caucus.

In the first part of this chapter we offer a theoretical overview of sponsorship networks by merging the insights of a political bounds approach with our theory of racial polarization. We then provide an overview of the rise of black legislative influence in Tennessee since 1965 and the TBCSL's emergence in 1975. Finally, we look closely at the legislative networks and subnetworks from 2003 to 2012 by relying on network-modeling statistical measures.

POLITICAL BOUNDS AND SPONSORSHIP NETWORKS

Throughout this chapter, we advance an argument called the political bounds thesis. The term "bound" here has a double meaning: not only is it the past tense of the verb "to bind," but it is also used to describe the act of surrounding a territory or geographic area. Because of the growing racial polarization in the state of Tennessee, we argue that (1) black legislators are connected (i.e., "bound" together) by a sense of shared struggle that produces commonalities in their political agendas, and (2) black legislators are "bounded" in the sense that they operate within highly constrained parameters of politics that are shaped by endogenous factors, such as race, partisanship, and leadership in the legislature, as well as exogenous activities, such as constituent services and efforts to collaborate with extralegislative advocacy groups. To address issues of polarization in Tennessee, black lawmakers need to navigate these exogenous and endogenous factors while cultivating strong yet fluid support networks that help them to leverage policies and to build alliances with nonblack legislators.

Black legislators operate in a racially institutionalized—if not racially hostile—environment that constrains legislative decision-making.[8] Haynie found that "racial considerations influenced evaluations of legislative behavior, and that these considerations had negative consequences for African American representatives."[9] The extent to which racial divisions or hierarchies limit black legislative decision-making is further affected by partisan politics. For example, Rocca and Sanchez claimed that congressional bills sponsored/cosponsored by whites had a higher rate of adoption than those sponsored/cosponsored by blacks. However, the adoption of bills sponsored/cosponsored by blacks increased when Democrats controlled Congress.[10]

Party leadership and committee appointments offer additional windows into racial politics inside legislative bodies.[11] Blacks have been able to ascend to leadership positions in legislatures controlled by the Democratic Party since the 1980s partly because of incumbency and their mastery of the legislative decision-making process. Black legislators who are more effective at building coalitions in support of policies are more likely to obtain leadership positions in legislatures.[12] Furthermore, some black legislators have eschewed positions on "interest committees," which are typically used to advance progressive policies, in exchange for influential positions on high-profile committees that have broad appeal to the general public.[13] Additionally, white Democrats representing racially conservative districts prior to the 1970s eventually learned to work with black legislators and grassroots activists, thus increasing the chances for blacks to ascend to influential leadership positions.[14]

Another way to interrogate the racial politics of state legislatures is to examine the cosponsorship networks that reinforce equity-based policies. Later in this chapter, we examine the support networks behind legislative measures, including racial equity, civil rights, and voting rights policies and elderly assistance or safety-net policies for senior citizens. These policies can reveal cleavages within the Tennessee General Assembly and the black caucus. In general, black legislators tend to push for social welfare, education, and equity-based policies much more often than their white counterparts do.[15] However, divisions often emerge within the state black caucus, mainly over a select number of "hot bills": controversial measures that draw a lot of attention from the public.[16]

Public activities exogenous to their legislative responsibilities are another challenge for black legislators. They include responding to constituent requests for assistance, participating in social service activities, and attending community events.[17] Public activities have been generally viewed as descriptive or symbolic forms of representation that are electorally profitable for legislators.[18] Constituencies on the receiving end of assistance from legislators are more likely to reelect those representatives regardless of their policy positions or production of bills.[19]

Even though public activity is rewarding for legislators, it is still an important aspect of their responsibilities, considering that many southern politicians represent resource-poor communities, and some state legislatures (such as Tennessee's) are in session for less than six months a year. Black lawmakers' constituent relations give them what Representative Johnnie Turner referred to as a "moral compass" for making tough decisions on policies.[20] Representative Barbara Cooper insisted that her connections to poor communities in Memphis gives her the resilience to take strong stands for marginalized people. Because of her extrainstitutional linkages, "I don't compromise the community," she stated.[21]

Much of the black caucus's involvement in the public sphere is measured not just by what they do in session, but by their ability to deliver goods and services during the out-of-session months. Representative Brenda Gilmore (D-Nashville) of the Fifty-Fourth District in Tennessee said that constituent services were more than 50 percent of her responsibilities. Between May 2010 and September 2011, she assisted with relief efforts for constituents whose homes were destroyed by the "great flood"; organized several community forums in response to gang shootings in her district; assisted with a series of forums educating African Americans about Tennessee's photo identification voter law; and aided district residents with legal problems.²² Gilmore was elected to the Tennessee Senate from the Nineteenth District in November 2018.

The impact of public activity on legislative behavior is twofold. On the one hand, it places demands on legislators' time and may influence their potential effectiveness. Legislators representing resource-poor communities are forced to address a different set of constituent concerns compared to those representing middle-class or affluent communities. On the other hand, public activity can inform what kinds of policies are sponsored by black lawmakers. For example, the NBCSL annual conferences and the TBCSL's weekly or monthly meetings serve as vehicles for aggregating constituent concerns and policies.

Black lawmakers' extrainstitutional linkages are further augmented by their alliances with social justice and civil rights advocates. At times, advocacy and social movement groups have coordinated protests at the state legislature in support of or in opposition to bills that reflect the positions of black lawmakers and other legislative allies. So far during the twenty-first century disability rights activists, the Occupy Wall Street movement, labor activists, civil rights groups, students, and health-care advocates have routinely organized sit-ins, demonstrations, and other actions at the state capitol. For instance, seven activists were arrested inside the capitol while protesting anti-union legislation in March 2011.²³ One of the Nashville 7, Ash-Lee Woodard Henderson, later became the first black woman to lead the Highlander Research and Education Center (previously called the Highlander Folk School).

In 2015 the Nashville Student Organizing Committee, led by Justin Jones, a prominent Fisk University activist, organized protests against the state's new voter identification law. A couple of years earlier, the state had changed the requirements for verifying prospective voters. The new law required residents to show a federal or Tennessee government-issued identification card as a prerequisite to vote. However, it prohibited students from using identification cards from state-run universities. Out-of-state students, who did not have a state-issued card, were hit the hardest.²⁴ Civil rights activists and government watchdog groups believed the new law further disenfranchised young, poor, and black voters.²⁵

Finally, it is important to discuss how geographic (rather than political and professional) boundaries shape black legislative politics. Tennessee's geographic isomorphism mitigates black legislative successes, but also creates opportunities for biracial coalitions in the General Assembly. African Americans are heavily concentrated in the western part of the state: in Memphis/Shelby County and an hour's drive eastward in rural West Tennessee counties. Nashville/Davidson County in Middle Tennessee also has a sizable black population, and smaller but concentrated black populations are in the urban communities of Chattanooga/

Hamilton County and Knoxville/Knox County in East Tennessee. The concentration of blacks in West Tennessee, to some extent in the mid-region, and in the cities virtually guarantees that many white and Republican legislators will come from overwhelmingly white-majority districts.

In the first decade of the twenty-first century, the Tennessee General Assembly experienced a partisan realignment. Democrats lost control of both chambers, and many Republicans won seats in overwhelmingly white and rural districts. As discussed in the previous chapter, beginning in 2002, Democrats experienced a steady decline in power. Republicans had a net gain of twenty-two seats between 2002 and 2010, and in the 2010 elections, the fourteen new representatives came from areas that were more than 90 percent white.[26] The surplus of Republicans had a twofold impact. It mitigated black political influence, and blacks lost leadership positions in the House of Representatives by 2010. Further, it constricted what is considered politically palatable policies. Democrats feared passing legislation that could ignite partisan rancor among Republicans, which could be used against them in election contests.

By the 107th General Assembly (2011–2012), Democrats had completely lost control of the state legislature. Republicans held nearly two-thirds of the seats in the House of Representatives, a number that would extend to a supermajority in 2014. The partisan shift in Tennessee reflected a trend of partisan realignment in state legislatures that dates to the 1970s. King-Meadows and Schaller documented how the growth in the number of black legislators in the South occurred simultaneously with the growth of the Republican Party in state legislatures. Black lawmakers essentially garnered influence in legislatures that were increasingly plagued by divisions and dominated by conservative constituencies.[27] This further constrained black legislative influence, especially in the South.

The intersection of race, partisanship, and geography is particularly relevant for this book, considering that black legislators were able to build linkages with some white Democrats to augment their support networks. These linkages were partially geographically based since white Democrats presiding over majority-white districts adjacent to black districts occasionally aligned themselves with the TBCSL's support networks. They were also racially based since white Democrats in "influence districts"—legislative districts that are less than 50 percent black, yet the black population is large enough to influence the election outcome[28]—were more likely to support legislation sponsored by African Americans.

Race, partisanship, public activities, and geographic isomorphism are all important factors for discussing racial polarization and the "bounds" of black legislative politics. Sponsorship networks can also enhance the success of black legislators. Next, we examine the TBCSL's rise from 1965 (before its formation) to the twenty-first century. Then we compare the sponsorship networks to similar patterns in the 103rd, 104th, 105th, 106th, and 107th General Assemblies. Finally, we look more closely at the black caucus's sponsorship subnetworks in the 103rd General Assembly.

THE RISE OF BLACK LEGISLATIVE INFLUENCE

Heading into the post–civil rights era, the most intransigent obstacle to black electoral influence in the Tennessee legislature was the archaic district maps that favored rural and white legislators as opposed to urban legislators. Although Tennessee underwent a process of urbanization and industrialization from the turn of the twentieth century to the early 1950s, most of the legislators in the General Assembly were from rural districts.[29] Thus, the major urban areas (Memphis, Knoxville, Chattanooga, and Nashville) and their suburban communities were underrepresented in the state legislature. The Supreme Court's *Baker v. Carr* decision in 1962 mandated that Tennessee's state legislative districts had to be reapportioned and drawn to accommodate the population shifts and changes.[30] The new district lines were not agreed upon, however, until the 1965 special session, just after the first black legislator since the Reconstruction era, A. W. Willis, entered the General Assembly. The court case opened the door for the possibility that more blacks could be elected to the state legislature.[31]

When the TBCSL was formed in 1975, it set out to advance policies that were beneficial to blacks and other marginalized groups, and it still functions as a solid coalition or bloc to maximize their influence. Establishing a cohesive and relatively unified group was seen as important even before the caucus's formation. The kind of partisan hyperpolarization seen in Tennessee politics during the twenty-first century was less noticeable in the early years of the black caucus. Governors of both parties and their senior administrators attended the caucus's annual legislative retreat, which was an important instrument for framing the TBCSL's agenda. For example, Republican governor Lamar Alexander issued an executive order on October 15, 1979, establishing the Governor's Advisory Committee on Equal Employment Opportunity and requiring state agencies to abide by an equal opportunity hiring policy.[32] The executive order reflected the internal advocacy of Francis Guess, a senior official in the Alexander administration. One month earlier, at the legislative retreat, Guess had presented a report on public sector employment for blacks, which called for a nondiscrimination executive order.[33] In 1981, as Alexander's commissioner of general services, Guess served as a liaison to the black caucus retreat so as to make black lawmakers "aware of actions of the Governor that have a special impact on black Tennesseans."[34] Among the updates was Alexander's support of the voting rights reauthorization bill, which was passed at the federal level in 1982. In his comments to the black caucus, the governor seemed to link the importance of black voter participation with devolution. He told the TBCSL that "with the devolution of some federal programs, projects, and responsibility to the states," electing state and local candidates that reflect the interests of their constituents was important to ensuring that they received their fair share of the resources.[35]

Political scientist Sharon Wright Austin outlined the TBCSL's growth in the 1980s and 1990s. She found that most black legislators shared the same socioeconomic backgrounds as the white legislators, yet they represented districts with a greater proportion of low-income households than those of their white counterparts.[36] Black legislators had high rates of incumbency, which allowed them to obtain seniority positions on legislative committees but made it difficult for insurgent candidates to challenge them in competitive elections. Whereas most black legislators during Reconstruction were Republicans, due to the party realignment of blacks between the 1930s and the 1960s, most black legislators since 1964 have been Democrats. However, one black legislator who is no longer in office, Charles "Pete" Drew of Chattanooga, was a member of the Republican Party.

Between 1965 and 2002, black legislators represented urban districts in Memphis/Shelby County, Nashville/Davidson County, Chattanooga/Hamilton County, and Knoxville/Knox County.[37] Two blacks have been elected from rural districts since 2000. Nathan Vaughn represented the mostly white Kingsport district in East Tennessee's Tri-Cities area.[38] Johnny Shaw represents a majority-black district in West Tennessee's Hardeman County, which was created because of a federal court case. When Vaughn and Shaw were elected, they were the only blacks to represent legislative districts outside the four metropolitan areas since Reconstruction.

Shaw was elected after black activists fought a rancorous six-year-long legal battle in *Rural West Tennessee African American Affairs Council Inc. v. McWherter*, which eventually led to the creation of a majority-black district in rural West Tennessee.[39] Activist Minnie Bommer, the Rural West Tennessee African American Affairs Council, and historian Phillip R. Langsdon initiated a political and legal battle that claimed that the state legislature had violated the voting rights of blacks in West Tennessee. Blacks made up 30 percent of that region's population, or one hundred thousand people, yet they had no representation in the state legislature.[40] The political wrangling began after the 1992 redistricting plan failed to create a majority-black district in rural West Tennessee. In 1998, a federal judge ordered the state legislature to redraw the district lines. His rationale was that the 1992 redistricting plan violated section 2 of the Voting Rights Act by refusing to offer legislative representation for blacks in the region. The decision, which eventually led to the creation of Shaw's district, was upheld by the Sixth U.S. Circuit Court of Appeals in 1998.[41]

Lois DeBerry, the highest-ranking black lawmaker in Tennessee's history, had to balance the interests of black lawmakers and the Democratic caucus, especially regarding legislative redistricting and committee assignments. She stated: "Your African American colleagues—they expect you to move mountains for them. If they want to be on certain committees, you have to fight for that. When it [comes] to redistricting, you have to make sure they're treated fairly. And you got to make sure that they get the committees that they want to be on. So, you have an obligation to them as well as to the Democratic caucus."[42] The redistricting battle after the 1990 Census was the most contentious. African Americans attempted to create a legislative district in rural West Tennessee. Resolving the intraparty divisions required intervention from Governor Ned McWherter.

In general, the TBCSL's legislative agenda has been shaped by three orientations. First, TBCSL members have focused on antidiscriminatory initiatives that directly affect blacks and other marginalized groups, such as disabled people and senior citizens. One example of antidiscriminatory policies was the caucus's efforts to convince each county legislative body to establish a Human Development or Human Rights Commission that would monitor discrimination. Other examples include initiatives to improve black college enrollment; strengthening civil rights compliance and monitoring procedures; securing funds for a civil rights education center and memorial; sponsoring legislation to offer medical services, legal counsel, and health care for indigent and disabled people; endorsing tax relief measures for disabled people and senior citizens; securing contracts and assistance for minority businesses; combating electoral laws that dilute or adversely affect the black vote; removing racial preferences in provisions relating to orphanages; sponsoring antidiscrimination legislation for nonblack minority groups; and calling for a moratorium on the death penalty.

In 2002, the black caucus also participated in an effort to stop the execution of Abu Ali Abdur'Rahman.[43] Related to voting rights and electoral reform have been the caucus's attempts to place a prohibition on the at-large election system for municipalities, county governments, boards, and commissions. Additionally, TBCSL members have sponsored legislation to restore voting rights for some people exiting the criminal justice system. In the mid-2000s, Representative Larry Turner (D-Memphis) sponsored a restoration bill that initially failed but was approved the following year.[44]

Universalistic programs that advocate for environmental and consumer protections and that attempt to ameliorate the social and economic conditions of poor and working-class Tennesseans have been the TBCSL's second area of focus. These programs include expanding educational opportunities; advocating for a home-buyer's loan fund pool, primarily for low-income residents; pushing for greater oversight of police departments that use deadly force; offering assistance for foster care parents; endorsing sales tax exemptions for Tennesseans who buy goods with food stamps and vouchers; lobbying for economic development projects for working-class residents; establishing protections for families needing assistance for dependent children; supporting welfare rights and family planning legislation; and advocating for food protection, road safety, and insurance programs.[45]

Finally, TBCSL members sponsor bills that reflect what Kerry Haynie called a "middle-ground strategy," which typically revolve around government reform or hometown-specific policies.[46] These initiatives are considered less divisive or offensive to moderate and conservative lawmakers.

The national gatherings for black legislators provide a vehicle for linking the endogenous tasks of legislative decision-making with their extralegislative activities. Between 2002 and 2004, TBCSL members sponsored twenty-two resolutions that were ratified at the NBCSL annual gatherings. Senator Thelma Harper made several proposals focusing on ballot and voter protections in 2002, and Representative Joe Towns advanced a resolution endorsing the restoration of voting rights for formerly incarcerated people. Senator Roscoe Dixon sponsored the most resolutions, almost all of them centering on health-care coverage. (See appendix 4.1 for a list of resolutions and sponsors.) The TBCSL's policies are further discussed at weekly or monthly meetings that allow for exchanges among public officials, senior-level staff in government agencies, and policy advocates. At these meetings, TBCSL members pass around sign-on slips, which are required for cosponsoring legislation.[47]

THE BLACK CAUCUS IN THE TWENTY-FIRST CENTURY

In the remainder of this chapter we focus on the black caucus's sponsorship networks across five legislative sessions: the 103rd (2003–2004), 104th (2005–2006), 105th (2007–2008), 106th (2009–2010), and 107th (2011–2012). The period of study is important for several reasons. First, it occurred after the redistricting battles of the 1990s created a black legislative district in rural West Tennessee. The court case, *Rural West Tennessee African American Affairs Council Inc. v. McWherter*, gave West Tennessee the first majority-black district since Reconstruction. This period also includes the last time Democrats had control of both chambers of the legislature. Democrats had control in 2003, yet by 2012 Republicans had nearly a supermajority in the legislature. The realignment of the legislature meant the loss of black political influence. This period also provides an opportunity to assess partisan polarization and whether black lawmakers were able to build alliances—as measured through sponsorship networks—with Republicans.

Furthermore, as we noted in the first two chapters of this book, there was some political instability that had a direct impact on the black caucus during this time, especially its Memphis/Shelby County delegation. In May 2005, a bribery investigation by the Federal Bureau of Investigation and the Tennessee Bureau of Investigation called Operation Tennessee Waltz eventually led to the convictions and departures of Roscoe Dixon and John Ford, the most influential black lawmakers in the Senate.[48] Kathryn Bowers, the former whip in the House of Representatives, was another Memphis lawmaker engulfed in the corruption scandal. She was elected to fill Dixon's seat, but had to resign a year later due to the scandal.[49] The FBI/TBI sting operation also forced the departure of Senator Ward Crutchfield (D-Chattanooga), a white lawmaker with close ties to TBCSL members.

Operation Tennessee Waltz weakened the Memphis/Shelby County delegation.[50] The lawmakers at the center of the scandal (Dixon, Ford, Bowers) were among the most progressive in the legislature and understood how to build policy coalitions with moderate and conservative Democrats. The Memphis/Shelby County delegation was further hurt by the deaths of several black Democrats: Representative Gary Rowe in February 2008, Representative Larry Turner in November 2009, and Representative Ulysses Jones in November 2010.

As already mentioned, by the end of 2010, the once Democrat-controlled legislature was dominated by Republicans. This shift, which occurred in the 106th session (2009–2010), ultimately contributed to increased racial polarization in the state. However, Kent Williams (R-Carter County) aligned with the Democrats, who elected him speaker of the House. Although Republicans held a 50–48 majority (one seat was vacant), this agreement allowed DeBerry to retain her appointment as speaker pro tempore.[51] Still, by the 107th session, Democrats were pushed out of power. In 2003–2004, they held a 54–45 majority in the 103rd session; in 2011–2012, Republicans had a 64–34 advantage with one lawmaker declared as an independent. In 2003–2004, Democrats had a slim majority of 18–15 in the Senate. By 2011–2012, the power was reversed: Republicans had an 18–14 advantage (one seat was vacant).

After the partisan realignment, some black lawmakers struggled to have their voices heard. Representative Johnnie Turner (D-Memphis) entered the legislature halfway through the 106th session in 2010 after the unexpected death of her husband, Representative Larry Turner. She was known across the state as "Ms. NAACP" because as executive director of the organization in Memphis, she had built the local branch into one of the largest in the country. Yet in her early years in the state legislature, she was ignored and prevented from speaking on bills deliberated on the House floor. Finally, she and a colleague protested her treatment: "one day, one of my colleague[s] and I, we got a mop and we put a yellow bag on it, and stood up with that mop.... The House just roared [laughed]. I said, 'I am not seen,' and I waved my mop and my yellow bag so I [could] be seen over there."[52] Although Turner's protest was awkward in the legislative body, it underscored the shifting partisan alliances. In her first full term (2011–2012), she and other black lawmakers still had difficulty gaining traction in the legislature.

METHODS AND DATA

We draw from our Legislative Political Network Profile database to analyze the sponsorship networks of black lawmakers. We use social network analysis (also referred to as dynamic network analysis),[53] analysis of variance, and regression analysis to investigate the sponsorship networks undergirding the 2,193 bills sponsored by the TBCSL from 2003 to 2012. We focus mostly on members of the House of Representatives, given its larger sample size. Our research approach allowed us to distinguish between resolutions (which include memorializing resolutions) and legislation (which is binding).[54] This is important because Sharon Wright Austin found that TBCSL members successfully passed more than 50 percent of their sponsored bills in the late 1980s.[55] By focusing only on binding statutes, we found a lower but nonetheless respectable passage rate for legislation (see below). Black lawmakers may have had an easier time building bipartisan coalitions or working with white lawmakers on nonbinding resolutions, thus overstating their success rate in bill passage.

The sponsorship networks allow for a closer examination of the interactions between African American lawmakers and Republican Party lawmakers, the success rate of legislative adoption, and the factors affecting legislative success. Identifying the cosponsors of legislative items is critical to evaluating legislative impact. Cosponsorship is a signaling device used by "institutionally disadvantaged" lawmakers to articulate policy preferences to their constituents, even though at times these measures may be rejected by legislative bodies.[56] The practices of cosponsorship or rejecting cosponsorship requests further reveal partisan and ideological divisions in legislatures.[57]

Network analyses allow us to measure the individual capacities of lawmakers to build policy coalitions. We conceive the black lawmakers in each legislative session as one comprehensive sponsorship network, or in the case of the five legislative sessions (103rd, 104th, 105th, 106th, and 107th) as five comprehensive networks. Social network analyses allow researchers to measure different kinds of relationships. We rely on the capability measure (using the ORA software) to explain sponsorship networks.[58] The algorithm for the capability measure "computes the number of connections for each entity" and "scales the value based on the variation from the average degree."[59] In simple terms, the algorithm allows researchers to evaluate how well an entity (in our case, a lawmaker) can perform certain tasks (e.g., sponsor legislation, recruit cosponsors, get legislation adopted). High scores indicate that the lawmaker has a unique set of connections or ties to other lawmakers in the legislature (or network), enhancing that politician's ability to influence legislation.

Capability scores are calculated for a lawmaker × bill adoption (1 = adopted, 0 = not adopted) network, and these scores serve as our dependent variables in the regression analyses. Our measure of bill sponsorship (this includes cosponsors) is our independent variable of interest, and it represents a tally of the number of legislators involved in the bill. For instance, a bill is scored 1 if advanced without any cosponsors. Likewise, the variable is scored 2 to count the sponsor and a single cosponsor of legislation; 3 to include the sponsor of the bill and two cosponsors; or 4 to count the sponsor and three cosponsors. Another independent variable, bill adoption, is scored 1 (passed) or 0 (rejected). At times, lawmakers obtained dozens of cosponsors, whereas in some cases, a lawmaker obtained no cosponsor for a piece of legislation. Additional independent variables for the regression are gender (0 = male, 1 = female); region as defined in the Tennessee Grand Divisions (1 = West, 2 = Middle, 3 = East); if the lawmaker was the chair of a full committee (1 = chair, 0 = not chair); if the lawmaker held an official leadership position in the House of Representatives or their party caucus (1 = yes, 0 = no); and if the lawmaker recruited Republican lawmakers to cosponsor legislation (a continuous variable tallying the number of Republican legislators involved in the bill).

In addition, we provide a snapshot look at the subsponsorship networks of influential black lawmakers with a more systematic investigation of the 103rd General Assembly (2003–2004). That is, we evaluate the sponsorship of bills by disaggregating lawmakers in both the House and Senate based on the following subnetworks:

- lawmakers representing districts below the state median income
- women lawmakers
- Republican lawmakers
- legislators representing crossover and influence districts (districts under 50 percent black)
- lawmakers representing majority-white districts
- support for racially egalitarian legislation
- senior citizen–related legislation

The 103rd session occurred when Democrats had slim majorities in the House and Senate, when the Democratic governor of Tennessee was in his first year of governance, and before the political instability that engulfed the legislature after 2004.

BLACK LAWMAKERS AND SPONSORSHIP NETWORKS, 2003–2012

We look at the sponsorship networks that anchored the decision-making processes of black lawmakers from 2003 to 2012. Tables 4.1 and 4.2 give an overview of these sponsorship networks. Legislation (a total of 2,193 bills) in the 103rd, 104th, 105th, 106th, and 107th General Assemblies received mean scores of 2.4, 1.8, 2.4, 3.2, and 3.9 sponsors/cosponsors, respectively. Black lawmakers recruited the most cosponsors in the 107th session, when the Republicans had a nearly 2–1 surplus. This legislative strategy, however, produced few rewards: whereas 28 percent of the black-sponsored bills in the 103rd General Assembly were adopted, only 11 percent of the black lawmakers' bills passed in the 107th session. Overall, the passage rate for bills was highest (28–31 percent) when Democrats controlled the House of Representatives in the Tennessee General Assembly.

TABLE 4.1 Characteristics of sponsorship networks

	103rd mean (SE)	104th mean (SE)	105th mean (SE)	106th mean (SE)	107th mean (SE)
Legislative cosponsors	2.4 (3.4)	1.8 (1.2)	2.4 (2.1)	3.2 (3.2)	3.9 (5.0)
Republican Party cosponsors	.13 (.34)	.13 (.33)	1.9 (6.2)	.13 (.34)	.53 (1.02)
Percentage of bills adopted	28	27	31	25	11
Capability of black lawmakers network (adopted legislation)	.32 (.31)	.29 (.36)	.28 (.31)	.29 (.36)	.27 (.38)

TABLE 4.2 Characteristics of the House of Representatives

	103rd	104th	105th	106th	107th
N = blacks in the House of Representatives	15	16	15	15	15
Total number of bills sponsored by black lawmakers	395	401	522	468	407
Party membership in the House of Representatives	54 D 45 R	54 D 45 R	53 D 46 R	48 D 50 R 1 vacancy	34 D 64 R 1 independent
Percentage of bills adopted	28	27	31	25	11

The low mean scores for Republican cosponsors of TBCSL legislation show the polarization between black lawmakers and the Republican Party. The one outlier is the 105th General Assembly. Representative Joe Armstrong (D-Knoxville) had the strongest ties to the Republican Party, recruiting twenty-five Republicans as cosponsors of his bills. In addition to being a seasoned lawmaker, Armstrong's bipartisanship reflected the context of his district. Knoxville is located in East Tennessee, the most conservative region of the state. Six lawmakers represented Knoxville in 2007–2008—four Republicans and two Democrats, including Armstrong. Hence, it is no surprise that he scored the highest on bipartisanship since he was building coalitions with lawmakers in his region.

The capability scores assess the combined influence of black lawmakers in each session. For example, the combined influence of the fifteen lawmakers in the 103rd session is evaluated as one capability network instead of fifteen individual networks. The most capable TBCSL network was the 103rd session. Black lawmakers scored .32 (out of 1) compared to .29 in the 104th, .28 in the 105th, .29 in the 106th, and .27 in the 107th sessions.

TABLE 4.3 Capability (network scores): Adopted legislation

Legislative session	103rd (2003–2004) B (SE)	104th (2005–2006) B (SE)	105th (2007–2008) B (SE)	106th (2009–2010) B (SE)	107th (2011–2012) B (SE)
Bill sponsorship	−.04 (.03)	.04 (.10)	.01 (.04)	.01 (.04)	.01 (.07)
Republican Party sponsors	.41 (.32)	.06 (.35)	−.01 (.02)	.15 (.38)	−.11 (.36)
Chair of a committee	.49 (.27)	.71 (.25)*	.64 (.23)*	.60 (.24)*	—
Leadership in the House of Representatives	.12 (.27)	.50 (.27)	.23 (.26)	−.08 (.37)	—
Gender	.50 (.22)†	.14 (.22)	.12 (.19)	.08 (.26)	−.29 (.25)
Region	.08 (.11)	.06 (.13)	.04 (.13)	.17 (.13)	.07 (.17)
Constant	−.62 (.46)	−.28 (.41)	−.16 (.32)	−.25 (.32)	.61 (.42)
N = blacks in the House of Representatives	15	16	15	15	15
Total number of bills sponsored by black lawmakers	395	401	522	468	407
Party membership in the House of Representatives	54 D 45 R	54 D 45 R	53 D 46 R	48 D 50 R 1 vacancy	34 D 64 R 1 independent
R^2	.48	.53	.53	.60	.14

Note: † = < 0.10; * = $p < 0.05$.

The regression analyses provide a closer look at the factors that contribute to the adoption of legislation. As already mentioned, the regression analyses control for sponsorship/cosponsorship, the recruitment of Republican sponsors, region, gender, and leadership (committee chair and senior positions) in the House. The capability score is the dependent variable.

The results in table 4.3 reveal that the committee chair variable is the most consistent statistically significant measure in the five legislative sessions. Black lawmakers were the most successful in the sessions where they chaired the highest number of full committees (the 104th, 105th, and 106th sessions). The other measures were statistically nonsignificant except for gender in the 103rd session. Black female lawmakers were more capable than their male colleagues of the same race when it came to advancing legislation to its full adoption during this period.

Throughout this book, we argue that the importance of black politics and the salience of a racially egalitarian agenda were adversely affected in the early twenty-first century. Certainly, partisan realignment weakened black political influence. At first, partisan realignment was gradual, but the shift from the 106th to the 107th session was dramatic. Attempts at comity by black lawmakers in the form of building bipartisan relations did not lead to the adoption of racially progressive legislation. Partisan realignment meant that black lawmakers lost their committee chairs.

BLACK LAWMAKERS, SUBSPONSORSHIP NETWORKS, AND THE 103RD GENERAL ASSEMBLY

To gain a clearer sense of the impact of black lawmakers, we focus attention on their subsponsorship networks in our snapshot of the 103rd General Assembly (2003–2004). During these two years, black lawmakers sponsored 395 bills, were appointed as chairs of influential committees, and held important leadership positions in their party.[60] Lois DeBerry (D-Memphis) was the speaker pro tempore of the House, and Larry Turner (D-Memphis) was the deputy speaker of the House. Democrats also controlled both chambers in the legislature and the governor's office.

In total, fifteen of the ninety-nine lawmakers in the House were African American, and three of the thirty-three senators were African American in the 103rd General Assembly. All but two of the black legislators represented majority-black districts, as indicated in table 4.4. Joe Armstrong represented a nonmajority-black, crossover district in Knoxville. Nathan Vaughn was the only black legislator to represent an overwhelmingly white (97 percent) district. This may explain the instability of his seat since he was elected and defeated twice, fi-

TABLE 4.4 Political and sociodemographic profile of TBCSL members, 103rd General Assembly

Lawmaker	County/region	Chamber of legislature	Race of district	Income	Gender	Leadership	Committee chair or vice chair
JArmstrong	Knox	H	CO	below median	M	Y	Y
KBowers	Shelby	H	B	below median	F	Y	N
HBrooks	Shelby	H	B	below median	F	N	Y
TBrown	Hamilton	H	B	below median	F	N	Y
BCooper	Shelby	H	B	below median	F	N	Y
JDeBerry	Shelby	H	B	below median	M	N	Y
LDeBerry	Shelby	H	B	below median	F	Y	Y
UJones	Shelby	H	B	below median	M	N	Y
ELangster	Davidson	H	B	below median	F	N	Y
LMiller	Shelby	H	B	below median	M	N	N
MPruitt	Davidson	H	B	below median	F	N	Y
JShaw	Rural West	H	B	above median	M	N	N
JTowns	Shelby	H	B	above median	M	Y	Y
LTurner	Shelby	H	B	above median	M	N	N
NVaughn	Tri-Cities	H	W	median	M	N	N
RDixon	Shelby	S	B	above median	M	N	Y
JFord	Shelby	S	B	below median	M	N	Y
THarper	Davidson	S	B	below median	F	N	Y

Notes: H = House of Representatives; S = Senate; B = black; W = white; CO = crossover district (entails white voter support); M = male; F = female; below median = below median family income of $36,145; median = at median family income of $36,145; above median = above median family income of $36,145.

nally being forced out of the legislature in 2008. Still, according to records of the TBCSL's weekly meetings, he was a regular participant in the group's activities.[61] Most black legislators represented districts with median family incomes below the state average of $36,145 at the time. Forty-five percent of the white-led districts had median family incomes below the state average. Eight representatives and the three senators (Dixon, Ford, and Harper) were chairs or vice chairs of standing committees.

Capability network scores measure the impact of black lawmakers while controlling for various subsponsorship networks. As indicated in table 4.5, among state representatives and senators serving districts with family incomes below the state median and among women lawmakers, TBCSL members were much more capable in advancing their legislation than were nonblack members. In other words, white lawmakers from poor districts and white women lawmakers were not as successful in advancing TBCSL policies as black lawmakers were, even though the TBCSL had a lengthy and favorable record of backing policies that were beneficial to low-income communities and women. Senator Harper was particularly influential (.99) among women lawmakers in the Senate.

TABLE 4.5 Capability network scores for subnetworks in the 103rd General Assembly

Subnetworks	House	Senate
Districts with income below state median	LMiller (.99) BCooper (.99) UJones (.99)	JFord (.99) THarper (.12) WCrutchfield (.04)
Women lawmakers	BCooper (.99) HBrooks (.99) KBowers (.93)	THarper (.99) RKurita (.07) CBurks (.02)
Republicans	THargett (.99) DGresham (.98) JHagood (.98)	CPerson (.99) TBurchett (.99) WClabough (.95)
Influence districts	BMarrero (.99) BTurner (.98) MKernell (.57)	SCohen (.99) WCrutchfield (.96) JKyle (.84)
White districts	HTindell (.99) MTurner (.84) JSontany (.75)	CPerson (.99) TBurchett (.95) JCooper (.90)
Racial equity, civil rights, and voting rights bills	LTurner (.99) BCooper (.98) UJones (.98)	RDixon (.99) JFord (.67) SCohen (.67)
Senior citizen bills	LDeBerry (.99) BMarrero (.99) BTurner (.99)	THarper (.99) RDixon (.50) JFord (.50)

Notes: The data were analyzed with the ORA software developed by Carnegie Mellon's CASOS. Italicized names are white legislators.

Overall few Republicans were considered capable cosponsors of TBCSL proposals. Republicans typically supported TBCSL policies that were noncontroversial. The legislative measures during the 103rd session that received the most attention from Republicans were H.B. 847, which prevented the sale of alcohol, tobacco, and lottery tickets to minors; a bill establishing a nursing program at a community college in Knoxville; and legislation awarding state contracts to call center companies that used U.S. citizens.[62] The first two measures were sponsored by Representative Joe Armstrong, a black legislator from Knoxville. Thus, it should come as no surprise that one of the Senate sponsors, Tim Burchett, was from Knoxville and the other cosponsor, Senator Bill Clabough, represented the neighboring city of Maryville.

Earlier in the chapter, we argued that black legislative politics are influenced by a highly constrained environment—an environment we refer to as having "political bounds." Race, partisanship, geography, and public or extralegislative activities influence both the success and failure of black lawmakers. When black legislators reached outside of the TBCSL infrastructure, they typically developed alliances with liberal lawmakers or white lawmakers from influence districts. They also developed alliances with some whites representing majority-white districts in urban counties. Representatives Beverly Marrero and Mike Kernell and Senators Stephen Cohen and John Kyle were all from influence districts in the largely black Memphis/Shelby County area. Senator Ward Crutchfield of Chattanooga/Hamilton County, another strong ally of black legislators, came from an influence district. Representatives Mike Turner and Janis Sontany were from Nashville/Davidson County districts with black populations ranging from 12 percent to 18 percent, and Harry Tindell was from Knox County.

Senator Cohen had particularly strong linkages to the TBCSL. As table 4.5 shows, he was the only white senator to score high on legislation that addressed racial equity, civil rights, and voting rights. For the most part, TBCSL members, such as Senators Roscoe Dixon and John Ford, were considered the most capable voices for these issues. Capability scores varied for senior citizen policies: Senator Harper was considered more capable than her Memphis counterparts. Speaker pro tempore Lois DeBerry, along with Representatives Beverly Marrero and Brenda Turner, both of whom represented influence districts, also received favorable scores for pushing TBCSL policies that addressed the needs of senior citizens.

CONCLUSION

In this chapter we have examined the activities of the Tennessee Black Caucus of State Legislators from 2003 through 2012. We have argued that political bounds—the constraints shaped by race, partisanship, public and extralegislative linkages, and geographic isomorphism—complicate black legislative success. As a result, the TBCSL has developed sponsorship networks to support its agenda, cultivate cohesion among black caucus members, and build alliances with nonblack legislators.

We focused specifically on five legislative sessions and gave additional attention to sponsorship subnetworks in the 103rd General Assembly. The findings reveal that partisan realignment diminished the power of black lawmakers. Notably, this shift removed them from the chairs of legislative committees that are critical to advancing legislation. Moreover, the capability scores and passage rates were the smallest for the 107th session, when the Republicans had an overwhelming majority.

The results demonstrate that black legislators, particularly legislators from the Memphis/Shelby County delegation, generally rely on each other to cosponsor bills. White legislators representing low-income districts are less likely to cosponsor black legislators' bills. Cross-racial alliances, however, are salient when considering geographic proximity and the racial composition of a district. White Democrats near large black populations and, more important, those representing influence districts were considered capable allies of the black caucus.

The sponsorship networks and subnetworks help to illustrate patterns of communication among TBCSL members and connections between the black caucus and nonblack legislators, particularly Republicans. The most effective examples of bipartisanship occurred when black lawmakers formed alliances with Republicans who were in close geographic proximity to their districts. The most striking characteristic of black lawmakers is their involvement in racially progressive and poverty-mitigation policies. Regardless of the partisan realignment, Representative Turner stated: "I'm not compromising my principles when it comes to helping poor people, when it comes to the least of these. I'm not compromising. Right is right."[63]

The story of polarization here is the gap between the political preferences of African American and white Tennesseans, which has been reflected in the party shift in the state legislature: as black officials lost ground to their white colleagues in political office, policies that were friendly to communities of color became harder to implement. In the next chapter, we examine how racial polarization shaped the debates about the state's budget and tax policies. We look at how black lawmakers advanced progressive tax reform legislation even though the Democratic politicians were divided in their opinions about a state income tax. We also show how black lawmakers connected the state's budget woes to the broader attacks by conservative legislators on social welfare policies.

APPENDIX 4.1

RATIFIED RESOLUTIONS BY TBCSL MEMBERS AT THE 2002–2004 NBCSL MEETINGS

NBCSL RESOLUTIONS RATIFIED (DECEMBER 2002)

Election Technology (Senator Thelma Harper, D-Nashville)
Standard Vote Counting Procedures (Senator Thelma Harper, D-Nashville)
Best Practices for Implementing the Help American Vote
  Act (Senator Thelma Harper, D-Nashville)
Consumer Health Assistance Programs (Senator Roscoe Dixon, D-Memphis)
Diabetes Insurance Coverage (Senator Roscoe Dixon, D-Memphis)
Community Health Centers (Senator Roscoe Dixon, D-Memphis)
Audit of the United States International Development Agency Regarding HIV/AIDS
  Prevention Funding (Representative Henri E. Brooks, D-Memphis)
Expanded Medicare Assistance for Low-Income Individuals
  (Senator Roscoe Dixon, D-Memphis)
Preferred Drug Lists and Data Collection for Patients
  (Representative Kathryn Bowers, D-Memphis)
Health Care and Prevention Programs for Obesity
  (Senator Roscoe Dixon, D-Memphis)
Voting Rights for People Exiting the Prison System
  (Representative Joe Towns, D-Memphis)
Condemnation of Senator Trent Lott (Representative Ulysses Jones,
  D-Memphis; Representative Henri E. Brooks, D-Memphis)
Botswana Educational Exchange Programs (Representative
  Henri E. Brooks, D-Memphis)

NBCSL RESOLUTIONS RATIFIED (DECEMBER 2003)

Preferred Drug Lists and Quality Care (Senator Roscoe Dixon, D-Memphis)
Remedies for Black Farmers (Representative Henri E. Brooks, D-Memphis; Senator
  John Ford D-Memphis; Speaker pro tempore Lois DeBerry, D-Memphis;
  Representative Henri E. Brooks, D-Memphis; Senator Roscoe Dixon,
  D-Memphis; Representative Ulysses Jones, D-Memphis; Representative Joe
  Armstrong, D-Knoxville; Representative Johnny Shaw, D-Memphis)
Health Care and Medicaid Coverage for Kidney Dialysis
  (Senator Roscoe Dixon, D-Memphis)
Eliminating Racial/Ethnic Bias in Health Care Coverage
  (Senator Roscoe Dixon, D-Memphis)
Treating Kidney Disease as a Health Disparity (Senator Roscoe Dixon, D-Memphis)

NBCSL RESOLUTIONS RATIFIED (DECEMBER 2004)

Programs for the Uninsured and Commending the Pfizer Helpful Answers
  and Pfizer PFriends Program (Senator Roscoe Dixon, D-Memphis)

Cervical Cancer Elimination Task Forces (Representative
   Kathryn Bowers, D-Memphis)
U.S. Department of Agriculture Loan and Credit Policies
   (Representative Henri E. Brooks, D-Memphis)
Commending the National Union of Families Organization
   (Representative Barbara Cooper, D-Memphis)

Sources: National Black Caucus of State Legislators, Resolutions Ratified in Plenary Session, Twenty-Sixth Annual Legislative Conference, Indianapolis, Ind., December 13, 2002; National Black Caucus of State Legislators, Resolutions Ratified in Plenary Session, Twenty-Seventh Annual Legislative Conference, Houston, Tex., December 5, 2003; and National Black Caucus of State Legislators, Resolutions Ratified in Plenary Session, Twenty-Eighth Annual Legislative Conference, Houston, Tex., December 3, 2004. https://nbcsl.org/public-policy/docs/category/39-1998-2015-ratified-policy-resolutions.html.

PART THREE
RACE AND POLARIZATION IN RECENT TENNESSEE POLITICS: THE ISSUES

CHAPTER FIVE

THE RACIAL POLITICS OF TAX AND SPENDING POLICIES

> It is a myth to think black people, poor people, do not want to participate as taxpayers.... I've not heard one constituent say he didn't want to pay his fair share. But nobody wants to pay more than their fair share.
>
> —STATE SENATOR JOHN FORD (2001)

On November 4, 2014, Tennessee voters adopted a constitutional amendment that created a permanent ban on a state income tax. The referendum occurred more than a decade after the state legislature was engulfed in heated and occasionally volatile battles over a series of income tax proposals during the 102nd General Assembly session (2001–2002). At the time, Republican governor Don Sundquist proposed a plan to tax personal income in order to erase a $350 million deficit that was expected to balloon to $1 billion.

Although Tennessee was one of a handful of states that did not tax personal income, the idea of a state income tax had been debated since the 1920s. Yet the state supreme court struck down attempts by the state legislature to tax income and related revenue streams.[1] Sundquist's proposal won support from centrist and liberal Democrats, who were assigned to shepherd the plan through the legislature during the budget hearings of 2001 and the legislative proceedings of 2002. The proposal failed, however, during both rounds of negotiations and ignited a conservative backlash that culminated with the 2014 passage of the constitutional amendment that banned a state income tax.

The highlight of the initial deliberations was a July 12, 2001, rally spearheaded by conservative talk show activists. It was attended by a reported 1,200 protestors who shouted "No new taxes! No new taxes!" throughout the event.[2] The rally was intended to sway a bipartisan conference committee, which was leading the budget negotiations, to exclude an income tax from the state budget. Some protestors became angry after they were prevented from entering the Senate chambers (where the deliberations occurred) due to limited seating. Some lawmakers claimed that they were "yelled at and spit on by some protestors" during the confrontation. Another wave of protestors outside the capitol building broke a window of the front door while demanding that lawmakers reject the income tax proposal.[3] The plan that eventually emerged from the conference committee, which was approved by both chambers, excluded any mention of an income tax.

In this chapter, we explore the debate over tax and spending policies in Tennessee, focusing on the role that devolution plays in polarizing whites and nonwhites on budgetary politics. Given the widely documented correlation between racial and economic issues, it makes sense that race has shaped dialogues about taxes and government spending in the Volunteer State. Senator John Ford (D-Memphis), a longtime proponent of a state tax on personal income, had to dispel arguments that the policy was solely a redistributive measure to benefit poor and nonwhite residents. As seen in the epigraph, Ford stated that he had "not heard one [black or poor] constituent say he didn't want to pay his fair share. But nobody wants to pay more than their fair share."[4] He and other members of the Tennessee Black Caucus of State Legislators helped to steer the tax debate during the 2001–2002 budget crisis.

Tennessee is an ideal case study for analyzing attitudes about tax and spending policies across multiple levels of government. The state allows us to examine what Smith and Seltzer refer to as the "racial divide" in attitudes toward budget deliberations.[5] African Americans were instrumental in shaping those deliberations and trying to negotiate an agreement between competing interests in the Tennessee legislature. And as demonstrated later in this chapter, black lawmakers have criticized fiscally austere policies that they believe adversely affect nonaffluent residents and communities of color.

We draw from two polls administered by the MTSU Survey Group in 2002 and 2007 to explore the racial politics of tax and spending policies in Tennessee. The MTSU polls were administered during the budget deliberations of 2001–2002 and shortly after the heightened debates over health care and education spending in the mid-2000s. The polls examined a host of race-related differences in attitudes about state- and federal-level taxation and spending practices.

In this chapter, we explain variations by race regarding tax and spending policies and in so doing highlight two important concerns. First, we investigate racial attitudes toward different features of budgetary politics. As Christopher Faricy and Christopher Ellis noted, research in this area tends to focus on public perceptions of *direct* (i.e., through budgetary appropriations) rather than *in-*

direct (i.e., via tax expenditures) spending.[6] Accordingly, we heed the recommendation of these authors by distinguishing between attitudes toward indirect types of tax expenditures and those pertaining to direct spending.

Second, most investigations of tax and spending issues tend to focus on federal instead of state-level policies.[7] Here, we move away from this conventional approach, for we acknowledge that the issues of taxation and spending have both national and subnational (state and local) trajectories. For instance, both the electorate and politicians fight over tax and spending policies that originate in Washington, D.C., but the consequences of these policies have bearing on the quality of state-level public services. For that reason, we examine tax and spending issues originating at both the federal and state levels.

Before proceeding with our analysis, we offer a brief overview of tax and budget disputes in Tennessee and how they have shaped state politics in the twenty-first century. We also look at how black lawmakers attempted to shape tax and spending policies in Tennessee.

POLARIZATION AND BUDGET POLICIES

Americans across the country express strong opinions about paying taxes and supporting government expenditures. Indeed, public opinion surveys show that some citizens loathe taxes and spending while others view these topics with an indifferent tolerance.[8] Earlier in the book, we argued that realignment politics, devolution, and political comity have contributed to the polarized identities that shape the state and that this has made it particularly difficult to advance a racially equalitarian agenda. Although Democrats had majority control of the legislature in the early 2000s, many feared that tax reform threatened the party in swing districts. For these reasons, Democrats were unable to use their seventeen-seat majority in the House to leverage support for tax reform. Sundquist was also unable to sway moderate Republicans to vote for the measure.

The budget crisis and ensuing debate over taxes in Tennessee are indicative of the challenges of managing state economies in the age of devolution. Indeed, Americans generally favor the transfer of federal responsibilities to the states, but this poses major problems for racial and ethnic minorities and poor residents in need of robust social spending and intervention programs. This is particularly the case for southern states, which are frequently left at the mercy of electoral coalitions that support fiscally austere measures.[9]

In addition, race is central to any discussion about tax reform. Blacks and whites are generally divided on these policies, but the polarization is more transparent in areas with severe patterns of racial segregation. For example, Alabama's Republican governor Bob Riley proposed a referendum in 2003 that intended to raise taxes to pay for education and other services in the state. The proposal consisted of an increase in the marginal tax rate for higher-income families, along with adjustments to property taxes, taxes on businesses, and exemptions.[10] The referendum was supported by 75 percent of the African American residents compared to 21 percent of white Alabamans, with the greatest divide occurring in the most racially segregated counties.[11]

Additional research found that progressive tax policies receive greater support when the poor and non-poor residents belong to the same racial or ethnic group. The "ethnic congruence" model contends that progressive tax measures receive the greatest levels of support in racially homogeneous areas, especially where there are smaller populations of people of color.[12] When blacks and whites are unevenly distributed across income categories (in contexts where, for example, blacks are disproportionately poor and whites are middle class), progressive taxes receive less support. To state this another way, in diverse counties or states where racial contact is common and involves blacks and whites from different income groups, there has been less support for a graduated income tax.[13] The overwhelming evidence thus suggests that tax and spending issues are racialized, but the racial differences intersect with a cross section of other issues, such as residential status and political context.

TAX AND SPENDING POLICIES IN TENNESSEE

Disputes over tax and spending policies have been at the forefront of American politics since the founding of the country,[14] and such disputes have influenced Tennessee's political development since the early nineteenth century. After the end of the Civil War, the constitutional convention in 1870 gave the state government the power to establish an income tax on stocks and bonds, but there was no explicit language that gave the state taxing powers on personal income. Other taxes were allowed under the state constitution and subsequent legislation, such as taxes on "privileges" and poll and property taxes.[15]

Although explicit language allowing for a personal income tax was not included in the state constitution, Tennessee attempted to pass an income tax measure in 1931. At the time, Governor Henry Horton pushed for a personal income tax because of economic upheaval stemming from the collapse of the banking industry in the state and in response to the Great Depression. Two years earlier, the Tennessee Supreme Court (TSC) had approved the "Hall income tax," which taxed only stocks and bonds, but the measure did little to resolve the state's deficit.[16] Shortly afterward, the state legislature agreed to a graduated tax on the personal income of higher earners. The TSC, however, overturned the tax in *Evans v. McCabe* (1932).[17]

Despite Tennessee's judicial history on tax reform, there was some disagreement with the TSC's conclusion. Although the TSC claimed that the state's 1870 constitution prohibited the establishment of a tax on personal income, the court ignored the official record of the constitutional convention's proceedings. As Lewis Laska pointed out, the delegates at the convention permitted taxes on "privileges," which they interpreted as taxes on personal income.[18]

Regardless of the TSC deliberations and the scholarly debate about tax reform, political observers claimed that if there were a prohibition on income tax in Tennessee, then it applied uniquely to a graduated instead of a flat tax. Hence, many of the various provisions for a state income tax proposed a flat rate. At the national level, a flat tax is widely supported by conservative antitax reformers. Yet at the state level—as a compromise between pro- and antitax reformers and in compliance with Tennessee jurisprudence—many Democrats and liberals have been willing to support a flat tax.

Several governors—from the Horton regime in the 1930s to Sundquist's tenure in the early 2000s—have supported a graduated or flat tax on personal income. In the 1970s, Republican Winfield Dunn and Democrat Ray Blanton endorsed different versions of an income tax on the recommendation of the Tax Modernization and Reform Commission of 1974. Calls for an income tax picked up steam in the late 1990s, even though Sundquist was initially lukewarm to the idea.

Sundquist surprised many political observers with his endorsement of an income tax. Tennessee was one of nine states with no income tax, and many lawmakers, including high-profile Democrats, signed an antitax pledge in the 1990s that was sponsored by conservative interest groups. However, the state faced a budget crisis with a deficit expected to exceed $350 million.[19] TennCare, the state Medicaid program discussed in the next chapter, also faced economic instability. The governor then received a favorable opinion about the constitutional legality of an income tax from the Tennessee attorney general's office. These factors encouraged Sundquist to reverse his position by 2001 and advocate for an income tax.

Opponents to an income tax argued that it would discourage businesses from moving into the state.[20] Antipoverty advocates and progressive policymakers, including members of the black caucus, insisted that budget shortfalls and poor delivery of services would continue unless an income tax was implemented to boost revenue. They further argued that since the state had one of the highest sales tax rates in the country, the tax burden was disproportionately carried on the backs of the working poor and communities of color.

Sundquist's tax proposals experienced two stunning defeats in 2001 and 2002. In 2001, the state legislature extended its session by two months—the longest in state history—to work out a budget agreement. Sundquist and pro-tax reform lawmakers proposed the income tax near the end of the legislative calendar; in response, conservatives organized a militant grassroots campaign that forced lawmakers to reject this proposal. Subsequently, the final budget implemented cuts to state programs worth hundreds of millions of dollars. Funds from the tobacco settlement were designated to fill the remaining $500 million budget gap. Sundquist then vetoed the budget agreement due to his belief that it failed to create long-term financial solvency for the state. Yet the state legislature overrode the governor's veto in a special session in August 2001. Afterward, the state was downgraded by the credit rating industry.[21]

Sundquist revitalized the tax plan the next year. Pro–tax reformers, mostly Democrats (who had a 58–41 majority in the House of Representatives and an 18–15 majority in the Senate), were ready to move the proposal through the legislature. Although many tax reform proposals were debated, the plan that had the potential to garner bipartisan support was a 3.25 percent flat tax coupled with a reduction in both the overall state sales tax and the sales taxes on food and other consumer goods. Speaker of the House James Naifeh proposed a 4–4.5 percent income tax, and he later added a tobacco tax to attract more legislators to his coalition. A graduated tax sponsored by Senator Robert Rochelle and Representative Tommy Head, both Democrats, received the greatest backing from liberal Democrats. It proposed to lower the sales tax while taxing middle- and higher-income residents. Their bill was cosponsored by Senator Roscoe Dixon, a black lawmaker from Memphis.[22]

Senator John Ford (D-Memphis), a prominent member of the black caucus, was a staunch advocate for progressive tax reform and had been working on the measure since the early 1980s. During the budget showdown in 2001, in a display of political comity, he proposed a flat tax to minimize political and racial discord in the legislature. He proposed a 2 percent rate on incomes, which was changed to a 3.1 percent tax combined with a significant reduction in the sales tax. He amended the proposal by adding deductions for poor families once progressives voiced opposition to it.[23] In reality, Ford was most likely lukewarm to the flat tax. Yet he was trying to win over centrists who understood the need to bring in revenue but would only be attracted to the more conservative-oriented flat tax.

Overall, the black caucus supported several income tax measures during the two-year debate. In 2002, it delayed its collective endorsement of a tax plan to negotiate with the governor and Democratic leaders for black representation on the Tennessee Regulatory Authority, which monitors the rates of privately owned gas and utility companies in the state.[24] The appointments are jointly considered by the governor and leaders of both houses of the General Assembly.

Kathryn Bowers, a Memphis legislator who was later elected to the state Senate, wanted guarantees that one of the seats that was opening on the three-person board (it now has a four-person board) would be filled by an appointee recommended by the black caucus.[25]

The Naifeh and Rochelle-Head proposals gave moderate and progressive lawmakers different tax reform options. Liberal and consumer advocacy groups also mobilized support for tax reform. On March 20, 2002, more than two thousand pro–tax reform advocates visited the capital to pressure lawmakers. The American Association of Retired Persons alone sent fourteen hundred people.[26]

These pressures notwithstanding, the General Assembly rejected both tax proposals. The final plan passed by the legislature increased corporate and businesses taxes in some areas, but it also increased the sales tax on some goods and items. No income tax measure was approved.[27] For these reasons, the revenue plan may have done more to hurt than to help the working poor. The measure split the black caucus: three members in the Senate (John Ford and Roscoe Dixon of Memphis and Thelma Harper of Nashville) supported it; however, all but two members in the House opposed it, with Joe Armstrong of Knoxville and Edith Langster of Nashville abstaining from the vote.[28]

The defeat of the income tax measure was a watershed event in the state. The income tax had the initial backing of an odd coalition: a conservative, states' rights governor; many liberal Democrats; and most members of the black caucus. But the coalition's defeat and the conservative angst about the tax ruined any chances for an income tax measure gaining momentum in the state legislature in the near future. The tax measure then became a litmus test for the 2002 gubernatorial election in which Phil Bredesen, a pro-growth Democrat who was Nashville's mayor in the 1990s, ran against Congressman Van Hilleary, a conservative Republican. Both candidates opposed the income tax.

Ironically, a graduated income tax was supported by Ed Sanders, an independent gubernatorial candidate and popular black minister from Nashville. Sanders was a peculiar candidate who did not fit squarely within the orthodoxy of the Democratic or Republican parties. Before campaigning for governor, he worked with public health advocates from both parties, especially on HIV/AIDS-related policies. His ideological positions were clearly on the left (more left than most Tennessee Democrats and just as progressive as the black Democratic legislators), although he also had public ties to the Republican Party.

In the next section, we explore how Tennesseans view tax and budget policies. The budget fights of the twenty-first century underscore why the state is an ideal case study of tax and spending attitudes, and they present us with an opportunity to explore residents' attitudes across several policy areas and at multiple levels of government. We examine the support for establishing a state income tax, attitudes toward the flat and graduated tax structures, views of state and federal spending, and racial polarization around these issues.

TENNESSEANS' VIEWS ABOUT AN INCOME TAX

We begin by looking for racial differences in attitudes about taxation. The first survey item in the spring 2002 MTSU poll gauged opinions about income taxes generally. A second item asked if respondents would be amenable to establishing a state income tax if doing so would ultimately lower sales taxes, and a final question asked Tennesseans if their viewpoint would change if the revenue from income taxes went toward funding education. In figure 5.1, we plot the number of whites (lighter bars) and nonwhites (darker bars) who opposed these three forms of income tax. Because of sample-size limitations, the racial comparisons that we make throughout this chapter are between white Tennesseans and nonwhite Tennesseans. Please note that the nonwhite category includes respondents who identified themselves as being African American, Asian, and Latino(a). We converted these numbers into percentages so that they can be more easily compared to one another. Overall, Tennesseans are more likely to oppose the income tax than to support it (see the first two bars in figure 5.1). This is true regardless of race. However, the percentage of white residents who oppose a general income tax is higher than that of their nonwhite neighbors.[29]

However, opinions changed when respondents were asked to consider the potential consequences of a higher income tax. Framing the creation of an income tax as an opportunity to lower the sales tax softens the viewpoints of Tennesseans. More than half of the respondents in the survey opposed an income tax in general, whereas less than one-fourth had that opinion if they believed the cost of an income tax would yield the benefit of a reduced sales tax.[30] Intriguingly, this policy frame was equally effective on white and nonwhite Tennessee residents. We find no statistically significant racial differences in opposition to this approach to tax policy,[31] which means that both whites and nonwhites were comparably susceptible to this framing of the question. A different pattern emerges, however, when exploring white versus nonwhite differences in opposition to an income tax plan that would finance education. On the one hand, it was useful to mention increased revenues for Tennessee schools when trying to persuade respondents to support an income tax. This is because the proportion of Tennesseans opposed to an income tax that excluded an education initiative was significantly higher than it was for a tax plan that indirectly benefited education.[32] However, unlike the "income tax can lower sales tax" policy frame, a

FIGURE 5.1 Racial differences in the opposition to a state income tax

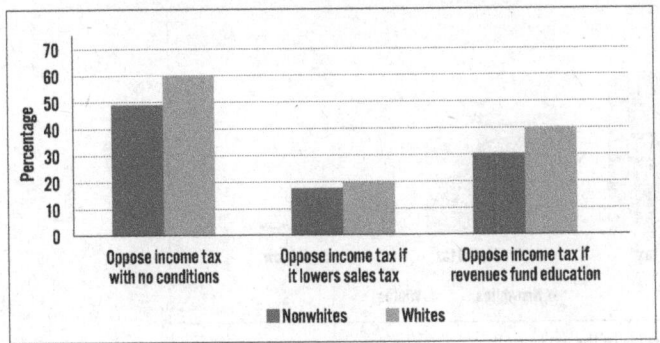

Source: Spring 2002 wave of the MTSU poll.
Note: N = 742.

greater percentage of whites (compared to residents of color) remained dissenters to income taxation even when it was paired with a public education plan.[33]

The results in figure 5.1 show that respondents were less opposed to higher income taxes if they thought the revenues were going to fund public education. However, this policy frame was not as convincing as the sales tax frame in decreasing opposition to an income tax. In other words, linking the income tax to school funding lacked persuasive force compared to the sales tax in reducing opposition to an income tax. The proportions of respondents who opposed an overall income tax and those who opposed one that lowers sales tax are .583 and .197, respectively, which constitutes a decrease of nearly 200 percent.[34] Conversely, the difference between the proportion of opposition to a plain income tax (.583) and to one that helps education (.388) is nearly 50 percent.[35]

Taken together, the results in figure 5.1 show that Tennesseans were generally resistant to the idea of a state income tax. However, this opposition weakened considerably if the rhetoric of passing an income tax was tied to the possibility of cutting the state sales tax. The prospect of spending income tax revenue on education inspired a similar (albeit smaller) boost in support.

The remaining set of items in the MTSU poll asked respondents to state their preference for either a flat (i.e., everyone is taxed the same amount or percentage, regardless of income) or graduated (i.e., Tennesseans with higher incomes are taxed at a higher rate) income tax. In figure 5.2, we illustrate that the flat tax option seemed to be more popular overall. Tennesseans tended to favor a tax structure that is applied equally to all residents rather than one based on income level.[36] We also uncover some fascinating racial differences in this set of opinions as the percentage of whites who favored a flat tax was significantly greater

FIGURE 5.2 Racial differences in preference for flat versus graduated tax

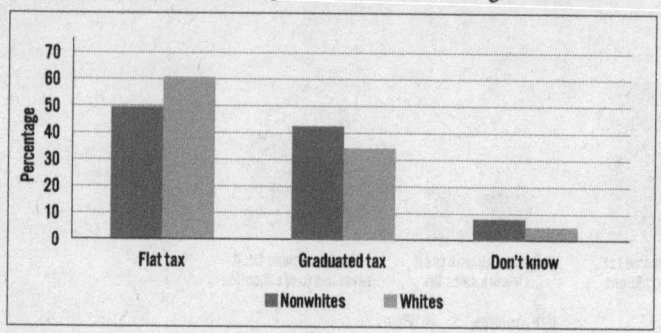

Source: Spring 2002 wave of the MTSU poll.
Note: N = 742.

than the percentage of nonwhites who preferred a flat tax.[37] Nonwhites outpaced their white counterparts when it came to expressing a preference for the graduated tax structure and claiming that they did not have a preference, but these differences do not reach conventional levels of statistical significance.[38] To summarize, the results in figure 5.2 demonstrate that if there has to be an income tax, Tennesseans would prefer a flat one.

In addition to assessing attitudes toward different tax plans, the spring 2002 wave of the MTSU poll embedded a question-order experiment within the survey. The experiment randomly queried half of the respondents about flat taxes before asking them a question about the graduated tax plan, while the order was reversed for the remaining respondents. In other words, the makers of the survey wanted to see if the answers to questions about taxes would change depending on whether flat-tax items came before graduated-tax ones or vice versa. Question-order experiments are common in public opinion research. Herbert Hyman and Paul Sheatsley conducted a well-known study in which they altered the order in which respondents received two survey items (one asked whether journalists from communist countries should be allowed to visit the United States to report the news, and the other checked to see if the same allowance should be granted to American journalists in communist countries). The authors demonstrated that respondents who got the communist version of this question before the American version were less inclined to welcome outside reporters.[39]

We take advantage of the MTSU poll's split-sample experiment to explore the influence of question order on the tax opinions of Tennessee residents. We discover racial differences across question order with respect to the level of opposition to the three questions about an income tax. Figure 5.3 provides visual evidence of these question-order effects. The figure is divided into two halves representing the results for nonwhites and whites. For each half, we report the percentage of respondents who opposed an overall income tax (darkest bars), an income tax that would lower sales tax (lightest bars), and an income tax that would funnel revenues into public education (medium bars). Overall, the patterns in this figure are familiar. Opposition among Tennesseans was highest for the unqualified variant of the income tax item, lowest for the item that proposed to lower sales tax, and moderate for the education-benefiting plan. More important, figure 5.3 tells us that question order had little influence on whites' opinions about the three income tax items.[40] This result holds true for nonwhite respondents when we consider the lower sales tax and funding education questions.[41] However, that is not the case when we explore attitudes about an overall income tax. Specifically, nonwhite respondents were significantly more accepting of a general income tax when they received the question about graduated taxes first.[42]

The fact that nonwhites expressed more tolerance for an income tax when the subject was introduced using ideas about a graduated (rather than a flat) tax structure suggests that we have found a circumstance in which race influenced the impact of question order on tax attitudes. Why were Tennesseans of color more susceptible to this question-order effect? We believe the answer lies in racial differences in demographic background. There is a long tradition of public opinion research confirming that people's attitudes about taxes reflect their economic self-interests, which, obviously, are influenced heavily by their social class. Likewise, extending the symbolic politics hypothesis, a line of reasoning developed by David Sears,[43] voters who abhor "big government" tend also to detest tax increases. We therefore expect Republican Tennesseans to oppose taxes of any kind more than their Democratic colleagues do. Furthermore, if we apply the rational calculus to Tennessee politics, then we could argue that affluent Tennesseans should prefer a flat tax system to a graduated one because the latter costs them more than the former.[44] Research by Kent Tedin and colleagues suggested that "group-based" considerations shape opinions about taxes. Younger respondents should be least pleased with income taxes, but the fervor of their opposition should wear down with age. Similarly, women are more tolerant of tax proposals because they tend to be more ideologically liberal than their male counterparts.[45]

When accounting for these demographic characteristics, we expect any racial differences in the respondents' opposition to an income tax to decrease, if not disappear. We marshal empirical evidence to support this claim. Table 5.1 contains two sets of analyses. First, we estimate a stripped-down multiple regression model of opposition to an income tax—with no control variables. Because the tax question is a binary dependent variable (1 = oppose income tax,

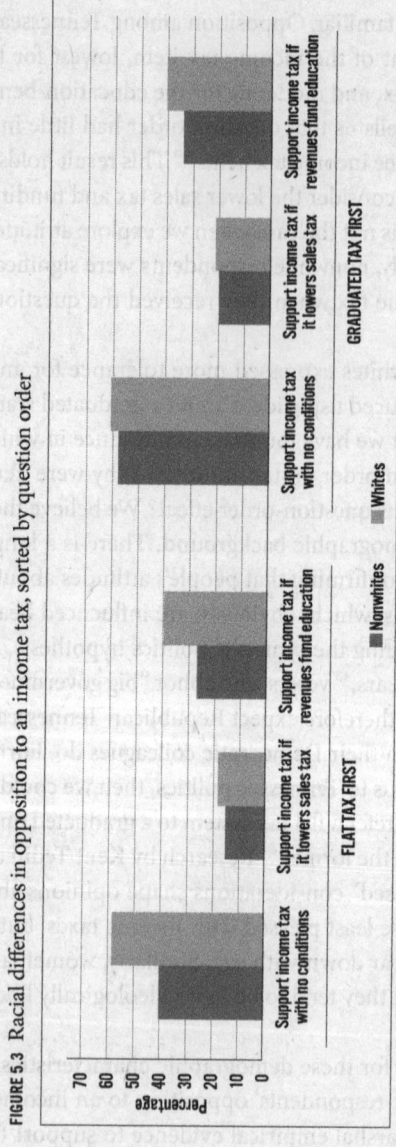

FIGURE 5.3 Racial differences in opposition to an income tax, sorted by question order

Source: Spring 2002 wave of the MTSU poll.
Note: N = 742.

0 = otherwise), we use logistic regression. The sole independent variable in the basic model is the race of the MTSU poll respondent, coded so that white Tennesseans get a score of 1, while nonwhites are scored as 0. This model specification enables us to explore the race gap in tax attitudes. A positive and statistically significant regression coefficient would tell us that whites are more opposed to an income tax than nonwhites are. A negative and significant estimate signals that nonwhites express the greatest disfavor. Regression values that are indistinguishable from zero (statistically nonsignificant) represent instances in which there are no racial differences in income tax attitudes. We break this basic model into two parts, each assessing the impact of race among the subsample of MTSU poll respondents for whom the flat tax or graduated tax discussion came first. The results in the basic model are consistent with previous findings. There were no white versus nonwhite differences (i.e., there was no race effect) in opposition to a state income tax when the tax question followed a discussion of graduated taxation. But white respondents (compared to their nonwhite colleagues) expressed significantly more opposition to an income tax when that polling question came after a survey item about the flat tax.

As expected, the race gap that was present in the flat-tax-first subsample of the basic model disappears in the fully specified regression model with control variables. To interpret this model, analysts should think of the race variable as representing the race gap in tax attitudes, holding several demographic, social, and political variables constant. We measure party identification with a pair of binary variables: each is coded as 1 for respondents who self-identify as Democrats (or Republicans) and 0 otherwise. Education is also a binary variable (1 = some college or trade school training, 0 = otherwise). So is gender (1 = woman, 0 = man). We also include several binary variables to distinguish Middle Tennessee's "doughnut" area (suburban counties that lean conservative and lie outside of the Democratic Party stronghold of Nashville–Davidson County) and "non-doughnut" area from the regions outside of Middle Tennessee. Income and age are continuous variables; the latter records a respondent's age in years, and the former keeps track of a respondent's income bracket (ranging from less than $20,000 per year after taxes to greater than $100,000 per year). We include a standard and squared version of the age variable to measure a potential curvilinear effect: the extent to which Tennesseans oppose the income tax might plateau and possibly decrease as respondents mature.

The results in the second half of table 5.1 show that whites and nonwhites are similarly opposed to a general income tax when a discussion of graduated taxes comes first.[46] We can see this because the previously positive and statistically significant regression coefficient for race is no longer significant after including all the control variables.[47] This is evidence that these background variables help to

TABLE 5.1 Predicting racial differences in the influence of question order on Tennesseans' opposition to a general income tax

Predictors	Flat tax first		Graduated tax first		Flat tax first		Graduated tax first	
	Logit estimate	SE	Logit estimate	SE	Logit estimate	SE	Logit estimate	SE
Race (1 = white, 0 = nonwhite)	0.73*	(0.31)	0.13	(0.31)	0.61	(0.36)	−0.04	(0.35)
Party ID (1 = Republican, 0 = otherwise)					0.62*	(0.29)	0.49	(0.28)
Party ID (1 = Democrat, 0 = otherwise)					0.54	(0.33)	0.14	(0.28)
Income level					−0.05	(0.03)	0.01	(0.03)
Some college/trade school education (1 = some education, 0 = otherwise)					−0.07	(0.27)	0.16	(0.26)
Age (in years)					0.15*	(0.05)	0.08*	(0.04)
Age squared					0.01*	(0.00)	0.01*	(0.00)
Region (1 = Middle Tennessee, doughnut, 0 = otherwise)					0.85	(0.52)	0.35	(0.42)
Region (1 = Middle Tennessee, non-doughnut, 0 = otherwise)					0.08	(0.49)	0.58	(0.47)
Region (1 = non–Middle Tennessee, 0 = otherwise)					−0.03	(0.42)	−0.13	(0.35)
Gender (1 = woman, 0 = man)					−0.98	(0.26)	−0.10	(0.23)
Constant	−0.39	0.28			−2.92	(1.09)	−1.57	(0.91)
Sample size	356		386		305		332	
Likelihood ratio chi-squared (χ^2)	5.91*		0.16*		35.92*		13.28*	

Source: Spring 2002 MTSU poll.

Notes: * = $p < 0.05$. For the education dummy variable, "no college" is the reference category. The reference category for the party identification variable is "independent." For the region dummies, the reference category is "Nashville suburb."

explain racial differences in the influence of question order on Tennesseans' opposition to the state implementing an income tax.

OPINIONS ABOUT STATE VERSUS FEDERAL GOVERNMENT SPENDING

Having explored opinions about taxation in the spring 2002 MTSU survey, we now focus our attention on racial differences in opinions about government spending. These differences, we anticipate, stem largely from the belief among Tennesseans that rises in government spending ultimately come out of the wallets of residents (sometimes in the form of increased taxes). This belief is understandable: economists have long debated the connection between government spending and taxation practices.[48] We explore these issues using the fall 2007 wave of the MTSU poll. This survey contained a battery of questions relating not only to specific taxes, but also to the more abstract notion of "government spending." This poll allows us to keep track of perceptions among Tennesseans regarding the government's use of taxes to finance a host of public works, defense, and health-care-related policies. In addition, the fall 2007 MTSU survey included an experimental manipulation in which half of its respondents were randomly assigned to receive questions about the spending practices of the state while the other half were asked about the spending practices of the federal government. This experiment gives us the opportunity to address the following question: Do Tennesseans believe that there has been too much, too little, or just the right amount of state or federal government spending? The answer to this question speaks directly to the role, if any, of respondents' preference for devolution on their policy attitudes.

As we show in figures 5.4 and 5.5, attitudes about government spending vary depending on the policy in question and the race of the respondent. The opinions of white respondents appear in the lighter bars, and those of minority residents are in the darker bars. In both figures, the bars reflect the number of Tennesseans (expressed as a percentage) who oppose government spending (those who responded that they believe there is "too much" government spending) on the policy or project in question.

Looking first at figure 5.4, we see that more whites (compared to nonwhites) were inclined to believe that the state government spends too much money. The only exceptions to this pattern were perceptions of spending on programs for residents with physical or cognitive disabilities, where more nonwhites expressed opposition than whites did. In several instances (spending on social welfare, highway construction, and mass transportation), the racial differences were so large that they are statistically significant.[49] There are also other cases—

FIGURE 5.4 Racial differences in opposition to various forms of state-level government spending

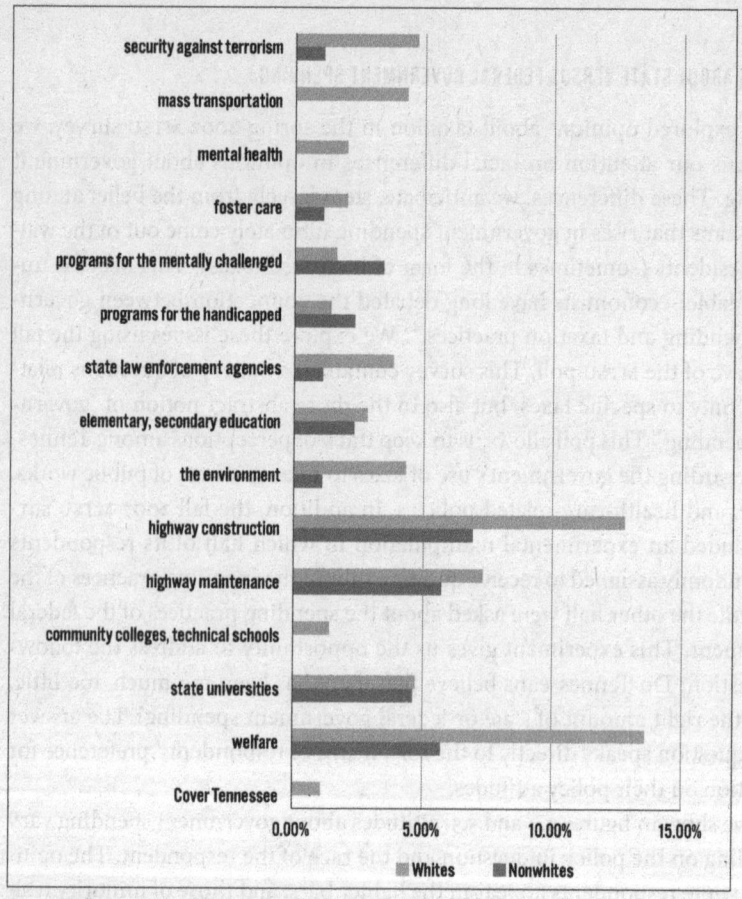

Source: Fall 2007 wave of the MTSU poll.
Note: N = 593.

spending on Cover Tennessee (the state's program for providing accessible and affordable health-care services to the uninsured), community colleges, mental health, and mass transportation again—in which there were not any nonwhite respondents who expressed opposition to state-level spending. In other words, nonwhites supported robust state spending on these initiatives.

The patterns become more complicated when we look at figure 5.5. What stands out most is that the race gap reverses: nonwhites were most likely to be unsupportive of government spending at the federal, rather than the state, level. When it comes to the topics of education (particularly spending for elemen-

FIGURE 5.5 Racial differences in opposition to various forms of federal-level government spending

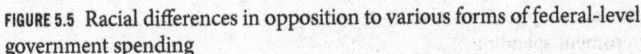

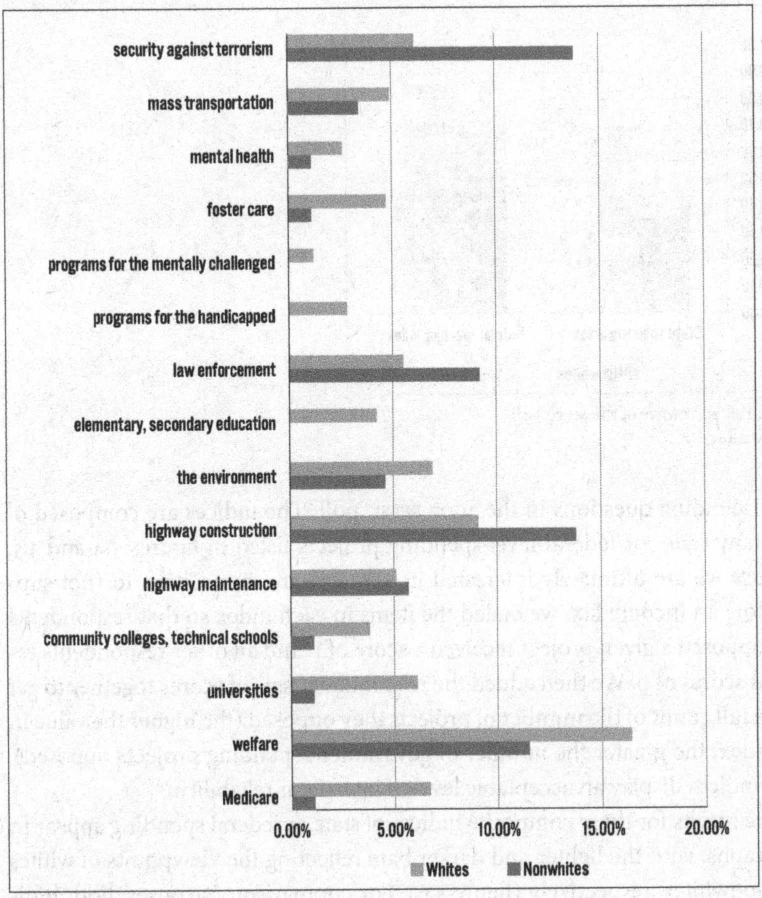

Source: Fall 2007 wave of the MTSU poll.
Note: N = 593.

tary schools and universities) and Medicare, these racial differences are both large in magnitude and statistically meaningful.[50] There are several instances in which there were no nonwhites opposing government spending. Interestingly, the largest racial gap was in attitudes about spending on security against terrorism, a policy domain in which nonwhites were clearly less sympathetic than their white counterparts.[51]

What do we make of these results? To explore further, it is useful to look not only at the individual survey items but also at an overall index of these spending opinions. Thus, we created additive indices of the state and federal govern-

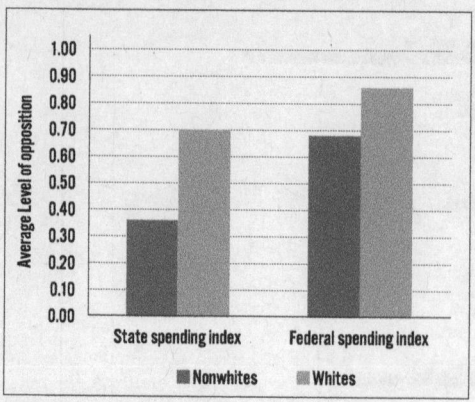

FIGURE 5.6 Racial differences in opposition to state- and federal-level government spending

Source: Fall 2007 wave of the MTSU poll.
Note: N = 593.

ment spending questions in the 2007 MTSU poll. The indices are composed of the many state- or federal-level spending projects listed in figures 5.4 and 5.5. Because we are ultimately interested in Tennesseans' opposition to (not support for) an income tax, we coded the items in each index so that respondents who opposed a given project received a score of 1, and all other respondents received scores of 0. We then added the respondents' sets of scores together to get an overall count of the number of projects they opposed (the higher the value in the index, the greater the number of government spending projects opposed). Both indices display an acceptable level of inter-item reliability.[52]

The results for these composite indices of state or federal spending appear in bar graphs, with the lighter and darker bars reflecting the viewpoints of whites and nonwhites, respectively (figure 5.6). For comparison purposes, both indices have been rescaled so that they range from 0 (low overall opposition toward government spending) to 1 (high opposition). The average levels of opposition toward state- and federal-level spending are .65 and .83, respectively, and a difference of means test reveals that opposition toward federal-level spending tends to outpace that of state-level spending by a substantial margin.[53]

We get an even clearer story when we separate the results of each composite index by race. As shown in figure 5.6, Tennesseans (regardless of race) were opposed to federal spending, but whites were consistently less tolerant of state-level government spending.[54] A similar trend emerges for the federal spending index, but the between-race differences are not large enough to reach statistical significance.[55]

CONCLUSION

We began this chapter with a discussion of one of Tennessee's more controversial issues in 2001–2002: an income tax. Some legislators had proposed to implement an income tax in the Volunteer State in order to resolve a crippling budget crisis. Several possibilities were considered, including using the money generated by income taxes to offset the state's similarly unpopular sales tax. Members of the Tennessee Black Caucus of State Legislators were instrumental in steering the agenda. Most believed that an income tax would boost revenues that could be used for social programs for their constituents, including the working poor. In other words, an income tax could help promote a liberal and racially egalitarian agenda, which has been traditionally supported by the black caucus.

As results from the 2002 MTSU survey show, the income tax was both a racial and a political issue. There is evidence that whites and nonwhites in Tennessee tended to perceive the issues of taxes and spending differently. These findings are not that surprising for, as we have noted throughout the chapter, there is anecdotal evidence to back up the statistical results.

The 2007 MTSU poll provides yet another perspective. The data show that Tennesseans of color felt differently than their white neighbors did about the role of government spending. Again, these differences of opinion are not surprising: they are further confirmation of the racial divide in public opinion. This divide arises from the divergent social and political experiences of whites and minorities. For example, Andrew Hacker spoke of "two nations": he argued that blacks and whites live in different Americas.[56] Hacker's description is an excellent point of departure for understanding race relations, and it makes sense that an analysis of tax and spending attitudes would consider the separate environments within which African American and white Tennesseans reside.

More generally, the findings we have presented in this chapter underscore how devolution and racial polarization have shaped Tennessee politics in the twenty-first century. Americans tend to support devolution in principle, despite being relatively skeptical of state governments' ability to enact and enforce various policies. Such skepticism is warranted when viewed from the perspective of U.S. race relations, for southern states like Tennessee have historically been ambivalent about (if not antagonistic toward) redistributive policies. In this chapter, we have shown not only that debates over taxes and government spending *reflect* this antagonism (in the sense that racial group competition and zero-sum perceptions fuel people's views about government funding priorities), but these debates may also *contribute* to it (by widening the opinion gap between white Tennesseans and residents of color).

CHAPTER SIX

THE RISE AND FALL OF TENNCARE

> Please reform the management of TennCare as you promised to do. Please restore health care for the sick and vulnerable people who have lost their TennCare and cannot get other insurance. Please allow TennCare patients to get medicine and other care that they urgently need.... People I know are hurting because of the TennCare cuts. Please do what is right and take care of the people who need it.
>
> —MEMPHIS RESIDENT TO GOVERNOR PHIL BREDESEN (2005)

Since the addition of the Title XIX provision in the Social Security Act of 1965, Medicaid (an option states can choose in which the federal government matches the funds that states allocate to medical goods and services) has worked to ensure that citizens with limited resources have access to quality health care. TennCare, which began in January 1994, was a unique health insurance plan. It was the first in the country to replace the state's Medicaid program with a "managed-care" bureaucracy. Tennessee implemented TennCare as an attempt to "expand Tennessee's Medicaid program by using managed-care principles to deliver health care to a larger number of people for the same amount of money."[1] Because of TennCare's innovative strategies, Tennessee attracted national attention from health-care advocates.[2] However, the experiment struggled. It faced routine opposition from fiscal conservatives and some insurance companies, but at the same time gave thousands of Tennesseans access to health care. As Carole Myers noted, we can attribute the rise and fall of TennCare to several factors.[3] These include allegations of bureaucratic mismanagement, the increasing costs of maintaining the program, and failed negotiations between government officials, various stakeholders in the medical industry, and advocates serving underserved communities in general and TennCare enrollees in particular.[4] Although we account for these factors, in this chapter we give particular attention to the role played by Governor Phil Bredesen in moving Tennessee away from this health-care plan and back to a more traditionally run Medicaid system.

On January 10, 2005, Bredesen, a Democrat, announced his final plan to reform TennCare. The governor's reform package was radical by any measure and included the most drastic cuts in the forty years since federal-state programs began delivering health care to the poor in Tennessee. He proposed the removal of almost half of the adults (323,000) from the TennCare program (this number was later reduced to 226,000 and then to 191,000) and reductions in benefits for the remaining 396,000 adult enrollees. These reductions included monthly and annual restrictions on prescription drugs, doctor visits, inpatient and outpatient care, and X-rays.[5] For sick beneficiaries facing the immediate loss of health care, the reforms were catastrophic.

The governor's reform package angered lawmakers, civil rights leaders, and health-care advocates. The county commission in Lawrence County passed a unanimous resolution opposing the cuts, pointing out that 3,566 adults, or more than one in ten adults in Lawrence County, would be cut from the TennCare rolls.[6] Ceci Connolly of the *Washington Post* reported that the "announcement sent shivers through health-care professionals nationwide who see ... TennCare's retreat as the start of a bleak trend to scale back government-paid care at the time the private sector is trimming benefits."[7] William Welch and Julie Appleby of *USA Today* wrote that doctors, therapists, and clinical social workers were worried that the governor's reforms "would create a second-class health system in which saving money, not healing the sick, is a primary concern."[8] "What is happening in Tennessee is profoundly cruel," noted *New York Times* columnist Bob Herbert.[9]

In response to his critics, Bredesen argued that Medicaid's payment scheme has more in common with a "socialist economy" than with "common sense economic and business principles."[10] After announcing the reduction plan, he tried to reassure residents that individuals who were disenrolled from TennCare would be able to receive medical assistance in alternative health-care programs—or what was often referred to in the media as the "health-care safety net," such as community health centers, hospital emergency rooms, employer-based insurance programs, and preventative and clinical services. According to the governor and his allies, the replacement of Medicaid with safety-net programs was an effective, cost-efficient trade-off. He insisted that these programs could absorb the working poor and chronically ill Tennesseans.

In this chapter we examine the debate over TennCare reform, focusing primarily on the period from the fall of 2004, when Bredesen proposed that TennCare be dissolved, to the winter of 2005, when the mass disenrollment of Tennessee residents from TennCare sparked considerable controversy. We assess how public actors (the governor and members of his administration, state lawmakers, health-care professionals, and health justice and civil rights advocates) shaped the debate about the program and how race and social class influenced perceptions about the TennCare reforms. In Tennessee, these actors constituted what Alan Abramowitz referred to as the "polarized public," the engaged citizens who advanced differing narratives about TennCare during this period.[11]

We give close attention to various rationales the governor used to justify the overhaul of TennCare and how the narratives polarized the public in Tennessee. Specifically, we look at the safety-net narrative the governor promulgated in order to examine whether voters in Tennessee believed his argument that this would mitigate the effects of losing access to TennCare health insurance. We rely on public opinion polls from the MTSU Survey Group and a survey-based experiment we conducted in the fall of 2008 and the spring of 2009, which measured the impact of the TennCare debate on social and political attitudes. We supplement these results with qualitative data drawn from primary and secondary sources, including documents obtained from the TennCare Saves Lives Coalition, the principal advocacy group that opposed the governor's reforms, as well as Bredesen's official records at the Tennessee State Library and Archives.[12]

First, we provide an overview of how the TennCare debate underscored deeper concerns about political polarization in Tennessee. This is followed by a historical summary of the TennCare program and the raucous battle over the governor's reform policy. We then investigate the degree to which the ideas underlying Governor Bredesen's safety-net narrative took hold in public discourse and shaped opinions about his reform of TennCare. We conclude by situating our results within broader discussions of the rise and fall of TennCare.

POLARIZATION AND TENNCARE

Debates over health-care reform tend to polarize the public. According to Douglas Blanks Hindman, partisanship tends to shape attitudes toward health-care reform more significantly than social status or class do. He argued that the public's views on health care will be more closely aligned to the preferences of their political parties than to the presumed predispositions of their social class.[13] Democrats have traditionally been the strongest supporters of Medicaid. Blacks have also been among the strongest supporters of Medicaid, since many blacks do not have access to adequate insurance and live in areas that have substandard medical care. In Tennessee, these conditions produce a context in which

African Americans disproportionately depend on Medicaid for their health and well-being.[14]

That attitudes toward health-care reform can be closely attached to political party membership and racial identity complicates the discussion of the TennCare reforms. Although it was a fellow Democrat, Governor Ned McWherter, who initiated TennCare in 1994, Bredesen was a fiscal conservative. He introduced his reform measures at a time when Democrats had a shrinking majority in both chambers of the Tennessee General Assembly. Thus, although progressives and many health-care professionals opposed Bredesen's measures, some Democratic Party elites attempted to curb such dissent because they were afraid that it would split the party's base and give Republicans an advantage in the 2006 midterm and gubernatorial elections.

There has been a growing racial divide at the national level over health-care reform.[15] Michael Henderson and D. Sunshine Hillygus found that racial minorities, especially blacks, tend to express the greatest support for universal or expanded health care.[16] These patterns also reflect party lines, for most blacks are firm members of the Democratic Party. Thus, the racial politics of the TennCare reforms presented a challenge to the Bredesen administration and his allies in the state legislature. Bredesen needed to be politically sensitive to African Americans: blacks were his most loyal bloc of supporters yet they had a lot to lose from his Medicaid reforms. Blacks were disproportionately represented in the program: although they constituted 17 percent of the state's population, the four hundred thousand black adults and children in TennCare constituted nearly one-third of the enrollees.

Bredesen needed to minimize opposition from health-care advocates and African American leaders. He attempted to convince prominent African Americans that the TennCare cuts would do little harm to their constituencies. This strategy relied on the notion that African Americans were beholden to what Frymer called "electoral capture";[17] they were trapped between a hostile Republican Party, which had been mostly opposed to TennCare since its creation, and the Democrats, whose principal leader in the state intended to downsize the program. The belief was that African American leaders would embrace political comity and offer little resistance to Bredesen's TennCare reform because they would deem it important to maintain (Democratic Party) unity. However, embracing political comity in this way can marginalize a racial equalitarian agenda or, as in the case of the TennCare debate, result in disregarding black opposition to public policies that hurt many African Americans. Bredesen had mixed success with this strategy. While some black lawmakers and interest groups attempted to shield the governor from criticism, there was a groundswell of opposition to his reform package.

It is important to highlight how devolution shaped the TennCare debate during this period. In contrast to Medicare, its sister program, Medicaid is a federal-state program that gives states the flexibility to adjust benefit limits and enrollment with oversight from Congress and from the Centers for Medicare and Medicaid Services.[18] In the early 1980s, President Ronald Reagan, under the banner of devolution, attempted to reduce Medicaid funding and give states more power to manage the program. In the early years of the program, section 1115 of the Social Security Act gave states waivers to initiate managed care and home- and community-based services, which were more cost-efficient than direct Medicaid spending.[19] Some observers believed that these waivers would give states too much authority in the provision of standard medical care and give them the power to exclude consumers in dire need of services.[20]

Despite the concerns about section 1115, President Bill Clinton expanded the waiver program in 1994 so that states could cover more uninsured populations.[21] This entailed the development of managed-care systems that would oversee the delivery of state-level Medicaid programs.[22] TennCare is an example of such a program. Although the traditional Medicaid program attempts to serve impoverished families, many individuals among the working poor or who are experiencing financial hardships due to disabilities and medical crises may not qualify because they do not meet the federal government's eligibility guidelines.[23] In 1994, Governor Ned McWherter began the process of expanding Medicaid coverage beyond the federal guidelines in order to provide health care to working-poor adults and children, disabled people, elderly residents who need financial assistance to pay for prescription drugs, individuals with mental health disabilities, and middle-class consumers with chronic long-term illnesses.[24]

Expanding Medicaid coverage to uninsured and ailing Tennesseans made the state eligible to receive federal funds: two dollars for every dollar the state spent on Medicaid. By some calculations, expanding Medicaid can contribute to the economic growth of a state. Because Tennessee has no state income tax, it routinely faces budget shortfalls, and lawmakers frequently call for cuts to much-needed programs and services. Many Democrats, health advocates, and social justice activists believe that supplemental dollars from the federal government could create a permanent funding stream and fix the chronic budget woes that the absence of a state income tax has created.

In the next section, we examine the rise and fall of TennCare. This discussion includes a description of the mobilization activities of those who worked to advance social justice through a more equitable allocation of resources related to health care. We also look at how race and, more specifically, African Americans shaped the debate over Medicaid and TennCare.

OVERVIEW OF THE TENNCARE DEBATE, 1994-2006

Medicaid (Title XIX) was created in 1965 as health insurance for the poor. It was negotiated as a political compromise between President Lyndon Johnson and the American Medical Association. The latter clearly wanted to increase physicians' ability to care for families with limited resources, and Johnson, seeking to bolster his appeal with voters, realized the importance of maintaining some of the momentum that the concept of a national health insurance program had gained as early as the Truman administration.[25] However, as Jonathan Engel noted, Medicaid has at times been referred to as the "orphan" of the War on Poverty initiatives.[26] The program was initially based on the medical vouchers that private insurance companies offered to poor people, but it quickly expanded into a robust insurance program.[27]

Blacks and other racial minorities were particularly supportive of Medicaid. Many lived in areas that lacked minority physicians and financially stable medical facilities.[28] Racial minorities looked to Medicaid to address their substandard health care and systemic exclusion from established medical institutions. Rural residents also benefited from Medicaid. Many lived far away from health-care facilities, which contributed to their alienation from the medical profession.

When TennCare was first initiated in 1994, health-care practitioners and African American leaders celebrated the program because of its potential to expand coverage to hundreds of thousands of uninsured and chronically ill patients. The program was initially conceived as a managed-care program: participating insurance companies were converted into managed-care organizations. These organizations were paid lump sums, or what was referred to as "capitation fees," to deliver and manage health care for thousands of patients.[29] The potential benefit for state Medicaid programs that use managed-care systems is that if medical costs in a given month or year for a group of patients are more than the fees allocated to a participating insurance company, that company must absorb the additional costs. For example, if TennCare allocated $1 million per year to Blue Cross/Blue Shield to supervise health coverage for forty thousand patients, the insurance company would have to pay the balance of the medical costs for its patients if the costs exceeded the capitated amount that TennCare allotted.

Some of the people who pushed for improved health care in Tennessee believed that managed-care systems contained costs by forcing providers and insurance companies to focus attention on preventative services.[30] Catastrophic illnesses, emergency room visits, and the overprescribing of drugs are common events for individuals who lack preventative care. These events add costs to Medicaid programs and can affix a financial burden to insurance companies. In theory, the potential risk of absorbing excessive medical costs encourages participating insurance companies to offer efficient services, disease management, and strict oversight of prescription drug use, all of which have the potential to stabilize costs and prevent Medicaid recipients from developing expensive medical conditions.

Within a few years of its implementation, TennCare expanded coverage to hundreds of thousands of working poor and chronically ill residents, people who otherwise would not have had any insurance. The state's uninsured population decreased by 30 percent, and the urban poor who used TennCare had greater access to private hospitals. Disabled residents could use TennCare to pay for private nursing and home health services; before the program was created, many had been forced to live in poorly run nursing homes.[31] Health coverage was expanded to residents with severe chronic conditions, such as HIV/AIDS, diabetes, cancer, and other illnesses that required long-term care.[32]

Despite evidence of TennCare's efficacy in reducing the number of uninsured Tennesseans, it faced many challenges. Fiscal conservatives and other opponents criticized TennCare for endangering the right of private physicians to provide or withhold their services as they choose and for giving the federal government too much influence over the state's health-care delivery system. They particularly opposed the program's managed-care system, and they questioned TennCare's capacity to control spending and the rising costs of prescription drugs.[33]

Governor McWherter responded to his critics by threatening to reduce existing Medicaid payments to hospitals, physicians, and nursing homes. He floated the ideas of levying a financing fee on hospitals or imposing a state income tax to raise revenue for medical care. The former strategy would have penalized hospitals (which typically have a tough time turning a profit) that tried to secure outside funding and/or merger partners, while the latter strategy would have meant that residents would pay higher taxes.[34] Private physicians and insurance companies were among TennCare's staunchest opponents.

The election of Republican Don Sundquist as governor in 1994, the same year the TennCare program began, created additional challenges for the program. During Sundquist's tenure (1995–2003), he made a failed attempt to remove thousands of beneficiaries from the TennCare program. He also restructured the contracts of managed-care organizations after several insurance companies threatened to leave the program and the state. The new agreements removed any risks for the insurance companies.[35] They no longer had to cover medical costs that exceeded the capitation fees; the state government absorbed these costs.[36] The combination of the exemption of insurance companies from financial risk, the rising costs of prescription drugs, and the large number of people with chronic conditions increased TennCare's annual costs.

In addition, Sundquist angered the state's black leaders when he canceled the TennCare contracts of two popular black-owned insurance companies, Xantus Corporation and Access MedPlus. Access MedPlus, founded and directed by Anthony Cebrun, was the second largest managed-care organization in the state and the largest minority-owned business in Tennessee. Cebrun had a close relationship with the state's black legislative caucus, health-care professionals, clergy, and civil rights groups. Although Access MedPlus was routinely criticized for mismanagement and financial insolvency, black leaders countered these claims by insisting that white-owned insurance companies also faced similar challenges yet escaped the criticisms that were levied against Cebrun's company.[37]

By the time Phil Bredesen became governor in January 2003, TennCare was a flashpoint for debates about the management and financial solvency of government-subsidized health care. His election was widely applauded by those in the health-care profession because throughout his campaign, Bredesen had insisted that he would draw on his experiences as a corporate health-care executive to fix the TennCare program. Many of the Tennesseans who supported Bredesen assumed that he would stabilize prescription drug costs, rein in insurance companies that were no longer obligated to follow the capitation-fee requirements, and solve TennCare's management problems without downsizing the program.

One of the first steps Bredesen took was to commission a study of the program by McKinsey and Company, a New York–based management consulting firm. Released in two waves (December 2003 and February 2004), the multimillion-dollar McKinsey Report analyzed the financial stability of the state's budget in the context of TennCare's annual spending growth.[38] Its authors predicted a dire scenario for the state budget: TennCare would consume 36 percent of state appropriations by 2008 if major reforms were not made to the program. The McKinsey Report catapulted TennCare to the top of the governor's agenda. From his standpoint, the study provided empirical evidence that TennCare would fiscally destabilize the state unless major reforms were implemented.[39]

Health-care advocates were troubled by the McKinsey Report. The study was mostly funded by Blue Cross/Blue Shield of Tennessee, the Hospital Corporation of America, Vanderbilt University, the Farm Bureau, and the Tennessee Hospital Association.[40] Virtually all these groups were critical of the TennCare program; the Tennessee Hospital Association, for example, openly endorsed TennCare reform even before the report was completed. Bredesen's critics charged that the study lacked the objectivity required to appropriately evaluate the TennCare program and that its underlying objective was to bias the evidence in order to justify the TennCare reforms.

The governor planned a two-stage blitzkrieg across the state to advocate for major changes to TennCare. Bredesen's initial reform plan entailed benefit reductions, limits on prescription drugs and doctor visits, and higher co-pays for adult enrollees. Children and disabled and pregnant beneficiaries were exempted from the reductions, although some observers complained that loopholes in the plan would force poor families to pay more for their children's medications or would force them to purchase the least expensive medications, even when those were known to have undesirable side effects.[41] The governor promised that disenrollments would only take place if health-care practitioners opposed the benefit cuts in the courts.[42] At the time, federal courts were supervising the TennCare program to ensure that it was adhering to consent decrees that protected the civil rights and due process of its beneficiaries. These decrees, which had been issued by federal judges in response to class-action lawsuits against the TennCare program, were major obstacles to disenrollment because they tied the governor's hands to some extent in terms of what he could do to change TennCare provisions.

The first stage of the tour, which was led by David Goetz, the state finance commissioner, coincided with the release of the first half of the McKinsey Report in December 2003. Governor Bredesen headed the second stage in late February 2004, after the second part of the report was released. During the tour, Bredesen and members of his administration met with the editorial boards of a dozen newspapers and other local media.[43] In the majority-black city of Memphis, Bredesen selected an "inner-city area" where a large number of people would be "facing the most initial shock/reorganization from the [TennCare] changes."[44] Bredesen had been advised that Memphis mayor Willie Herenton and Shelby County mayor A. C. Wharton had "higher profiles than General Assembly members" and that they could be used to leverage support for the reforms.[45] In East Tennessee, where the tour began, he wanted to fend off potential opposition from prominent Republicans, many of whom were reluctant to replace a Medicaid program that had a proven track record with a managed-care system that they saw as a "Cadillac program" that was rife with "too much fraud and abuse."[46]

Polling data revealed that the medical community in Chattanooga had concerns about the TennCare reforms. Managed-care programs like TennCare allow health-care providers to cover poor and disabled Medicaid enrollees in return for a fixed payment from taxpayers. That is good from the standpoint of stabilizing a government's budget. However, some health-care analysts believe that managed-care programs create potential conflicts of interest: the less care delivered by these health-care companies, the more money they can make, and such an incentive may ultimately compromise the health-care services residents receive.[47]

In March and April 2004, the Tennessee legislature began deliberations of the reform plan.[48] Representative Kathryn Bowers, a leading black lawmaker from Memphis, was among the most vocal critics of the plan. As the vice chair of the TennCare Oversight Committee, the legislative body tasked with reviewing changes to the program, she submitted fifty questions to her colleagues that called attention to the lack of legislative supervision over the reform measures and the adverse impact the governor's plan would have on people with chronic illnesses.[49] Senator Doug Jackson (D-Dickson), chair of the oversight committee, raised similar concerns.

The bill to reform TennCare included restrictions on hospital visits, X-rays, prescription drugs, and inpatient and outpatient care. Conservatives celebrated it. Representative Beth Harwell, chair of the Tennessee Republican Party, said that it "included elements of previous Republican proposals."[50] The bill received unanimous approval in the Senate, which included three black senators (Thelma Harper of Nashville, John Ford of Memphis, and Roscoe Dixon of Memphis). In the House, only eight of ninety-nine members voted against it; that group included three of the fifteen members of the Tennessee Black Caucus of State Legislators.[51] The bill thus passed overwhelmingly in both the House and the Senate, and the new law went into effect on May 17, 2004.

In addition to reducing benefits to TennCare clients, the legislation centralized oversight responsibilities for TennCare inside the executive branch by removing monitoring of the program from the legislature's jurisdiction. The new law gave the governor's office, the State of Tennessee Bureau of TennCare (created during the McWherter administration as part of the Division of Health Care Finance and Administration), the TennCare Advisory Commission (part of the state legislature), and the newly created TennCare Foundation (a nongovernmental office that was later closed for unknown reasons) primary responsibility for determining TennCare eligibility. As the legislation was written, the governor would make appointments to the TennCare Advisory Commission and the TennCare Foundation.[52] However, Bredesen amended the bill in the last hour to permit some legislative consultation regarding appointments to the advisory commission.

Another controversial aspect of the new law was that, at the urging of Bredesen, it changed TennCare's definition of the term "medical necessity." Medical necessity, a conceptual framework used by medical professionals and insurance programs, defines how much treatment health-care providers can give their patients. States that have expanded their Medicaid programs have the capacity to develop either a restrictive definition of medical necessity or an expansive one that offers broad treatment to patients—with the approval of the Centers for Medicare and Medicaid Services.[53] A restrictive definition could mean that Medicaid beneficiaries would only receive the least costly treatments for medical conditions instead of the standard of medical care.

The new definition used a four-part model to determine medical necessity: the treatment needed to be necessary for diagnosing a condition, it needed to be "safe and effective" (that is, "the reasonably anticipated medical benefits of the item or service must outweigh the reasonably anticipated medical risks"), it needed to be the least expensive mode of treatment, and it needed to have "adequate" scientific evidence of its safety and effectiveness.[54] Under Bredesen's definition of medical necessity, treatment could include "observation, lifestyle or behavioral changes, or where appropriate, no treatment at all."[55] This new definition applied to all TennCare enrollees, including children.[56]

Advocates of equal access to quality health care argued that this definition of medical necessity was among the most austere in the country, and a Kaiser Family Foundation survey of definitions of this concept across the country found that Tennessee's was substantially more restrictive than those used in other states.[57] The survey report pointed out that under Tennessee's definition, a standard of care that prioritized the treatments that were most appropriate and safe was no longer sufficient; in Tennessee, treatment also had to meet the criterion of least costly. In 2004, there was no precedent in the United States for delivery of care under this type of mandate.[58] Representatives of the American Association of People with Disabilities, the Children's Defense Fund, the National Women's Law Center, and the American Association of Retired Persons insisted that this definition paved the way for a two-tiered health-care delivery system in which consumers with private insurance received standard medical care while those on Medicaid did not.[59] Ted Shaw of the NAACP Legal Defense and Educational Fund, Inc., believed that the new definition of medical necessity would have a disparate impact on blacks in Tennessee. In a letter to the governor, he stated:

> [The Legal Defense and Educational Fund] anticipates that this change [the revised definition of medical necessity] could have serious and disproportionate adverse effects on the quality of health care available to low-income African Americans in Tennessee. We are also concerned that this definition could establish a harmful precedent that would further depress the already substandard quality of health care

available to minorities across the country. This legislative change could set a precedent for other states across the country which would further depress the quality of health care available to low-income African Americans and other minorities.[60]

It was reported that Ron Pollack, the director of Families USA, a national public health-care advocacy group, worried that Bredesen's definition would cut services to the poor and that other states would follow Tennessee's example if the federal government approved the proposed change.[61]

In remarks before the House of Representatives, Kathryn Bowers said that the TennCare Oversight Committee and the Government Operations Committee, both of which were committees of the Tennessee General Assembly that reviewed procedural changes, would amend the governor's plan in ways that would soften its impact on the working poor and those with acute medical conditions.[62] However, the amendment process Bowers anticipated did not happen, mainly because the statute handed over some of the traditional responsibilities of these two committees to members of the executive branch, whose loyalties were to Governor Bredesen.[63] Moreover, many of the committees' members, especially those on the Government Operations Committee, were supporters of the governor or represented constituents who were skeptical about universal health insurance.

Another source of controversy was the status of federally supervised consent decrees that monitored the civil rights of TennCare enrollees. Shortly after the program was created in the mid-1990s, state officials and the legal representatives of TennCare participants, chiefly the Tennessee Justice Center, a nonprofit organization that represented tens of thousands of beneficiaries who had been abused by health-care providers, negotiated several legal settlements for TennCare enrollees, both adults and children. These decrees (*John B. v. Goetz, Rosen v. Commissioner, Grier v. Goetz,* and *Newberry v. Goetz*) were supervised by the U.S. District Court of Middle Tennessee and the Sixth Circuit Court of Appeals. They ensured that TennCare did not discriminate against applicants for Medicaid who had been on public assistance; that the program met the federal standard for early and periodic screening, diagnostic, and treatment for children; that improvements in the appeals process were implemented; and that the appeals process for children in state custody was monitored.[64] In other words, the federal government had stepped in to ensure that the rights of the most vulnerable were protected.

The consent decrees created a unique power dynamic for the Bredesen administration. Although approval from the federal courts was required for changes to TennCare benefits, the courts had limited authority to prevent a wholesale disenrollment of beneficiaries if the governor and the state legislature approved such a move. The consent decrees did not prevent public officials from removing beneficiaries from TennCare nor from eliminating appropriations that funded the program. Considering this legal circumstance, the governor presented two options to advocacy groups: they could agree to major benefit reductions and to modifications to the consent decrees or they would be forced to accept a massive disenrollment of beneficiaries. Both options would curtail TennCare's spending growth, which the governor projected to be $2.5 billion by 2008. From the standpoint of health-care advocates, Bredesen's proposal was a devil's bargain. Either option would jeopardize low-income and high-risk beneficiaries and eliminate legal safeguards against maltreatment.

By August 2003, Governor Bredesen had renegotiated the terms of the agreements in the four statewide class-action lawsuits the Tennessee Justice Center had previously won. This was a victory for Bredesen because the new settlement agreements would save the state millions of dollars. Although Bredesen had the power to modify the consent decrees, he did not have the power to eliminate them completely. The federal government could sanction the state or shut down TennCare if Tennessee did not agree to the consent decrees. Thus, the Tennessee Justice Center successfully used the courts to block the governor's plans to have the four consent decrees set aside.[65]

After efforts to remove the consent decrees failed in the courts, the state turned to the U.S. Congress. In the summer of 2005, Lamar Alexander, Tennessee's junior senator, sponsored a bill designed to reduce the effectiveness of federal consent decrees. The governor's finance commissioner, Dave Goetz, was also invited to testify before a U.S. House of Representatives subcommittee to discuss the harmful impact of consent decrees. He said, "As the Tennessee experience illustrates, when consent decrees are allowed to exist perpetually, state officials with the responsibility for administering the program at issue are unduly constrained by plaintiffs' attorneys and federal judges."[66] The bill failed, but if it had been implemented, it would have curtailed the ability of TennCare enrollees to have adequate legal representation in medical-care-related grievances.

By the fall of 2004, tensions between the governor and the Tennessee Justice Center had reached a crisis point. The deadline for negotiating a settlement agreement over new court cases involving the alleged mismanagement of TennCare enrollees was early January 2005, when the legislative session began. During this period, the administration discussed various ways to respond to the concerns of medical-industry stakeholders and community advocates regarding the unsatisfactory state of TennCare reform. In a confidential document titled "Framing the TennCare Contingency Plan," which was circulated among members of the governor's staff on October 15, 2004, the Bredesen administration outlined changes in the way it would discuss the TennCare reforms. This entailed going beyond benefit reductions to include the possibility of a major overhaul of the program: "If we are solving for full FY06 budget success (TennCare expenditures approaching 30 percent of state budget), early analysis suggests that only one contingency plan with reasonable odds of success may exist, i.e., return to traditional Medicaid with full disenrollment of all optional enrollees, due to operational, legal and CMS [Centers for Medicare and Medicaid Services] realities."[67]

In this confidential document, the administration discussed three options for reforming TennCare. The first entailed only instituting the benefit restrictions that had been approved by the state legislature in September 2004. The second was full disenrollment, which the governor admitted would be the "worst for enrollees" since it would move residents into a more traditional Medicaid program, thus limiting the services that were available to them (or that they could afford). The third option was to freeze enrollment for standard Medicaid, essentially limiting the number of Tennesseans who could receive government-assisted health-care benefits.[68] The administration believed that health-care stakeholders would not oppose the first option but that the second and third options would generate resistance.

Negotiations between stakeholders and the governor failed in November 2004. In a good-faith effort, the Tennessee Justice Center offered a deal: the court would extend the deadline for the stakeholders and Bredesen to reach a resolution (which would be advantageous for the governor because it would, in essence, dilute the consent decrees) in exchange for the governor's promise that a certain agreed-upon number of enrollees would still be covered in the event that TennCare ended and was replaced with traditional Medicaid.[69] If the governor agreed to this proposal, the delay would last two years. Although the Tennessee Justice Center, in effect, was willing to renegotiate the consent decrees, the governor believed that this deal would not curtail enough spending on TennCare.

On November 11, the governor announced a major disenrollment of hundreds of thousands of TennCare beneficiaries. Referring to the negotiation between himself and the Tennessee Justice Center, Bredesen said that "persistent lawsuits have tied our hands. The sad reality is we can't afford TennCare in its current form. It pains me to set this process in motion, but I won't let TennCare bankrupt our state. This is the option of last resort."[70] A week later, the governor backed away from this disenrollment plan and resumed talks with the Tennessee Justice Center. However, after another round of negotiations that extended to December 15, both sides left the bargaining table without an agreement.

On January 10, 2005, the start of the legislative calendar year, the governor again proposed a major overhaul of the TennCare program. This version entailed the disenrollment of 323,000 beneficiaries and benefit reductions that implemented the cuts authorized in the 2004 statute.[71] At the same time, the governor asked the courts for modifications to the consent decrees. In April, the Sixth Circuit Court of Appeals ruled that the governor could move forward with the disenrollments without penalty for violating the consent decrees.[72]

These and related events underscore the governor's unique role in TennCare reform. While it is tempting to believe that the governor had the power to unilaterally downsize TennCare, Bredesen leveraged the support of medical experts to validate his plans. For example, to the surprise of many, President John Maupin Jr. of Meharry Medical College publicly backed the governor's proposed reform measures. Specifically, Maupin downplayed the impact of the TennCare cuts in testimony on July 13, 2005, before U.S. District Court judge John Nixon, the chief arbitrator who determined the constitutionality of the governor's request to downsize TennCare.[73] Having the support of a highly regarded member of the state's medical community added a level of legitimacy to the proposed reforms, and Bredesen used the advocacy of Maupin and other medical experts in his efforts to persuade his constituents to accept the reforms. Trudy Lieberman argued that Bredesen's involvement in health-care reform—and his need for experts to back these reforms—was an attempt by the governor to boost his reputation nationally and perhaps advance his political career.[74]

The TennCare appeals process was overly complex and was biased against residents who lacked expertise in the intricacies of health-care policies, rules, and procedures. Appellants had to complete a seven-page appeals form that included complex medical terminology. In a controversial decision, the governor, with approval from the Senate Government Operations Committee and the House Fiscal Review Committee, shifted the venue of the appeals hearings from the TennCare Bureau to the state's Department of Human Services. Appellants found that the Department of Human Services hearing examiners who were assigned to represent TennCare recipients were unfamiliar with the details of Medicaid policy.[75] After the disenrollments began, only 350 of the 70,000 appeals were approved.[76]

PROTESTING THE TENNCARE REFORMS

Health-care advocates and grassroots activists mobilized against the TennCare reforms from 2004 to 2006. The mobilization activities were coordinated by the TennCare Saves Lives Coalition, an alliance that included the Tennessee Justice Center, the Tennessee Health Care Campaign, and the Tennessee Disability Coalition. Other groups joined these advocates, including the Nashville Peace and Justice Center; the Nashville-based Grassroots Organizing Committee; the

Tennessee Alliance for Progress; the Ad Hoc Committee for Equity; the state chapter of the Southern Christian Leadership Conference, based in Memphis; Solutions, a Knoxville-based antipoverty group; the Memphis Center for Independent Living; and the state chapter of the American Association of Retired Persons. Together, these advocates organized a series of town halls, protests, and organizer trainings in at least thirty cities and a seventy-seven-day sit-in at the governor's office to protest the cuts.

Beginning in the summer of 2004, the TennCare Saves Lives Coalition convened meetings with black grassroots leaders and health-care professionals in Nashville to discuss how they could work together to resist the impending TennCare cuts. In September of that year, members of the coalition met with the governor to present a list of recommendations for addressing TennCare's financial problems. They also explained that the reforms would disproportionately harm black Tennesseans, who made up roughly 30 percent of TennCare enrollees.[77]

In October 2004, the Tennessee State Conference of the NAACP adopted a resolution urging the governor to "make appropriate changes to his reform proposal to ensure that TennCare enrollees receive health care as prescribed by competent health care professionals."[78] Over the next year, other black activists and members of the civil rights community expressed opposition to the reform plan. Marian Wright Edelman of the Children's Defense Fund, the nation's foremost child advocacy group, and Theodore Shaw, the NAACP Legal Defense and Educational Fund's director-counsel, warned that the TennCare reforms would pave the way for other governors to initiate similar cuts to their state Medicaid programs.[79]

At the annual African American Church Day on Capitol Hill in Nashville on March 1, 2005, some faith leaders renounced the governor's reform plan.[80] The organizers of African American Church Day also lobbied members of the TBCSL that year. Representatives from the NAACP, the Southern Christian Leadership Conference, the Coalition of 100 Black Women, and the Missionary Baptist Convention attended the meeting. However, the meeting turned into a verbal slugfest between the health-care advocates and caucus members, especially chair Johnny Shaw. Shaw was a close ally of the governor, and his district had received a multimillion-dollar health-care facility a year earlier. Nashville pastor Victor Singletary, a strong opponent of the governor's reform plan, harshly criticized Shaw for his performance on that occasion.[81]

A month later, more than 300 mostly black activists rallied in Nashville to protest the governor's cuts.[82] Later in the year, Memphis activists brought Sandra Gadson of the National Medical Association and U.S. delegate Donna Christensen of the Virgin Islands to the city to explain the harmful impact of the TennCare cuts.[83]

Most members of the black caucus expressed reservations about the TennCare reforms. They wanted to support the governor as a display of party unity, as they had done when they supported the 2004 vote for benefit reductions, but many of their constituents would be adversely affected by the sweeping cuts. Because of protests and the general opposition to the proposed cuts, some lawmakers wanted the governor to call a special legislative session in the fall of 2005 to develop a proposal for mitigating the impact of the cuts. The governor countered these pressures in letters to lawmakers that blamed health-care advocates for his actions: "I want to remind you that my original [2004] reform proposal kept everyone on TennCare. I am not happy about disenrolling anyone from this program, but we have been left with no choice due to the intransigence of legal advocates."[84] Members of the black caucus were unmoved by the governor's response, and most of them supported a special legislative session.[85]

Black activists and members of the black caucus raised concerns about the adverse and racially disparate impact of the reforms on low-income residents, blacks, and high-risk populations. During the two-year battle, the governor repeatedly attempted to shut down reform opponents who were making racial equity arguments about the impact of the cuts by claiming that TennCare reform would do more harm to rural and white residents than to black residents. Bredesen sent a letter to local officials in the summer of 2005 titled "The Truth about TennCare Changes," which stated that the TennCare cuts would mostly impact working-class counties in East Tennessee rather than the urban areas where many blacks resided. He said that blacks made up only 15 percent of the people who would be disenrolled from the program and that the health-care practitioners and advocates for TennCare enrollees had created a disinformation campaign that exaggerated the impact of the proposed cuts on blacks.[86] The governor's claims were problematic because they set up a false dichotomy: since many black Tennesseans are working class, dissolving TennCare would indeed have a disparate racial impact.

It is difficult to determine the accuracy of the governor's numbers. Since children were spared from the worst of the TennCare reforms and since many of the four hundred thousand black TennCare enrollees were children, it is possible that he was correct. Yet it is nearly impossible to objectively evaluate the racial dimension of the governor's reforms—at least when assessing how many blacks were in the disenrolled populations—because it is difficult to obtain sociodemographic data on the beneficiaries who were removed from the program.[87]

Another problem is that most analyses and debates of the TennCare reforms, from both opponents and supporters, focused exclusively on the 200,000–300,000 beneficiaries who were disenrolled. Those who were able to remain in the program but were forced to accept benefit reductions and limits were frequently left out of the discussion. The number in this category ranged from 400,000 to 500,000. It is not possible to obtain a racial breakdown of this population. What we do know is that the TennCare appeals process treated blacks and whites differently. An investigation of 55,000 appellants (8,000 of whom were black) found that whites were more likely than blacks to receive a timely hearing. Blacks who were affected by the curtailment of benefits were also the least likely to be treated fairly by hearing examiners in the TennCare Bureau.[88] Advocates believed that other aspects of the TennCare reforms, such as the increase in co-payments for enrollees, changes to the medical necessity framework, and the adverse impact of the changes on public hospitals, had a disparate impact on blacks.[89]

To counter concerns about racial inequities, the governor sent his health commissioner, Kenneth Robinson, a black doctor and the pastor of St. Andrew AME Church in Memphis, to community meetings and venues across the state, trying to minimize opposition to the reforms. In September 2004, Robinson attended a community forum sponsored by Nashville's Interdenominational Ministerial Fellowship on the impact of the TennCare cuts on the black community. At the forum, he downplayed the harmful effects of the benefit cuts and insisted that TennCare was too expensive to maintain and that the governor had no alternative but to introduce benefit cuts.[90]

Robinson was in an unenviable position. He had a strong reputation as an advocate for poor people and was equally respected as a health equity specialist. He was also the highest-ranking black official in the Bredesen administration at a time when Republicans were gaining ground in Tennessee politics. Bredesen had not mentioned major cuts to TennCare during the 2002 gubernatorial election, so Robinson had not known of these plans when he was appointed to his position. In addition, the Department of Health, which Robinson oversaw, did not supervise the Medicaid program; the TennCare Bureau did that. Yet his role in state government put him right in the middle of the political debate over TennCare. In addition, he had important goals that he wanted to accomplish while in office; he and Bredesen had started an initiative designed to reduce Memphis's infant mortality rate, which was the third highest in the country in 2005.[91]

Robinson is a good example of how black leaders routinely embrace political comity in order to mediate political disputes that may polarize the electorate. This is usually done through private negotiations between black politicians and white moderates and conservatives. For Robinson, this strategy was best exemplified by his involvement in the debates between those who wanted to keep TennCare and those who sought to dismantle it, believing that a safety net would catch people who were disenrolled. Realizing the potential political fallout from the TennCare cuts, he coordinated a "soft landing cabinet group" that began developing strategies to address the urgent care needs of disenrollees. The group was put together a week after Bredesen's January 10 announcement that at least three hundred thousand more people would be disenrolled from TennCare and that benefits would be cut for those who remained in the program. The energies of the new group were channeled into the Governor's Task Force on the Health Care Safety Net, which was established on January 24, 2005, by executive order. Chaired by Robinson, the task force had four working groups: one focused on clinical services, one focused on providers, one focused on best practices, and one focused on special populations (e.g., individuals with serious mental health conditions, HIV/AIDS, alcohol and drug addictions, and mental disabilities).[92] Robinson set an ambitious deadline of May 1 for coming up with recommendations for the safety net.

The final plan proposed by the task force, which the state legislature adopted, entailed $100 million of additional spending on health care. The funds were used to expand county health department clinics, increase the number of doctors, provide prescription drugs for those with serious mental illnesses, and help people with chronic medical conditions.[93] However, these were stopgap measures that did not guarantee annual appropriations.

Despite the safety-net initiatives, many black leaders were critical of the TennCare cuts. Pastor Dwight Montgomery, the state president of the Southern Christian Leadership Conference, was a vocal critic of Bredesen. Another critic was Pastor Henry Blaze, the chair of the Ad Hoc Committee for Equity and the cochair of the TennCare Saves Lives Coalition. Blaze and Montgomery traveled to Washington, D.C., to speak with members of the Congressional Black Caucus about the efforts to oppose TennCare reform. In 2005, Montgomery attempted to convince the Memphis Baptist Ministerial Association to endorse the protest campaign, but ministers who were the governor's allies defeated the endorsement plan. Despite this setback, Montgomery organized several protests against the TennCare reforms that drew support from black ministers in Memphis, including representatives from the National Baptist Convention, and other groups, such as the Association of Community Organizations for Reform Now, the Nation of Islam, labor unions, and the Center for Independent Living.[94]

These mobilization activities had various objectives. As already mentioned, Bredesen's critics wanted the governor to call a special legislative session that would specifically address TennCare's financial problems. (The governor rejected this demand.) Those who fought on behalf of TennCare enrollees wanted the state legislature to reject any budget proposals that defunded line items in the TennCare budget. When the governor rejected these demands, advocacy groups shifted their strategy, asking the state legislature to exempt chronically ill beneficiaries from the budget cuts.[95]

In response to these mobilization activities, the governor tried to downplay the adverse impact of the TennCare reforms and prevent defections from his base of Democratic Party supporters. He offered the Democrats who opposed his reforms a deal: a pay increase for members of the Tennessee State Employees Association in exchange for their support for the TennCare cuts. Bredesen then signaled to Democratic Party leaders that he would use the revenue savings from TennCare to fund his expanded preschool education program. Early in the discussions of TennCare reform, on November 18, 2004, the governor had addressed the black caucus at its annual legislative retreat. He had informed the group that the creation of the preschool program was dependent on whether his TennCare reforms were implemented. However, Representative Kathryn Bowers told the press at the time that there was enough money in the budget to pay for both programs. "It [the preschool program] does not have to be at the expense of TennCare," Bowers stated.[96]

Several months later, Bredesen sent a letter to House leader Jimmy Naifeh and Senate leader Douglas Wilder that explained his position on the TennCare reforms. Rejecting his reforms, he warned, would lead to a cut in education spending "by $191 million, for a total cut to K-12 of $278 million." He also stated that there would be "no raises, state shared return, [or] other optional improvements" for the 2005–2006 fiscal year unless the additional cuts to TennCare happened. He told the two leaders that "these are obviously unacceptable scenarios" that "could not be allowed to come to pass."[97] The governor pressured Naifeh and Wilder to support the TennCare reforms if they wanted funding for core education programs.

Despite the grassroots lobbying initiatives of advocacy groups, the House and the Senate overwhelming approved a state budget in May 2005 that included additional cuts to the TennCare program. Surprisingly, two vocal critics of the TennCare reforms were conservative Republicans: Joey Hensley of Hohenwald in East Tennessee and Senator Jim Bryson of Middle Tennessee's Williamson County. They were reluctant to endorse the governor's reforms because both had dual careers as legislators and medical professionals and had patients who were adversely affected by the TennCare cuts. They introduced an amendment to the proposed budget that would have kept sixty-seven thousand patients who had chronic medical conditions (and were thus uninsurable) in the TennCare program.[98] A bipartisan coalition of lawmakers supported the amendment, which would have used the proposed $100 million safety-net funds to pay for

TABLE 6.1 Residents' assessment of the biggest problems in Tennessee

Number one problem facing Tennessee	Spring 2005 (%)	Spring 2006 (%)
High crime	4.50	5.16
Inefficient/wasteful government	3.78	8.39
Poor education	14.77	11.61
Flawed health care/insurance/services	36.04	28.39
High taxes	6.67	3.55
Government corruption	2.90	8.39
Poor economy	7.39	8.71
Other	21.08	18.71

Sources: Spring 2005 and spring 2006 waves of the MTSU poll (in 2005, $N = 555$; in 2006, $N = 310$).

Note: Sample sizes (N) represent the number of respondents who answered the "number one problem facing Tennessee" question.

the uninsurable population. However, the effort failed after the governor made a "rare visit to a meeting of the House Democrats" to pressure legislators to support his plan.[99]

Together, the reform measures of 2004 and 2005 (disenrollment of beneficiaries, reorganization of TennCare oversight, benefit reductions, changes to the federal consent decrees, the redefinition of medical necessity, and changes to the appeals process) radically altered the TennCare program and shifted the state's delivery system for health care from an innovative experiment to a program more reminiscent of Medicaid in other states. TennCare was a major issue in Tennessee state politics in 2005 and 2006. As table 6.1 shows, more than 36 percent of the electorate in 2005 and more than 28 percent in 2006 said that the health-care crisis was the number one problem facing Tennessee.

The debate about access to health care polarized the electorate. The governor used talk of a safety net to downplay the adverse impact of the TennCare reforms. He asserted that community health centers, community- and faith-based health initiatives, and emergency room care would provide health care for former beneficiaries. In 2004, he had issued an executive order establishing the Governor's Office of Children's Care Coordination to comply with a federal consent decree. This new body coordinated health-care services for children affected by public health risks and those in low-income communities.[100] He also established the TennCare Task Force to evaluate the health-care alternatives to TennCare.

Other narratives were used to garner support for the TennCare cuts. Conservative proponents of the reforms routinely accused TennCare enrollees of abusing the program and taking more prescription drugs than were needed for their infirmities. This narrative was like the rhetoric President Reagan used to demonize "welfare queens" to rationalize the retrenchment of social welfare programs.[101] Another narrative, the cost-savings argument, insisted that TennCare would shatter the state's budget if cuts were not made to the program. This argument was outlined in the McKinsey Report, which laid the groundwork for the reforms.[102]

Clearly, Governor Bredesen was very active in creating messages meant to justify his cuts to TennCare. Underlying these efforts is an assumption about the role played by elite-level rhetoric (in this case, arguments coming from the governor's office about the health-care safety net) in mass-level opinions. After all, the idea that elite discourse can influence public perceptions is so widely recognized that Matthew Gabel and Kenneth Scheve characterized it as a central feature in the study of political behavior.[103] But did Bredesen succeed with his safety-net rhetoric and persuade Tennesseans to accept the reforms? In the next section, we offer what may be the first empirical analysis of the extent to which Bredesen's messages took hold among voters.

POLLING RESULTS RELATED TO THE TENNCARE CONTROVERSY

In the remainder of the chapter, we rely on survey data to analyze how the TennCare controversy polarized the public. We use polls conducted by the MTSU Survey Group in the spring of 2005 and the spring of 2006.[104] The spring 2006 survey is particularly useful because it asked a question pertaining to the safety-net narrative. Specifically, the survey item assessed the degree to which the Tennesseans who participated in this survey believed that former TennCare enrollees would obtain alternative medical care that would be comparable to that of the TennCare program. This is the exact wording of the survey item:

> About what portion of the people cut from TennCare do you think will find some other way of meeting their essential medical needs? Will nearly all, most, only some, or nearly none of them find some other way of meeting their essential medical needs—or don't you know?

Since the safety-net narrative was an elite-level message used to counter critics who were skeptical about the TennCare reforms, we were curious about the effect of such elite-driven rhetoric on the attitudes of rank-and-file Tennesseans about public health care. We hypothesized that residents who received the safety-net justification would be less anxious about the TennCare rollbacks. Results from the 2006 MTSU poll suggest that the safety-net argument was plausible to voters because support for TennCare reform tended to increase as perceptions increased that a safety net existed. In table 6.2, we combine the survey item about the health-care safety net with an item asking respondents to rate their approval of Bredesen's TennCare cuts. Here is the exact wording of the TennCare reform question:

> Governor Phil Bredesen has removed nearly two hundred thousand people from TennCare, the state's medical care program for the poor, disabled, and uninsurable. Bredesen says the cuts were needed because the state could no longer afford the program in its original form. From what you've heard, how much do you approve of how the governor is handling TennCare?

As table 6.2 shows, only a small percentage of the respondents approved of Bredesen's decision to reform TennCare when they believed that "nearly none" of the people cut from the program would find alternative ways to meet their health-care needs. For those who thought that "most" or "nearly all" Tennesseans cut from TennCare would land successfully within the safety net, the percentage that supported Bredesen's TennCare reforms was much higher. The patterns in table 6.2 reveal that support for TennCare reform increased if there was a perception that alternative safety-net programs were accessible to those who needed health care. These findings lend some credence to the idea that perceptions about the strength of the safety net influenced public opinion.

Next, we considered whether the safety-net narrative had similar impacts on Tennesseans from different socioeconomic groups. We had reason to doubt that it would, for there are many accounts of a class divide in terms of TennCare's impact on Tennesseans. Shortly after the first wave of disenrollments, reports of medical emergencies and premature deaths emerged throughout the state, especially in working-poor communities and among the state's sickest populations. For example, more than one thousand HIV/AIDS patients were possibly left without coverage because of the cutbacks.[105] Many hospitals that relied on Medicaid reimbursements experienced budget shortfalls and rising costs due to the number of uninsured patients using their emergency rooms. Nashville's St. Thomas and Metro General hospitals, Memphis's Regional Medical Center, and Chattanooga's Erlanger Hospital all experienced an influx of emergency room patients

TABLE 6.2 Relationship between assumptions about the existence of a health-care safety net and approval of cuts to TennCare

Participants' responses about the portion of Tennessee residents who would find other ways of meeting their health-care needs	Do you approve of cuts to TennCare?	
	No (%)	Yes (%)
Nearly all	30.61	69.39
Most	26.96	73.04
Only some	63.50	36.50
Nearly none	90.15	9.85

Source: Spring 2006 wave of the MTSU poll ($N = 626$).

who were TennCare disenrollees.[106] Urban Ministries in Clarksville reported an increase in the number of people coming to its food bank: 55 percent of all the people who came to the food bank were TennCare enrollees whose health insurance had been completely eliminated or partially downsized.[107] The burdens placed on hospitals and community organizations are examples of how cuts to TennCare had a disproportionately adverse impact on the state's less-affluent residents.

Given the rising costs of medical insurance, it stands to reason that lower-income residents were particularly sensitive to the safety-net narrative. Not surprisingly, the spring 2006 MTSU poll pointed to a class divide among Tennesseans regarding support for the TennCare reforms. We differentiated between respondents with lower incomes (earnings at or below the 25th percentile); moderate incomes (25th–75th percentiles); and higher incomes (at or above the 75th percentile). In table 6.3, the third column shows that people with higher incomes displayed consistently strong support for TennCare downsizing measures, regardless of what they believed about the availability of a health-care safety net. The other columns show that lower- and moderate-income respondents offered greater support for the TennCare reforms only if they believed that the safety net was large enough to catch most or nearly all residents who got dropped from the state's Medicaid program. This pattern makes sense, considering that less-affluent residents were likely to perceive their group as being disproportionably dependent on TennCare and would therefore believe that members of their group would be adversely affected by the reforms.

We posited that economic risk was the main reason that income shaped this gap in perception about how effective a health-care safety net would be. For example, participants who had lower incomes were at risk in the sense that they would likely struggle to pay for quality health care. Because of their precarious

TABLE 6.3 Relationship between assumptions about the existence of a health-care safety net, income level, and approval of cuts to TennCare

Participants' assumptions about the portion of Tennessee residents who would find other ways of meeting their health-care needs	Approval of cuts to TennCare by income level		
	Lowest quartile (≤ 25th percentile) (%)	Middle quartiles (25th–75th percentile) (%)	Highest quartile (≥ 75th percentile) (%)
Nearly all	46.51	14.89	41.06
Most	25.58	36.17	32.17
Only some	18.61	29.79	36.52
Nearly none	4.65	6.38	31.13

Source: Spring 2006 wave of the MTSU poll ($N = 626$).
Note: We divided income levels into quartiles. The lowest quartile is defined as an annual net income (after taxes) of less than $24,000; the middle quartile represents net income levels ranging from $25,000 to $90,000; and the highest quartile includes incomes above $90,000.

economic situations, we expected at-risk residents to be relatively more concerned about reforms to TennCare and more inclined to be persuaded by the safety-net narrative.

We also had reason to believe that the safety-net narrative had a differential impact on Tennesseans based on their racial/ethnic background, especially considering the racial dimension of Medicaid. As mentioned earlier, African American and civil rights groups raised concerns about the racially disparate impact of the cuts. As early as September 2004, even before the disenrollments were announced, the TennCare Oversight Committee heard testimony about the disproportionate impact of the cuts on African Americans, who constituted a third of the TennCare enrollees.[108] Governor Bredesen and Commissioner of Health Robinson downplayed the racially disparate impact. Their arguments that most TennCare enrollees were children (who had been spared from the cuts) and that only 15 percent of the beneficiaries who would be removed from the program were African American explain only part of the story, even if their claims were accurate. It is important to also consider the impact of the reforms on those who were still enrolled in TennCare, such as benefit reductions, changes to the definition of medical necessity, the racially biased appeals process, and the decrease in funding for high-risk urban hospitals. When all these factors are considered together, it becomes clear that blacks were disproportionately and adversely affected by the reforms.

Since blacks in Tennessee relied on TennCare more heavily than other residents did, we anticipated that they would evaluate Bredesen more critically than whites would, even though blacks were a large voting bloc in the coalition that elected him. We also doubted that Bredesen's safety-net narrative would improve his standing with blacks. However, as table 6.4 shows, the spring 2006 MTSU poll did not provide sufficient evidence of a racial gap in respondents' support for the TennCare reforms. We predicted that compared to white Tennesseans, African Americans would be less likely to change their opinions about TennCare reform even after hearing about the alleged safety net. The results in table 6.4 get us only partway toward verifying our hypothesis since we could not

TABLE 6.4 Race of respondents and approval of cuts to TennCare

	Disapprove (%)	Approve (%)
Black/African American ($n = 47$)	52.26	47.74
White, non-Hispanic ($n = 422$)	76.60	23.40
Other ($n = 20$)	70.37	29.63

Source: Spring 2006 wave of the MTSU poll ($N = 626$).
Note: Sample sizes (n) are the number of survey respondents who answered the question about cuts to TennCare.

properly test for racial differences using the survey data. In addition to the fact that there were few African American participants in the MTSU poll,[109] any inferences we draw from this data source are necessarily tentative: there is no way for us to conclude that contested narratives about health care *caused* Tennesseans to have certain attitudes about TennCare.

These limitations underscored the need for further data collection. To probe more deeply into the linkages between the safety-net narrative and attitudes toward TennCare reform differentiated by race, we devised an innovative field experiment that allowed us to look at the causal relationship between that narrative and public opinion.

EVIDENCE FROM THE 2006 TENNCARE FIELD EXPERIMENT

The field experiment was conducted at Middle Tennessee State University in Murfreesboro in the fall of 2008 and the spring of 2009. This experiment sought to determine the level of approval for Bredesen's handling of TennCare reform among various groups of Tennesseans. Our measure of "approval" differed slightly from the question in the MTSU poll. Whereas the MTSU poll asked whether respondents approved or disapproved of the way the governor had handled cuts to TennCare, we used a continuous variable to evaluate levels of support for Bredesen's handling of the TennCare program. We asked the participants in our experiment to respond to a version of the survey question mentioned above. Participants rated their approval of TennCare cuts on a scale that ranged from 0 (no approval) to 10 (highest approval).

We predicted that the main variable associated with participants' approval of Bredesen's policies would be their perception about how many TennCare recipients would be included in the purported health-care safety net (that is, absorbed into other medical care programs). Using the survey item from the MTSU poll as a template, we built different levels of responses into the question in our experimental treatment. We modified the wording so that it included different descriptions of how many of the former TennCare beneficiaries ("nearly all," "most," "only some," or "nearly none") would have access to health care through alternative medical services. The control group in the field experiment was presented with the original wording of the question without any of the variations we used with other subjects. We provide more information about this question-wording experiment in appendix 6.2.

In addition, we recorded the race of the participants so that we could examine black-white differences in the impact of the experimental manipulation of attitudes toward Bredesen's handling of TennCare. A sizable portion of the individuals who took part in our field experiment identified themselves as "[non-Hispanic] whites" ($n = 375$) or "African Americans (or blacks)" ($n = 155$). The sample sizes of Hispanics ($n = 9$) and Asians ($n = 18$) were too small, so we limited our focus to the two primary racial groups.

Finally, we drew from the insights of Michael O'Grady and Gooloo Wunderlich to create an Economic Disadvantage Index based on responses to four yes-no questions related to respondents' relationships to health-care costs in the previous year:[110]

1. Did you not visit the doctor when you were sick because of medical costs?
2. Did you have to choose between paying for health care and other essential needs?
3. Have you had problems paying or were unable to pay your medical bills?
4. Have you run up debt because of medical costs?

The index ranged from 0 (low economic risk) to 4 (high economic risk).[111] Our prediction was that economic risk would influence the attitudes of Tennesseans toward Bredesen's approach to TennCare and that those who were the most economically vulnerable would tend to disagree with Bredesen's approach to resolving the health-care crisis in Tennessee.

As discussed earlier, one of the principal narratives Governor Bredesen used to legitimize his TennCare reforms emphasized the availability of a health-care safety net. Figure 6.1 summarizes the overall results of the experiment, listing the average levels of participants' approval of Bredesen's handling of TennCare by race and across experimental conditions, on a scale of 0–10 in which 0 indicated no approval and 10 indicated the highest approval. The figure includes the number of participants within each condition to show that the random assignment to the variously worded questions produced similar group sizes.[112]

Did approval of Bredesen's handling of TennCare vary by experimental condition? We expected approval levels to increase in tandem with a person's belief about the extent of the purported safety net that would service TennCare disenrollees. Perhaps the most obvious finding in figure 6.1 is that blacks (represented by the darker bars) were significantly less approving of Bredesen's approach to TennCare than were whites (lighter bars).[113] Overall, however, the approval ratings did not vary significantly by belief about the extent of the safety net. Regardless of race, none of the results for the groups that received experimental treatments were significantly different from the results for the control group.[114] These results indicate that regardless of racial background, the participants in our study were generally unaffected by beliefs about how many TennCare disenrollees would be able to find other sources of health care.

FIGURE 6.1 Race of participants and assumptions about how many disenrolled TennCare clients would be able to find alternative sources of health care

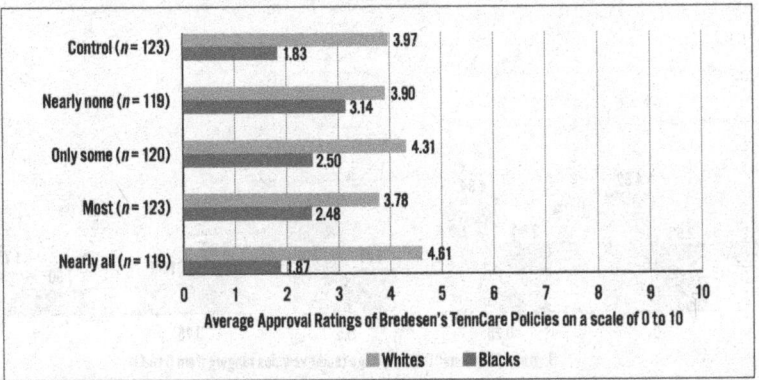

Source: Authors' 2008 TennCare study (N = 604).
Notes: Estimates are averages by racial group and across experimental conditions.

This "nonfinding" was not surprising to us. Arguments about safety-net options largely occurred within policy networks and were debated among health-care professionals, lobbyists, and legislators. Notwithstanding the salience of the TennCare debate of 2004–2006, these arguments were mostly articulated by opinion leaders—both supporters and opponents of Bredesen—and health-care practitioners who had a professional interest in and were active participants in the TennCare struggle. Given the fact that TennCare debates were largely conducted within elite circles, such arguments may not have trickled down to the masses.

Our next goal was to determine the extent to which blacks and whites varied in their level of support for Bredesen's reforms based on their degree of economic risk. Our intention was to confirm the argument that downsizing TennCare was a pressing concern among Tennessee's economically vulnerable populations. Our survey results confirmed the importance of the relationship between degree of economic risk and support for Bredesen's handling of TennCare. As figure 6.2 shows, the higher were white subjects' levels of economic disadvantage, the lower was their approval of Bredesen's downsizing of TennCare.[115] In general, black subjects were less supportive of Bredesen's reform plan than whites were.[116] However, blacks had low approval ratings of Bredesen's policies regardless of their degree of economic disadvantage.[117]

In figure 6.3, we show the degree to which the effect of economic vulnerability on approval of Bredesen's handling of TennCare varied by the race of the participant and beliefs about the extent of the safety net. For each experimental

FIGURE 6.2 Degree of economic disadvantage by average level of approval of cuts to TennCare, by racial group

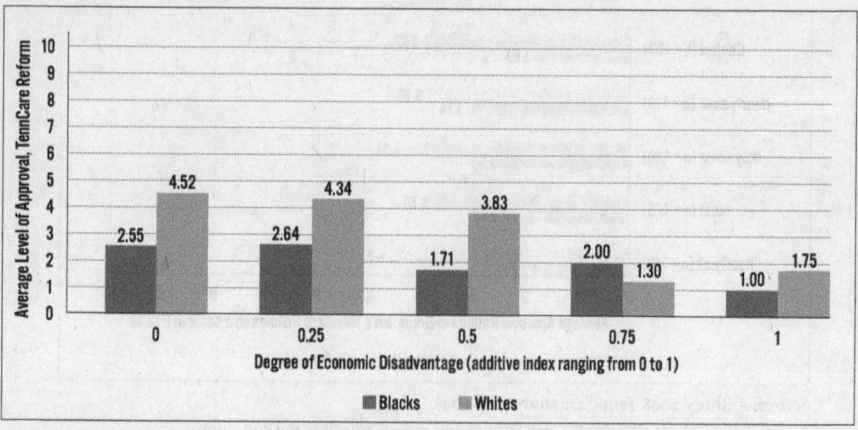

Source: Authors' 2008 TennCare study (N = 604).
Notes: Estimates are averages by race and across values of the Economic Disadvantage Index.

condition, we plotted the average levels of approval of the TennCare cuts among the white (lighter lines) and black (darker lines) participants. For ease of interpretation, we collapsed our Economic Disadvantage Index into two categories: we classified all participants who got a score of 0 on our additive index as having "no economic disadvantage," while we classified all other participants as having "economic disadvantage" (because these survey respondents got an index score that was greater than 0).

By organizing the information this way, we can demonstrate that respondents' approval of Bredesen's handling of TennCare was relatively higher among those who were not at risk financially—that is, among those who scored a 0 on our Economic Disadvantage Index. Conversely, participants who were at economic risk (in this case, subjects who scored anything greater than 0 on the Economic Disadvantage Index) gave lower approval ratings for Bredesen's TennCare policies. We can see this by examining the slopes of the lines in figure 6.3. Each mini-graph represents the results for each experimental condition, and we compare the level of approval for Bredesen's TennCare policies among participants who were not at risk financially to those who were. The patterns in figure 6.3 indicate that participants were generally less approving of Bredesen's approach to reforming TennCare if they were economically at risk with respect to health-care access.[118] This underscores the point that financial status shaped participants' attitudes toward Bredesen's rhetoric about how many TennCare disenrollees would be able to access other types of health care.

The slopes of the lines for whites and blacks in each mini-graph reveal clear

FIGURE 6.3 Racial differences in approval of TennCare reform by economic disadvantage and perceptions of proportion of disenrolled TennCare clients who would find alternative health care in the purported safety net

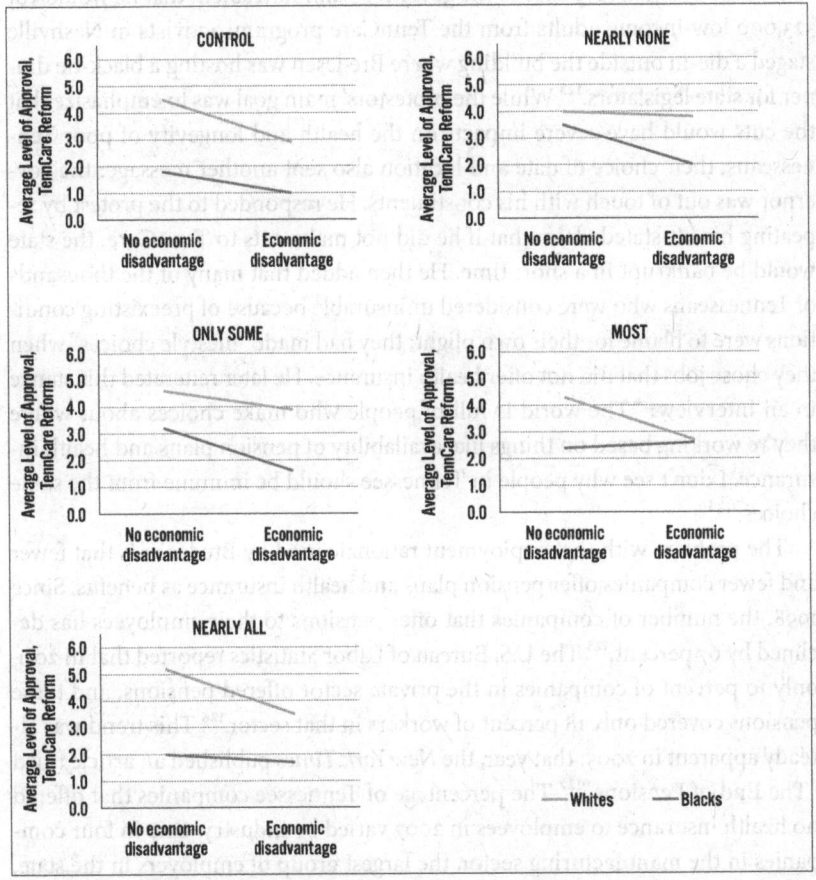

Source: Authors' 2008 TennCare study (N = 604).
Notes: Estimates are averages by race and across values of the Economic Disadvantage Index.

evidence of racial differences. Compared to their white colleagues, black Tennesseans were significantly less approving of the TennCare cuts.[119] That said, the approval ratings did not vary significantly by race across the experimental conditions.[120] We did find racial gaps in the degree to which economic disadvantage informed approval of TennCare reform. An increase in white subjects' level of economic disadvantage was correlated with a significant decrease in their approval of the TennCare cuts.[121] Black subjects were less supportive of the reforms in general, and economic disadvantage had no meaningful impact on blacks' level of approval of the TennCare cuts.[122]

CONCLUSION

In January 2005, in response to the governor's announcement that he would cut 323,000 low-income adults from the TennCare program, activists in Nashville staged a die-in outside the building where Bredesen was hosting a black-tie dinner for state legislators.[123] While the protestors' main goal was to emphasize that the cuts would have severe impacts on the health and longevity of poor Tennesseans, their choice of date and location also sent another message: the governor was out of touch with his constituents. He responded to the protest by repeating his oft-stated claim that if he did not make cuts to TennCare, the state would be bankrupt in a short time. He then added that many of the thousands of Tennesseans who were considered uninsurable because of preexisting conditions were to blame for their own plight; they had made "lifestyle choices" when they chose jobs that did not offer health insurance. He later reiterated this stance in an interview: "The world is full of people who make choices about where they're working based on things like availability of pension plans and health insurance. I don't see why people in Tennessee should be immune from the same choices."[124]

The problem with the employment rationale used by Bredesen is that fewer and fewer companies offer pension plans and health insurance as benefits. Since 1998, the number of companies that offer pensions to their employees has declined by 67 percent.[125] The U.S. Bureau of Labor Statistics reported that in 2011, only 10 percent of companies in the private sector offered pensions, and these pensions covered only 18 percent of workers in that sector.[126] This trend was already apparent in 2005; that year, the *New York Times* published an article titled "The End of Pensions."[127] The percentage of Tennessee companies that offered no health insurance to employees in 2007 varied by industry. One in four companies in the manufacturing sector, the largest group of employers in the state, provided no health insurance to employees. In the second and third largest sectors, 48 percent of employers in the retail trade and 25 percent of employers in entertainment provided no health insurance. More than 50 percent of companies in the health-care industry itself provided no health insurance.[128] The activists were right. The governor was out of touch. At least in his rhetoric, he relied on a world of work that had already disappeared.

The governor's chief opponent in the battle over TennCare, Gordon Bonnyman, the director of the Tennessee Justice Center, thought that Bredesen was out of touch in other ways. He found the governor to be "very divorced from a whole realm of human, medical, social, and political realities." Bonnyman felt that instead of considering the long-term consequences of his policies, Bredesen focused on the bottom line of the state budget in the short term, just as a CEO would. This perspective ignored significant long-term implications of the cuts he made, such as "causing patients to become wards of the state, failing to control the spread of communicable diseases, and overburdening the criminal justice system with mentally ill patients."[129]

Advocates of the TennCare program consider the reforms of 2004 and 2005 to be a tragic failure of politics. Before the cuts, the program was viewed as a pathbreaking model for federal-state partnership in the delivery of comprehensive health care to vulnerable populations. Gordon Bonnyman described the hallmarks of the program as "wall-to-wall capitated managed care and coverage expansion to a broad population of uninsured Tennesseans."[130] After the cuts, Tennessee plummeted from "among the top-ranked states [in the delivery of health care to poor people] to the bottom on many measures." In Bonnyman's view, "TennCare failed not because the original design and operations were flawed—they were successful—but because political decisions made by the state ultimately made it unsustainable."[131]

Even after he was out of office, Bredesen still saw himself as a lone warrior in a just battle to protect the state budget. Yet his uncompromising, dogmatic style made it clear to those on the other side of the negotiating table that he would not compromise. Each proposal from advocates for the state's poor was met with even harsher responses. At one point, Bredesen seemed to hold the children of the state hostage, threatening to make cuts to education if advocates for poor people insisted on fewer cuts to TennCare enrollment. Bonnyman found that the governor "personalized what were honest disagreements about public policy. . . . He treated the TennCare issues as if I and a few other advocates were willfully trying to damage his administration."[132] The governor's words corroborated this perspective; he felt that "basically nobody would work with me."[133]

In 2010, Bredesen stated that the 2005 cut of nearly two hundred thousand people from the TennCare rolls was "my largest mistake from my time as governor."[134] It is not clear what he meant by those words, but many Tennesseans would certainly agree with them. After the cut, the financial burden on hospitals, which were forced to treat uninsured patients, increased substantially. Disenrolled diabetics made repeat trips to emergency rooms because they could not afford to buy insulin. Some pharmacies lost 20–30 percent of their business. One advocate insisted that people died from lack of health care, a claim that was supported by an analysis from the University of Tennessee Center for Health Services Research.[135] That analysis projected that there would be a preventable death in Tennessee every thirty-six hours because of the cuts.[136]

In addition to examining the political debate over TennCare and the racial politics undergirding the tension between health-care advocates and Bredesen, in this chapter we also explored the potential impact of the governor's safety-net rhetoric on the attitudes of Tennesseans. Overall, we found that Tennesseans who endorsed the TennCare cuts and gave Bredesen higher approval ratings tended to be economically stable and tended to believe that the safety net was comprehensive and would provide services to most TennCare disenrollees. However, the answers participants gave to this question as it was framed in our experimental design demonstrated that people's attitudes about the TennCare cuts were generally unaffected by beliefs about the extent of the health-care safety net. We attribute this finding to the fact that the safety-net debate occurred mostly within policy networks and did not filter down into the public dialogue of most Tennesseans.

We also found that economic risk shaped Tennesseans' perspectives about the TennCare reforms. The respondents who did not visit a doctor because of medical costs, who had to choose between paying for health care and paying for other essential items, who had problems paying medical bills, and who ran up debt because of medical costs were the most disapproving of how Bredesen handled TennCare.

Thus, the TennCare debate is instructive for examining the degree to which people base their assessments of political events on what they believe: in this case, beliefs about the proportion of disenrolled residents who presumably would find alternative ways to meet their health-care needs. We were particularly interested in how these beliefs changed once we took into consideration the experiences of African Americans and economically at-risk populations. The race- and class-based differences we uncovered in residents' receptivity to Bredesen's narrative speak to the willingness of people to believe in political rhetoric when the issue does not threaten their access to key goods and services.

This chapter took a closer look at the implications of the rise and fall of TennCare. In addition to deepening racial polarization in residents' viewpoints about the implementation and administration of health care and related services, Bredesen's decisions also contributed to increased racial disparities in health outcomes in the state. In the next chapter, we examine another debate that has polarized the electorate: immigration policy. Similar to the disputes over taxes and TennCare, the immigration debate underscores broader narratives about state spending and public policy. These narratives have also been instrumental in how Tennesseans assess "new" Americans in a state that has long been characterized by the black-white divide.

APPENDIX 6.1

TENNCARE TIMELINE, 1994-2005

1 January 1994	TennCare is implemented, replacing the state's Medicaid program. TennCare covers three groups: those ineligible for Medicaid; uninsured people; and uninsurable people who had been turned down for health insurance because of a health condition.
31 December 1994	Because TennCare is approaching capacity, enrollment in the uninsured category is closed.
26 August 1996	A consent decree known as *Grier v. Goetz* is implemented by the court. *Grier* covers appeals of service denials.
1 April 1997	Enrollment is reopened in the uninsured category for children under eighteen. There is no income limit, but households with incomes over the poverty level must share costs.
21 May 1997	Enrollment is opened to dislocated workers, defined as people who lost their jobs through a plant closing. There is no income limit, but households with incomes over the poverty level must share costs.
1 January 1998	The age limit for uninsured children is raised to nineteen. In addition, children living in households with incomes 200 percent of the poverty line can enroll, even if the parents have access to insurance.
March 1998	*John B. v. Goetz* consent decree is signed. This decree requires the state to meet federal early and periodic screening, diagnostic, and treatment standards for children in the TennCare program.
March 1999	Xantus, the third largest managed-care organization in the TennCare program, is placed in receivership.
January 2001	Tennessee Justice Center files a complaint in federal court regarding the state's contempt of the *John B. v. Goetz* consent decree.
1 August 2003	Tennessee terminates its contract with Xantus.
26 August 2003	Tennessee reaches an omnibus consent decree settlement with the plaintiffs in *Grier v. Goetz*, *John B. v. Goetz*, and two other court cases.
11 December 2003	The first part of the McKinsey and Company report concludes that limiting TennCare access to individuals eligible for Medicaid would produce only marginal savings that would be erased by the loss of federal matching funds. It cites the "relatively generous" coverage of the program.
11 February 2004	The second part of the McKinsey and Company report outlines benefit cuts that would produce savings of $1.1 billion over four years. It recommends that an advisory group be created to review benefits and eligibility criteria.

Chapter Six

17 February 2004	Bredesen announces his proposals for "TennCare transformation" in a speech. Saying that the state had been "far too easy to get along with" and that it needed to "stop being... just a checkbook and become a purchaser," Bredesen proposed that the TennCare program start cutting benefits, require more cost-sharing from enrollees, and take greater control over delivery of care, particularly with regard to prescription drugs. Work groups are developed to formulate specific recommendations to implement the governor's proposals.
6 May 2004	The state legislature passes Bredesen's reform package. The new law limits the number of doctor visits to ten per year, limits the number of prescriptions to six per month, eliminates coverage for antihistamines and medications that reduce gastric acid, mandates the use of the lowest-cost prescription drugs, and creates a new definition for "medical necessity" that will determine which medical treatments are permitted under the insurance plan.
June 2004	Gordon Bonnyman of the Tennessee Justice Center takes the state to federal court, arguing that the TennCare reforms violate four consent decrees that ensured that the TennCare program complied with federal mandates in areas such as eligibility, home health visits, and medical screening for children.
10 November 2004	Bredesen announces that unless the Tennessee Justice Center gives the state "immediate relief" from complying with the TennCare consent decrees, restructuring of the TennCare program cannot move forward. He also announces that the state will begin phasing out TennCare and will return to the traditional Medicaid program.
10 January 2005	Bredesen proposes an alternative plan for modifying TennCare that eliminates the uninsured and uninsurable adult categories and reduces benefits for adult enrollees. Bredesen says these moves will make it possible to keep children on the program.
24 March 2005	The Centers for Medicare and Medicaid Services announce approval of the state's request to disenroll uninsured and uninsurable adults and to close enrollment in the medically needy adult categories (except for pregnant women).
29 April 2005	Tennessee closes enrollment in the medically needy adult categories (except for pregnant women).
June 2005	After the state wins a five-month battle in the courts over whether it is legal for TennCare to drop enrollees, TennCare begins the disenrollment process.
8 June 2005	The Centers for Medicare and Medicaid Services approve a waiver amendment allowing the state to place a limit on prescription drug coverage for non-institutionalized adults and to eliminate dental and methadone clinic services for adults.

July 2005	Tennessee announces that 191,000–200,000 adults will be disenrolled from the TennCare program and that benefits will be cut for the 97,000 adults still in the program.
1 August 2005	The waiver amendment limiting prescription drug coverage and eliminating dental and methadone clinic services goes into effect.

Sources: Christina Bennett, *TennCare: One State's Experiment with Medicaid Expansion* (Nashville, Tenn.: Vanderbilt University Press, 2014), 78–79; "Bredesen Says TennCare Cutbacks Necessary," *Chattanoogan*, February 17, 2004; Cyril F. Chang and Stephanie C. Steinberg, "TennCare Timeline: Major Events and Milestones from 1992 to 2016," Methodist Le Bonheur Center for Healthcare Economics, University of Memphis, September 2016, http://www.memphis.edu/mlche/pdfs/tenncare/tenncare_bulleted_timeline.pdf; Governor's Communications Office, "State Moves toward Medicaid: 'Persistent Lawsuits' Block TennCare Reform Effort" (news release), November 10, 2004, https://tnjustice.org/wp-content/uploads/2011/01/Bredesen-release-re-consent-decrees.pdf; Leighton Ku, "Will the New TennCare Cutbacks Help Tennessee's Economy?," July 8, 2004, Center on Budget and Policy Priorities, http://www.cbpp.org/archiveSite/7-8-04health.pdf; Carole R. Myers, "Failed Promises: The Demise of the Original TennCare Vision," *Managed Care Interface* 20, no. 2 (2007): 24–25.

APPENDIX 6.2

METHODOLOGY: TENNCARE EXPERIMENT ANALYSIS

We conducted a field experiment at Middle Tennessee State University (MTSU) in Murfreesboro, Tennessee, in the fall of 2008 and the spring of 2009. To collect the data, teams of research assistants visited well-known places where students congregate (e.g., dormitories, student union, library) to recruit subjects into the study. The subjects who agreed to participate read and signed a consent form, which was stored separately from the other data. The research assistants then gave the students a ten-minute questionnaire to complete. The subjects were informed that their participation in the study would provide valuable insights about health care and that their responses would remain confidential. In all, 604 subjects completed the questionnaire.

DEPENDENT VARIABLE

Our dependent variable in the field experiment was perceptions of the health-care safety net. We used the wording from a question in the spring 2006 MTSU poll as a template:

> About what portion of the people cut from TennCare do you think will find some other way of meeting their essential medical needs? Will nearly all, most, only some, or nearly none of them find some other way of meeting their essential medical needs—or don't you know?

As noted in the chapter, we used a continuous variable to evaluate support for the governor's position. Specifically, we asked the subjects to respond to the following question: "Governor Phil Bredesen has removed nearly 200-thousand people from TennCare, the state's medical care program for the poor, disabled, and uninsurable. Bredesen says

TABLE A6.1 Summary of the experimental conditions in the 2008 TennCare study

	Control group	Treatment groups (perceived amount covered by health-care safety net)			
	No rhetoric	Nearly none	Only some	Most	Nearly all
Sentence 1	Governor Phil Bredesen has removed nearly two hundred thousand people from TennCare, the state's medical care program for the poor, disabled, and uninsurable.	Governor Phil Bredesen has removed nearly two hundred thousand people from TennCare, the state's medical care program for the poor, disabled, and uninsurable.	Governor Phil Bredesen has removed nearly two hundred thousand people from TennCare, the state's medical care program for the poor, disabled, and uninsurable.	Governor Phil Bredesen has removed nearly two hundred thousand people from TennCare, the state's medical care program for the poor, disabled, and uninsurable.	Governor Phil Bredesen has removed nearly two hundred thousand people from TennCare, the state's medical care program for the poor, disabled, and uninsurable.
Sentence 2	Bredesen says the cuts were needed because the state could no longer afford the program in its original form.	Bredesen says the cuts were needed because the state could no longer afford the program in its original form.	Bredesen says the cuts were needed because the state could no longer afford the program in its original form.	Bredesen says the cuts were needed because the state could no longer afford the program in its original form.	Bredesen says the cuts were needed because the state could no longer afford the program in its original form.
Sentence 3	N/A	It is estimated that **nearly none** of the people cut from TennCare will find some other way of meeting their essential medical needs.	It is estimated that only **some** of the people cut from TennCare will find some other way of meeting their essential medical needs.	It is estimated that **most** of the people cut from TennCare will find some other way of meeting their essential medical needs.	It is estimated that **nearly all** of the people cut from TennCare will find some other way of meeting their essential medical needs.
Sentence 4	From what you've heard, how much do you approve of how the governor is handling TennCare?	From what you've heard, how much do you approve of how the governor is handling TennCare?	From what you've heard, how much do you approve of how the governor is handling TennCare?	From what you've heard, how much do you approve of how the governor is handling TennCare?	From what you've heard, how much do you approve of how the governor is handling TennCare?

Note: The **bold** text in the third sentence is the only thing that varied across subjects. Subjects in the control group received no such text.

the cuts were needed because the state could no longer afford the program in its original form. From what you've heard, how much do you approve of how the governor is handling TennCare?" Respondents were asked to rate their approval of TennCare cuts on a scale (0 = no approval, 10 = highest approval).

THEORETICALLY CENTRAL INDEPENDENT VARIABLE

Our main predictor of the respondents' approval of TennCare cuts was their perception of how many TennCare recipients would be assisted by the health-care safety net. Still using the same question from the MTSU poll, we built into the question different levels of our experimental treatment, that is, we modified the wording so that it included different descriptions of how many former TennCare recipients ("nearly all," "most," "only some," or "nearly none") would have access to health care through alternative medical services. The control group in this field experiment was composed of subjects who received no modified wording and were presented only with the original survey question.

As illustrated in table A6.1, subjects were randomly assigned to one of four treatment groups or the control group. It is worth emphasizing that we were manipulating the perceived extent of the health-care safety net for former TennCare recipients. The logic here is that a large safety net implies that many people will find alternative health-care sources. Conversely, a small safety net implies that few people will find alternative ways to meet their medical needs. The wording of sentences 1, 2, and 4 were identical. Sentence 3 presented varying descriptions of the safety net according to the condition. Because we were careful to vary only the text in the third sentence, the differences we observed in subjects' Bredesen approval ratings can be attributed to subtle changes in question wording. We encourage readers who seek to know more about the logic of random assignment to read Donald Campbell and Julian Stanley's timeless primer *Experimental and Quasi-Experimental Designs for Research* (Boston: Houghton Mifflin, 1963).

MODERATING VARIABLES (RACE AND ECONOMIC RISK)

In addition to predicting that Bredesen approval would vary by safety-net rhetoric, we also expected the effect of safety-net perceptions on Bredesen support to differ according to a subject's demographic group. Because many blacks relied on TennCare, we expected African Americans to evaluate Bredesen more critically than whites would, and we doubted that safety-net rhetoric would improve Bredesen's standing with blacks. Accordingly, we recorded the race of the subjects so that we could examine differences in the effect of the experimental manipulations on Bredesen approval. The racial/ethnic breakdown of the subjects was as follows: self-identified "[non-Hispanic] whites" ($n = 375$), self-identified "African Americans (or blacks)" ($n = 155$), self-identified Hispanics ($n = 9$), and self-identified Asians ($n = 18$). Due to small sample sizes for Hispanics and Asians, we limited our analyses to blacks and whites.

As discussed in the chapter, we used an additive index based on the following questions to assess economic risk:

1. [In past year]: Did you not visit the doctor when you were sick because of medical costs?

2. [In past year]: Did you have to choose between paying for health care and other essential needs?
3. [In past year]: Have you had problems paying or were unable to pay your medical bills?
4. [In past year]: Have you run up debt because of medical costs?

CHAPTER SEVEN

IMMIGRATION AND THE NEW TENNESSEANS

> They go out there like rats and they multiply.... I am not going to try and be politically correct with everything I say. If I offended [immigrants] I am sorry. But the truth is the truth. A spade is a spade.
>
> —TENNESSEE REPRESENTATIVE CURRY TODD (2010)

Since the late twentieth century, some of the federal government's traditional authority over immigration has devolved to the states. Several legal scholars have pointed out that the devolution of immigration policy has contributed to an increase in state-level initiatives targeting immigrant populations.[1] In April 2010, Arizona enacted what was arguably the strictest set of anti-immigration measures at the time. State lawmakers adopted the Support Our Law Enforcement and Safe Neighborhoods Act (Senate Bill 1070), a statute that required, among other things, that immigrants carry proof of their legal status. It also allowed law enforcement officials to target individuals who were suspected of having undocumented status.[2] Opponents argued that the standard established in the law allowed for the racial profiling of Latinos. According to van Zeller and Ross, S.B. 1070 was an open invitation for harassment and discrimination against Latinos, regardless of their citizenship status.[3] Despite the national controversy it created, 55 percent of Arizonans endorsed the bill,[4] and the profiling portion of it was upheld by the Supreme Court in *Arizona v. United States* (2012).

Immigration has been a contentious issue in U.S. politics, especially since the wave of protests in 2005 and 2006 pushed President George W. Bush to acknowledge the need for comprehensive immigration reform. The growing power of the Latino vote in national elections and the association of Latinos with immigration politics have also kept immigration reform at the forefront of U.S. politics. The debate about immigration reform has extended beyond the traditional Latino and immigrant strongholds of the West Coast, Southwest, and Florida. In the U.S. South, a region historically characterized by the black-white encounter, immigration is now part of state and local political debates.[5] In Tennessee, as noted by Alapo, politicians "wrestl[ed]" with several legislative bills in 2010 that resembled Arizona's S.B. 1070.[6]

In this chapter, we assess immigration politics in Tennessee in the early twenty-first century. The main argument is that immigration politics became an increasingly polarizing issue in Tennessee at that time. The growing political capital of immigrants—or at least the long-term prospect that immigrants will emerge as a power base given their rapid growth in the state—has partially fueled the anti-immigrant animus. The devolution of immigration policy to the states further exacerbated polarization in the early 2000s. African Americans in Tennessee, whose political and social history has been mostly shaped by black-white interactions, were also routinely pulled into the immigration fights of this period.

We argue that the polarization of immigration politics in Tennessee has been undergirded by contests over how immigrants and immigration-related issues are framed by political elites. A wide range of studies have indicated that certain framing strategies by media and political elites engender support for restrictive immigration policies.[7] When immigration is associated with illegality, moral turpitude, or criminality, then immigration politics will foment racial and partisan polarization. These frames are wedded to broader struggles of partisanship and racial equity, and they have become central to state policymaking, given the increasing role state and local officials have assumed in regulating immigration.

Certainly, immigration politics have been adversely affected by hostile rhetoric in Tennessee. This was exhibited at a November 2010 legislative hearing when Republican Curry Todd described undocumented pregnant women as "rats" that "multiply."[8] When questioned about the tone of his rhetoric, he stated (as can be seen in the epigraph): "I am not going to try and be politically correct with everything I say.... But the truth is the truth. A spade is a spade."[9] Todd's statement reflected a growing animus toward Tennessee's immigrant population.

We give special attention to the attitudes among Tennesseans about immigration in the early twenty-first century. This period saw the emergence of national protests in 2005 and 2006 organized by immigration and Latino civil rights groups to pressure Congress to pass comprehensive immigration reform. It ended with the closure of the 287(g) program in Nashville in 2012. This program was perhaps the most controversial immigration policy in the state because it mirrored, though on a lesser scale, Arizona's S.B. 1070.

We begin with a theoretical overview of why immigration became contentious in Tennessee during this period. We briefly look at how the politics of realignment, devolution, and race shaped the debate. Most of this discussion focuses on issue framing, or how immigration was discussed by political elites. We rely on several polls to assess immigration-related framing strategies. The findings, discussed at the end of the chapter, underscore the relationship between issue framing, polarization, and race in Tennessee.

POLARIZATION AND IMMIGRATION POLITICS

Throughout this chapter, we suggest that issue framing, especially by elites, influenced how Tennesseans viewed immigration politics. Yet issue framing did not occur in a vacuum. During the early twenty-first century, the political context augmented the arguments of advocates of immigration reform and those of state lawmakers and public officials, thus allowing them to uniquely affect immigration politics and the rhetoric surrounding proposed reform measures.

Immigration policy has generally been placed under the jurisdiction of the federal government, although much of this changed after the passage of the Illegal Immigration Reform and Immigrant Responsibility Act (IIRIRA) of 1996. This federal law tightened restrictions on undocumented immigrants. It bolstered border security, created a tracking system for monitoring undocumented residents, and established more penalties for employers who hired this class of workers.[10]

Although the IIRIRA was seemingly harsh, the law countered more strict state-level measures, such as Proposition 187, California's draconian ballot initiative that would have imposed severe restrictions on undocumented immigrants. In addition to potentially denying immigrants social and health services, the proposition would also have limited their access to public education.[11] The protests against the measure, along with questions about its constitutionality, prompted federal officials to establish more uniform federal procedures for regulating immigration.

A decade after the passage of the IIRIRA, immigration and Latino civil rights activists organized national protests to counter legislation by Congressman Jim Sensenbrenner (R-Wis.) that proposed to build a 700-mile fence along part of the Mexico border and that criminalized charitable and civic groups that assisted undocumented residents.[12] The House of Representatives approved the bill in 2005, but it failed to pass the Senate. By 2006, mass marches attracting millions of participants were organized by immigrant rights activists across the country, culminating with a national day of protest on May 1.[13]

The national debate over immigration reform in the 1990s and 2000s was partially shaped by concerns over party realignment. Certainly, most Latinos voted heavily for Democrats in the 2000, 20004, 2008, and 2012 presidential election cycles. Yet George W. Bush's moderate success among Latinos—he garnered 40 percent of the vote, according to some reports[14]—was encouraging to moderate Republicans and pragmatists who were interested in mobilizing nonwhite voters to make up for the shrinking white vote. Bush's senior strategist Karl Rove "envisioned building a stronger long-term Republican coalition by adding [Latino] voters."[15] The president even endorsed comprehensive immigration reform in the mid-2000s.[16]

At the same time, partisan polarization has increasingly fueled anti-immigration policies despite attempts by moderate Republicans to downplay this phenomenon.[17] In fact, the most restrictive policies since 2000 have been advanced by Republican Party officials at the national and state levels. Gyung-Ho Jeong and colleagues contended that an intraparty division between social-racial conservatives and economic conservatives best explains the triumph of the anti-immigrant wing of the Republican Party since the civil rights and civil liberties revolution of the 1960s.[18] Economic conservatives are generally more supportive of immigration reform because they view undocumented immigrants as a source of cheap labor. This group was the main driving force inside the Republican Party behind the passage of the Immigration Reform and Control Act of 1986.

Civil rights and other identity-based movements have been used as wedges to divide Democrats and to mobilize social and racial conservatives into the Republican Party. Indeed, anti-immigrant attitudes among whites converge with partisanship: those who identify with the Republican Party are more apt to embrace nativist policies.[19] The social-racial conservative wing is now the main power source of the party, overshadowing the economic conservatives who are sympathetic to immigration reform. The September 11, 2001, terrorist attacks "made it easy for social conservatives to frame immigration as an issue of national security and national identity rather than as a way of providing cheap labor as Reaganite Republicans once viewed it."[20] The consequence of this intraparty battle—which has been won by social-racial conservatives—is that Republicans have difficulty fulfilling Rove's dream of building a broader electoral coalition.

Concerns about party realignment dovetailed with a major shift in immigration enforcement with the passage of the IIRIRA, which devolved some powers to state and local officials.[21] One of the IIRIRA's most controversial provisions, especially for Tennessee, was the 287(g) program, which deputized local law enforcement officials to enforce immigration laws through federal-state-local agreements.[22] In 2002, the U.S. Department of Justice's Office of Legal Counsel authored a legal opinion explaining that state and local officials have the statutory power to arrest undocumented residents for transfer to federal authorities.[23] This legal opinion countered an earlier Justice Department opinion from 1996 opposing this power.

Immigration reform usually is considered a federal issue. A principal objection to California's Proposition 187 in 1994 was that it would accelerate too much state action and would create uneven policies by states across the country.[24] The devolution of immigration enforcement has made it increasingly difficult to develop uniform policies. Hundreds of immigration-related bills were sponsored or passed in state legislatures in the 2000s. By some accounts, local governments considered adopting at least 370 measures between 2006 and 2011.[25] Hence, devolution has augmented the power of state and local officials around immigration enforcement. And, as Curry Todd's commentary about "rats" in the epigraph indicates, these officials are instrumental in helping to frame the viability of immigration reform and the social and political status of legal and undocumented residents.

The anti-immigrant rhetoric and the devolution of immigration policies have placed blacks in the middle of the immigration debate. This is because some racial conservatives opposed to traditional civil rights are also at the forefront of anti-immigrant initiatives. Blacks have mixed feelings about undocumented immigrants. Although some blacks hold nativist views,[26] most have come down on the side of protecting immigrants' rights. As an act of coalition building, black politicians and civil rights groups typically support progressive immigration reform. The NAACP, the nation's leading and oldest civil rights organization, adopted a resolution opposing sanctions on employers that hired undocumented immigrants as early as 1990.[27] The National Black Caucus of State Legislators authored a resolution in 2011 opposing Arizona's S.B. 1070.[28]

Political scientist Katherine Tate argued for a more complex understanding of immigration policies. She found that while African Americans are more progressive than whites on immigration reform, they are also more politically conservative than Latinos on this topic. Black people are open to amnesty (a path to citizenship) and guest-worker programs yet are receptive to tough penalties on undocumented residents and to initiatives that reduce immigration flows.[29] Robert C. Smith raised concerns that the flow of undocumented immigrants has eroded black political strongholds, such as South Los Angeles, and limited blacks' access to working-class jobs, which are presumably filled by undocumented workers.[30]

Despite the complex views about immigration policies among the black masses, the black leadership and civil rights establishment remain committed to progressive immigration reform. Even Smith concedes this point: "in general there is a consensus in the African American leadership group in favor of liberal immigration reform."[31] Much of this is due to coalition politics, partisanship, and the belief that the anti–civil rights and anti-immigration forces work hand in glove to promote white supremacy.

We hypothesized that the politics of realignment, devolution, and race have influenced immigration politics in Tennessee. The politics of realignment have placed Latino voters and immigration at the center of partisan struggles. While moderate Republicans and economic conservatives may be receptive to immigration reform—and are opposed to racially animated attacks against legal and undocumented immigrants—social and racial conservatives are supportive of nativist policies. The devolution of immigration policy, which was historically under the jurisdiction of the federal government, gave state and local officials a more authoritative voice in framing the issues. Furthermore, race remains at the forefront of immigration policies. Blacks, in particular, are perceived to be natural allies to immigrant rights activists due to the advocacy of black leaders, elites, and civil rights groups that are wedded to the progressive wing of the Democratic Party.

ISSUE FRAMING AND IMMIGRATION

As mentioned earlier, issue framing is critically important to understanding immigration politics in Tennessee. Dennis Chong and James Druckman's comprehensive treatise illustrated that framing involves the strategic picking of symbols and rhetoric to encourage specific interpretations while discouraging others.[32] Other research on issue framing has indicated that citizen responses to policies, in terms of their support and opposition, vary depending on how the contents of such questions are described.[33]

Regarding immigration policies, support for progressive or judicious reforms depends on how elites, including state officials and advocates, frame these issues. For example, sociologist Hana Brown distinguished between racial and legal frames.[34] The racial frame deems immigrants as unworthy or undeserving residents. It also associates immigrants with criminality. The legality frame, which engenders more judicious attitudes about immigration reform, focuses on legal versus illegal or unauthorized immigrants. From the standpoint of immigrant rights activists, immigration rhetoric is toxic when the term used is "illegal" immigrants.[35]

Despite its wide usage, the "illegal" frame is problematic on several fronts. First, it ignores the fact that many immigrants are exploited by U.S. companies that benefit from low-wage labor. If, for instance, political elites framed the issue around the illegality of employers' actions instead of those of immigrants, the public would have a different perception of the immigration debate. More important, the behavioral script associated with the term "illegal" and criminality misconstrues the nature of the lawbreaking of many unauthorized residents in the United States. Individuals who enter the country outside formal channels are committing offenses that are qualitatively different from those who commit severe procedural crimes.[36] There is also a troubled history of crime being racialized,[37] such that associating illegal immigration with criminality is likely to prime whites toward the adverse consequences of both legal and unauthorized immigration. Finally, the "illegal" frame minimizes the economic and cultural contributions of immigrants. Some analysts believe that comprehensive immigration reform that creates a pathway to citizenship for undocumented immigrants would add more than a trillion dollars to the U.S. economy over the course of a decade.[38]

Another common term used to describe unauthorized immigrants is "undocumented." Rinku Sen of the Race Forward group was an early advocate for replacing the term "illegal" with "undocumented." She and other racial justice activists insisted that the media frame of "illegal" fomented negative racial scripts about Latinos and other immigrants of color. In 2010, her organization launched the "Drop the I-Word" campaign to counter media and elite narratives that framed the immigration debate as a problem of "illegals."[39] Many advocates and an increasing number of mainstream news organizations have dropped the "illegal" frame in exchange for terms such as "unauthorized" or "undocumented."[40]

Unlike the "illegal" frame, which connotes criminality or moral turpitude, the characterization "unauthorized" or "undocumented" has a more wholesome interpretation.[41] It describes individuals who entered the country without permission in order to search for better economic opportunities or those displaced because of military and civil conflicts. It also describes individuals who legally entered the country but remain on expired visas, as well as children who were illegally brought to the United States by their parents. These terms also decriminalize undocumented residents and attempt to reduce the racial animus associated with immigrants. Later in the chapter, we illustrate that Tennesseans' diverse attitudes toward immigration are partly a function of issue framing.

IMMIGRATION POLITICS IN TENNESSEE

The issue of immigration is particularly important for Tennessee residents because of the demographic trends. According to the 2000 U.S. Census, Tennessee had the fifth fastest-growing foreign-born population; other states with fast-growing immigrant populations include North Carolina, Georgia, Arkan-

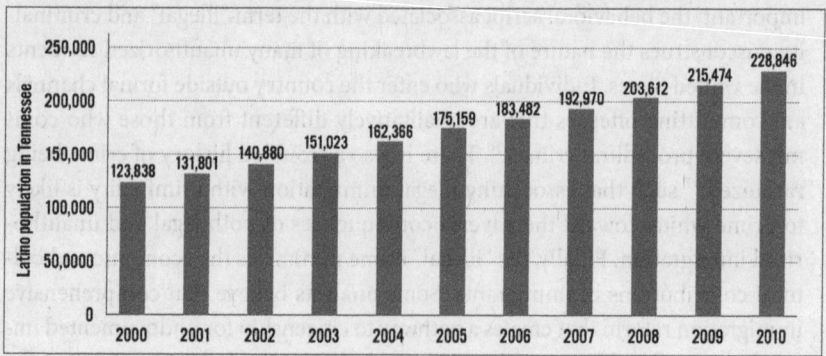

FIGURE 7.1 Latino population trends for Tennessee, 2000–2010, as projected in 2004

Source: University of Tennessee, "The Growing Hispanic Population in Tennessee" (2006), https://extension.tennessee.edu/publications/Documents/PB1762.pdf.
Note: These population numbers are estimated projections.

sas, and Nevada. Furthermore, Tennessee had the fourth fastest-growing Latino population. In the first decade of the twenty-first century, the state's Mexican-born population expanded faster than that of any other state in the country.[42] Figure 7.1 shows that the state's Latino population increased by nearly 85 percent, from 123,838 to 228,846, between 2000 and 2010.

Immigration population growth, principally from newly arriving Latinos, thrust the issue to the forefront of Tennessee politics. Between 2006 and 2012, dozens of bills were sponsored by Tennessee lawmakers, most of which attempted to restrict immigration. In 2006, the state passed a bipartisan law prohibiting businesses from receiving state contracts if they knowingly hired undocumented residents.[43] Other state laws were passed during this period that attempted to prohibit the transportation of undocumented residents in the state; to regulate driver's licenses for the targeted population; and to restrict the hiring of undocumented immigrants. Katherine J. Bogle offered an exhaustive treatment of immigration policies. After assessing survey data and forty-eight bills sponsored by state lawmakers, she found that immigrants were routinely scapegoated by Tennessee officials. She also discovered racial divisions in attitudes toward undocumented immigrants, with whites embracing the most restrictive policies.[44]

Polling data provide additional evidence of the salience of immigration in the state (figure 7.2). In an exit poll of the 2006 Senate race matching Congressman Harold Ford Jr. against Chattanooga mayor Bob Corker, the findings indicate that immigration politics figured prominently into voters' choice for senator. Approximately 42 percent of the respondents reported that illegal immigration

FIGURE 7.2 Perceived importance of immigration in U.S. Senate race

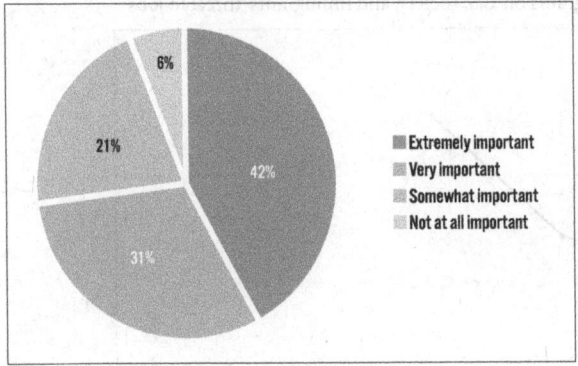

Source: Edison Media Research/Mitofsky International, 2006 Tennessee Senate race exit poll (N = 2,600).

was "extremely important" to their vote for U.S. senator, while only 6 percent claimed that the issue of immigration was "not at all important."

Considering the recent influx of immigrants (particularly those from Spanish-speaking countries) into Tennessee and thus the increased salience of immigration, it is not surprising that political elites and the public in the state were polarized around immigration-related issues.[45] Survey data from 2000 to 2008 reveal a good deal of diversity of anti-immigration attitudes among Tennesseans. Figure 7.3 indicates that between 2000 and 2006, the number of people in the state who believed that immigrants worsen the lives of U.S. citizens increased. On the other hand, the fear that immigrant workers were taking jobs lessened slightly from 2004 to 2008, and there was declining support for guest-worker programs for immigrants.

Nashville, the state capital, was the epicenter of the most controversial immigration battles. In 2007, the Nashville/Davidson County Sheriff's Department signed a 287(g) agreement with the U.S. Department of Homeland Security. The agreement gave the department broad discretion to target immigrants for detainment. Civil libertarians and civil rights groups alleged that the program profiled Latinos. The Nashville program garnered national attention in 2008 after the detainment of Juana Villegas, who was pregnant at the time. She was taken to a local hospital and "shackled to her bed until the final stages of labor." After giving birth, she was taken back to jail, and her newborn developed jaundice.[46] The furor over the Villegas case and a subsequent lawsuit over the constitutionality of 287(g) forced the sheriff's department to close the program.

Immigration rights advocates and groups such as the Tennessee Immigrant

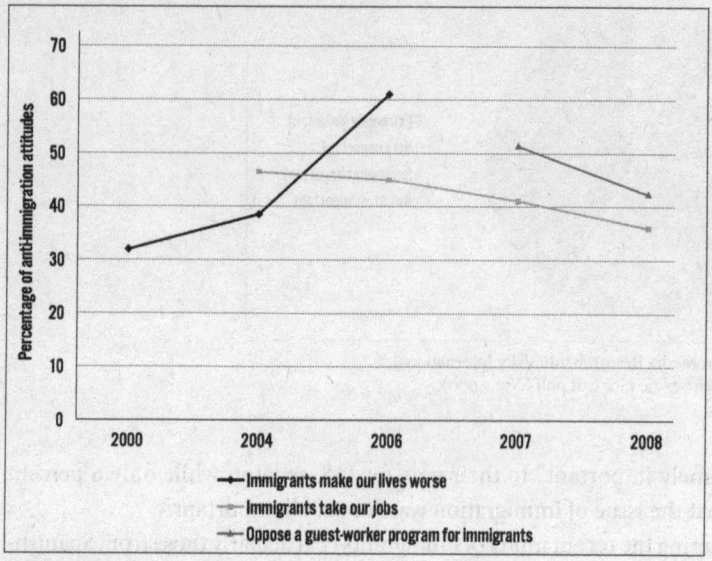

FIGURE 7.3 Trends in Tennesseans' viewpoints regarding guest-worker programs, the impact of Latino immigrants on U.S. society, and immigrants' threat to jobs

Sources: MTSU poll: fall 2000, spring 2004, fall 2006, spring 2006, spring 2007, and fall 2008 waves.
Note: Estimates are the percentages of participants expressing the anti-immigration response of interest.

and Refugee Rights Coalition and Nashville for All of Us were particularly angered by the "English-only" charter referendum in 2009. If adopted, the proposal would have "require[d] all government communications and publications to be conducted in English, though the [metropolitan Nashville] council could make specific exceptions for health and safety."⁴⁷ African American groups joined the opposition to the English-only provision by organizing a rally on January 9, 2009. The Urban League of Middle Tennessee, the Nashville NAACP, and the Urban EpiCenter all protested the measure. State representative Brenda Gilmore, who represented a mostly black legislative district (District Fifty-Four), said that "the passage of the charter amendment would look strange to the rest of the world after the election of Barack Obama, an African-American."⁴⁸ The referendum was defeated 57 percent to 43 percent.

THE INFLUENCE OF ISSUE FRAMING ON TENNESSEANS' VIEWS TOWARD IMMIGRATION

In the remainder of the chapter, we take a closer look at the impact that issue framing has on immigration attitudes and, more generally, on racial polarization in the state. As mentioned earlier, we expected issue framing to be more im-

FIGURE 7.4 Summary of the conditions in the MTSU survey experiment on issue framing and immigration attitudes

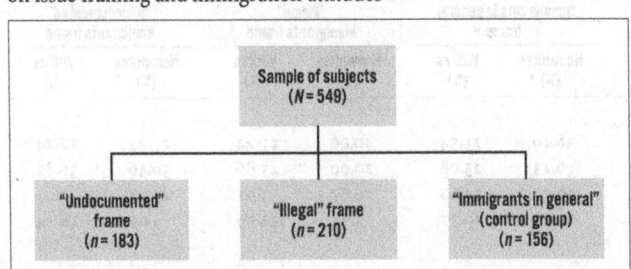

Source: Fall 2006 wave of the MTSU poll.

pactful in twenty-first-century Tennessee politics, given the devolution of immigration regulation, and we expected that such polarization would be moderated by race.

We draw from the fall 2006 poll by the MTSU Survey Group. This wave included an experimental design that randomly assigned the respondents ($N = 549$) to different frames or narratives for describing immigrants. All the other survey questions were identical across the experimental conditions.

As shown in figure 7.4, 38 percent of the respondents ($n = 210$) received a question frame that characterized unauthorized immigrants as "illegal"; approximately one-third ($n = 183$) received the "undocumented" frame; and 28 percent ($n = 156$) were asked about their support for "immigrants in general." For our study, the "immigrants in general" condition served as the control group to which the other framing approaches (calling immigrants "illegal" versus "undocumented") were compared. This allowed us to measure the direct influence of the frames on exacerbating anti-immigration sentiment. We also evaluated if anti-immigration attitudes are conditioned by frames such as "illegal" and "undocumented." Both measures suggested that anti-immigrant attitudes vary by the types of frame that are used to leverage Tennesseans' attitudes about immigration politics. We differentiate between the impact of these frames ("direct" versus "conditional") later in the chapter.

As indicated in table 7.1, the respondents in the fall 2006 poll represented a variety of sociopolitical backgrounds; they were diverse in race/ethnicity, gender, ideological partisanship, and education.[49] They were not distributed evenly across the framing conditions.[50] However, the random assignment procedure did eliminate differences across the experimental manipulations in terms of the respondents' sociodemographic and political backgrounds.[51]

As noted earlier, we are concerned with how various frames polarized the public about immigrants in Tennessee. We refer to the dependent variable as

TABLE 7.1 Social and political background of participants in the fall 2006 MTSU poll

	"Immigrants in general" frame		"Illegal" immigrants frame		"Undocumented" immigrants frame	
	Nonwhites (%)	Whites (%)	Nonwhites (%)	Whites (%)	Nonwhites (%)	Whites (%)
Age						
18–34	38.46	21.54	40.00	17.24	27.27	18.24
35–49	19.23	23.08	20.00	25.86	36.36	30.82
50–64	30.77	34.62	26.67	33.91	27.27	32.7
65 or older	11.54	20.77	13.33	22.99	9.09	18.24
Gender						
Man	46.15	55.38	40.63	50.00	47.83	43.75
Woman	53.85	44.62	59.38	50.00	52.17	56.25
Political ideology						
Far left	7.69	1.54	6.25	1.12	0.00	0.00
Liberal	15.38	12.31	18.75	12.92	4.35	0.63
Middle of road	42.31	33.08	37.5	34.27	8.7	11.25
Conservative	15.38	41.54	21.88	35.96	43.48	38.13
Far right	3.85	5.38	6.25	5.62	26.09	38.75
Party identification						
Republican	0.00	50.00	15.63	34.27	8.7	39.38
Democratic	42.31	23.85	37.5	29.78	47.83	26.88
Independent	26.92	14.62	31.25	24.16	39.13	19.38
Other	19.23	5.38	12.5	8.99	0.00	9.38
Education						
≤ High school grad	46.15	39.68	38.71	37.85	54.55	35.03
Some college or trade	30.77	23.81	16.13	25.99	22.73	25.48
≥ College grad	23.08	36.51	45.16	36.16	22.73	39.49

Source: Fall 2006 wave of the MTSU poll.

the Anti-Immigration Attitudes Index (AIAI). The index is composed of the responses to three immigration questions:

1. Should immigration be increased, decreased, or remain the same?
2. Do you believe immigration is a good or bad thing for the country?
3. Have immigrants made your life better or worse?

As seen in table 7.2, the answers to the questions were collapsed into two categories (0 and 1) with higher values representing viewpoints that were more negative toward immigration and immigrants. The index, created from combined responses to the three questions, was then converted to a three-item dependent variable ranging from 0 (none of the respondent's viewpoints were anti-immigrant) to 3 (all of the respondent's opinions were anti-immigrant). Race/ethnicity is a moderating variable of interest. Yet the survey had only a small sample of nonwhites disaggregated by race/ethnicity (blacks, whites, Latinos, Asians, etc.). Like our approach in chapter 5, the small sample size limitations

TABLE 7.2 Summary of the theoretically central variables in the immigration framing experiment

	Sample mean	Standard deviation	Minimum value	Maximum value
Dependent variable				
Immigration rates should decrease	0.54	0.50	0	1
Immigration is a bad thing	0.34	0.47	0	1
Immigrants make our lives worse	0.23	0.42	0	1
Anti-Immigration Attitudes Index (AIAI)	1.11	0.97	0	3
Moderator variable				
Respondent's race (1 = white, 0 = nonwhite)	0.85	0.35	0	1
Experimental condition				
"Immigrants in general" frame ($n = 156$)	0.28	0.45	0	1
"Illegal" immigrants frame ($n = 210$)	0.38	0.49	0	1
"Undocumented" immigrants frame ($n = 183$)	0.33	0.47	0	1

Source: Fall 2006 wave of the MTSU poll.
Notes: $N = 549$. All experimental manipulations are coded so that 1 = frame of interest and 0 = otherwise. We use a similar coding logic for the race variable. Means for dichotomous variables represent proportions.

motivated us to dichotomize our measure of racial group identification in order to facilitate comparisons between white and nonwhite respondents.

The impact of issue framing is exhibited in figure 7.5, which displays the average values for the AIAI variable across the experimental conditions, sorted by respondents' race (white versus nonwhite). For the full sample, there was no difference between the "immigrants in general" and "undocumented" frames regarding the intensity of respondents' anti-immigration attitudes. However, the "illegal" frame produced more negative attitudes about immigrants. The patterns of anti-immigration responses among whites look similar to the findings for the full model. But the labels "undocumented" and "illegal" both heightened the negative immigration attitudes of nonwhite respondents. These findings suggest that issue framing can polarize attitudes and, in extreme cases, foment anti-immigrant responses.

The regression models provide a closer examination of the effect of race and issue framing on the respondents' anti-immigration attitudes in the fall 2006 survey.[52] The first model in table 7.3 shows the direct effect of issue framing on anti-immigration attitudes. The second model evaluates the conditional effect of issue framing, or whether anti-immigrant attitudes vary by the type of frame used to influence the public. The regression analyses include interaction terms that allow us to account for race. Any statistically significant interactions that emerge would suggest racial group differences (between whites and nonwhites) in the impact of issue framing.

The finding for the race variable in the first model is both positive and sta-

FIGURE 7.5 Average levels of the Anti-Immigration Attitudes Index across experimental conditions, sorted by respondents' race

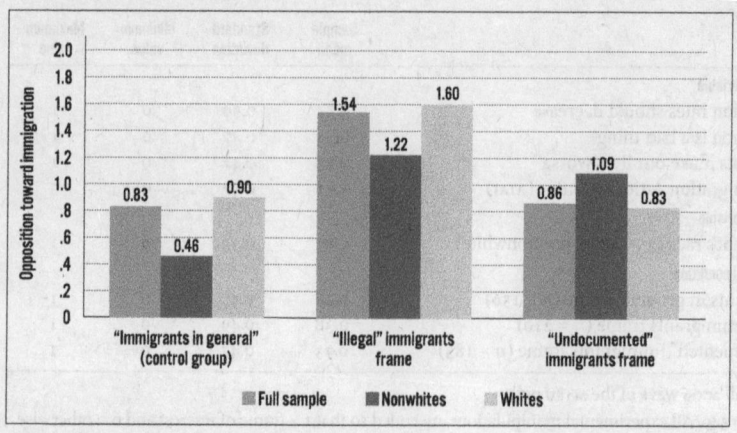

Source: Fall 2006 wave of the MTSU poll.
Note: Mean values on the AIAI among minority (darker bars) and white (lighter bars) respondents, with higher values representing greater overall opposition toward immigrants and immigration policies.

TABLE 7.3 OLS regression models of the influence of issue framing on Tennesseans' opposition toward immigration

Independent variables	Model 1 (direct effect)		Model 2 (conditional effect)	
	OLS estimate	SE	OLS estimate	SE
Subject race (1 = white, 0 = nonwhite)	0.21*	(0.11)	0.44**	(0.19)
"Illegal" immigrants frame	0.71**	(0.10)	0.76**	(0.24)
"Undocumented" immigrants frame	0.02	(0.10)	0.63**	(0.26)
Race × "illegal" frame	—	—	−0.06	(0.26)
Race × "undocumented" frame	—	—	−0.70**	(0.28)
Constant	0.65**	(0.12)	0.46**	(0.18)
Number of subjects (N)	549		549	
Model fit (adjusted R^2)	0.12		0.13	

Source: Fall 2006 wave of the MTSU poll.
Notes: The dependent variable is our three-item AIAI, coded so that higher values represent greater overall opposition toward immigrants and immigration policies. Dashes (—) indicate portions of the model for which estimates were not calculated. * = $p < .05$; ** = $p < .01$, one-tailed test.

tistically significant.[53] Regardless of framing, and compared to nonwhites, white Tennesseans expressed viewpoints that were typically more anti-immigration, holding the other variables constant. The average level of whites' and nonwhites' AIAI scores, regardless of framing, are 1.14 and .93, respectively. This leaves a racial difference of approximately 1.14 − .93 = .21. The statistically significant result of white-nonwhite differences in immigration attitudes is consistent with the argument that white Tennesseans are generally antagonistic toward immigrants, and it provides clear evidence of racially polarized opinions.[54] The regression coefficient for the "illegal" immigrant frame is also positive and statistically meaningful.[55]

Model 2 (conditional effect) in table 7.3 explores how race shapes the effect of issue framing on immigration attitudes. The estimate for the constant shows that the respondents' answers were significantly different from those of Tennesseans in other experimental conditions.[56] The race coefficient is positive and statistically significant,[57] revealing a difference in the effect of framing as the value of the race variable moves from nonwhite to white in the control group. In other words, this estimate records the race effect when the "illegal" and "undocumented" frames are set to a value of 0. Compared to nonwhites (average = .46), white respondents in the control group had an average AIAI score of .90, which is .44 points higher than that of nonwhites. The coefficient estimate for the "illegal" immigrants frame represents the effect of this framing manipulation on nonwhites.[58] Moreover, a coefficient for the "undocumented" immigrant frame reveals that a shift from the control group to this manipulation caused nonwhites' average AIAI score to rise.[59]

A closer assessment of the interaction variables (race × "illegal" and race × "undocumented") in table 7.3 shows negative results for both; however, only one of these interactions (race × "undocumented") is statistically significant. The effect of the "illegal" frame is larger, though insignificant, for whites, while the "undocumented" framing effect is greater for nonwhites. This provides further evidence that the magnitude of the effects of the framing manipulations differed across racial groups.

To highlight the results for the interaction variables, we plotted the conditional impact of race on anti-immigration attitudes across the experimental conditions. Specifically, the data points in figure 7.6 tell us what respondents' average AIAI scores would be if varied by race (white versus nonwhite) and framing condition ("immigrants in general," "illegal," and "undocumented"), while holding other variables at their modal values. The general patterns reinforce the significance of the direct impact of immigration frames. Regardless of race, the "illegal" immigrants frame produces the strongest anti-immigration attitudes, followed by the more neutral phrasing "immigrants in general"; the label of "undocumented" immigrant appears to be the least offensive to Tennesseans.

Finally, we found some interesting white-nonwhite differences in the effect of issue framing on immigration attitudes. Overall, nonwhite respondents were significantly more positive in their perceptions of immigration.[60] A similar pattern emerged for the "illegal" immigrants frame, in that whites (compared to nonwhites) expressed attitudes that were less accepting of Latino immigrants, although the racial difference is not statistically meaningful.[61] Intriguingly, the

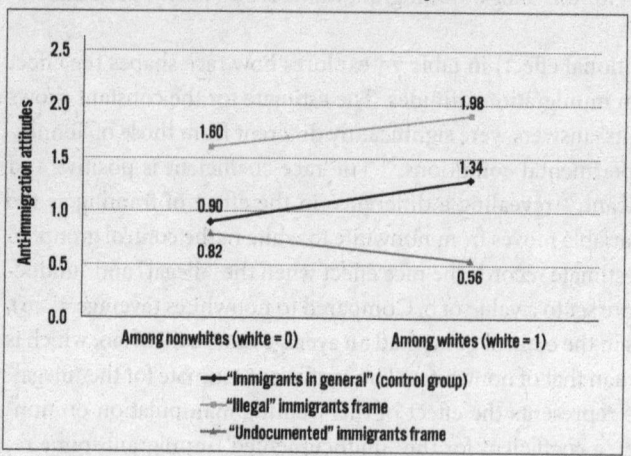

FIGURE 7.6 Post-estimation results: How the effect of race on respondents' immigration attitudes differed across the framing conditions

Source: Fall 2006 wave of the MTSU poll.

"undocumented" condition findings contradicted our expectations: it was nonwhites who expressed the greatest antagonism toward immigration in this experimental condition. Yet it is important to note that the "Drop the I-Word" initiative, which was principally sponsored by racial justice groups, emerged four years after the administration of this survey.

CONCLUSION

Like in the explorations of racial polarization presented in previous chapters, the evidence here tells a story about whites and nonwhites moving away from each other when it comes to the extremity of their viewpoints about the "new Tennesseans." Compared to their neighbors of color, white Tennessee residents tend to be more antagonistic in their attitudes about immigration (as a social topic) and immigrants (as newcomers to the state). We also demonstrated that the degree to which anti-immigrant/anti-immigration attitudes are polarized depends on the manner in which this topic and the people involved are presented. Scholars refer to these differences of presentation as "issue framing," and our chapter joins this body of research to demonstrate further the power of framing effects.

We began this chapter with a commentary by Representative Curry Todd, who castigated immigrants as "rats" while rationalizing his decision to deny them prenatal care. The statement offers some indication of how issue frames—elite-driven narratives that have the consequence of polarizing the electorate—influence immigration politics. The relevance of issue framing was augmented by partisan and ideological disputes in Tennessee, the devolution of immigration policy, and the centrality of race in the immigration debate.

More important, the analyses provided in this chapter show not only that immigration attitudes are susceptible to framing effects, but that the extent to which framing shapes beliefs about immigration varies by race. The population growth of Latinos has influenced Tennessee politics, which has historically been characterized by a black-white struggle. The emergence of Latinos raises the general concern of how Tennesseans will respond to the burgeoning diversity of the twenty-first century. On the one hand, Tennesseans may embrace the changes and tolerate diversity. On the other hand, increased diversity may lead to perceptions of heightened racial/ethnic threat and thus more intergroup polarization.

The findings in this chapter underscore the importance of devolution and racial polarization and emphasize how immigration is at the forefront of Tennessee politics. Current and future immigration patterns, partisan rhetoric, and the federal government's delegation of responsibility to the states create an environment that is highly conducive to racial and political polarization in Tennessee. Politicians and media pundits can exploit this context by using divisive messages. Compared to their white counterparts, nonwhites are differentially sensitive to such framing attempts. In other words, race affects the influence of issue framing. Among nonwhites, the terms "undocumented" and "illegal" both trigger anti-immigration attitudes. Among whites, it makes a difference whether immigrants are called "undocumented" or "illegal"; specifically, using the latter frame triggers greater negativity in whites' immigration attitudes as reflected in respondents' average AIAI scores (holding other variables at their medians). In the next chapter, we discuss sentencing reform in Tennessee and racial polarization in another hot-button issue: the death penalty.

CHAPTER EIGHT

CONTROVERSIES AND CONFLICTS OVER SENTENCING POLICIES AND THE DEATH PENALTY

> How can the rehabilitation component of the correctional institution be effectively restructured?
>
> —TENNESSEE BLACK CAUCUS OF STATE LEGISLATORS (1976)

In 2016, the Tennessee Black Caucus of State Legislators (TBCSL) sponsored a legislative package to reform the state's criminal justice system. The legislative items included a "ban the box" hiring policy (also called the "fair chance" hiring policy), which removed the question on state employment applications asking job candidates to identify their criminal histories; several bills expunging the records of people with criminal histories; and proposals to alter the state's sentencing laws for adults and juvenile offenders.[1] The approximately thirty bills signaled a remarkable turnaround in the state legislature's approach to criminal justice reform. Two decades earlier Tennessee, like other southern states, had instituted a set of zero-tolerance policies that expanded incarceration and state spending on the penal system.

The shift in Tennessee's approach to criminal justice, though modest, occurred because of several factors. First, renewed attention to criminal justice reform was sparked by national social movements, such as those emerging out of the Black Lives Matter protests, and grassroots organizing that were fueled, in part, by the publication of Michelle Alexander's *The New Jim Crow: Mass Incarceration in the Age of Colorblindness*. Alexander argued that the criminal justice arena—which includes criminal convictions, plea deals, policing strategies, and strategies of political elites—has been largely positioned against communities of color.[2] Community activists and legal advocates in Tennessee used her book as a mobilizing tool to pressure lawmakers to reconsider zero-tolerance policies that exacerbate incarceration.[3]

Second, advocacy and civil rights groups pressured state lawmakers for criminal justice reforms. In 2007, the American Civil Liberties Union of Tennessee organized the "Right to Vote" campaign to relax the state's felony disenfranchisement law.[4] One organization, Tennesseans for Alternatives to the Death Penalty (TAPD, which was previously known as the Tennessee Coalition to Abolish State Killing), was especially effective in educating the electorate about the politics of the death penalty. Specifically, TAPD launched a multifaceted campaign—which supplemented community outreach events with a strong media presence—while cultivating partnerships with other sympathetic grassroots organizations.[5]

A third factor that contributed to a renewed focus on criminal justice reform was the shifting positions of conservative libertarians in the state. Libertarian groups (such as the Beacon Center of Tennessee, whose mission is to "promote policy solutions that will reduce the burdens government places on individuals and businesses") endorsed criminal justice legislation, including some of the TBCSL's bills.[6] Moreover, the Beacon Center joined forces with the ACLU of Tennessee to form the Coalition for Sensible Justice in 2016 to advance a legislative agenda.

The fourth and perhaps most important reason that criminal justice reforms occurred in Tennessee was the work of the frontline activists, attorneys, faith leaders, families, and incarcerated and formerly incarcerated people involved in the reform efforts. As we showed in chapter 2, Tennessee has a rich history of social activists laboring in penal institutions and advocating for reentry initiatives. Advocacy around the death penalty, wrongful convictions, imbalanced sentencing, felon disenfranchisement, and post-sentence employment opportunities has been the focus of these activists.[7]

In this chapter we examine racial and political polarization around criminal justice reform in Tennessee. The mistreatment of blacks and poor people in the criminal justice system has been a central concern of black politics in Tennessee for decades. As early as 1972, Governor Winfield Dunn appointed Charles Traugher to the Board of Pardons and Parole, the highest-ranking African American in the state's criminal justice system, due to concerns about the mistreatment of black people and poor people in the executive commutation process. The governor further concluded that "excessive sentencing in cases involving black defendants" may be a problem in the state.[8] Five years later, the TBCSL asked officials in Governor Ray Blanton's administration to answer a "criminal justice questionnaire" in anticipation of its legislative retreat.[9] Questions and concerns about rehabilitation, police brutality, bail reform, the death penalty, excessive sentences, and executive clemency were part of the policy agendas of black lawmakers for decades.

Despite these earlier reform attempts, racial disparities and the (mis)treatment of poor people and black people in the criminal justice system remained central concerns of black lawmakers, grassroots activists, and legal advocates in the late twentieth and early twenty-first centuries. As we mentioned in previous chapters, in the twenty-first century Republicans gained a supermajority in the state legislature, thus contributing to the loss of African American power in the legislative body; the retrenchment of labor and consumer protections by state lawmakers; the downsizing of TennCare; and fierce debates over balanced budgets and taxes. In this chapter we continue the conversation about black Tennesseans losing political power by focusing specifically on racial disparities in residents' attitudes about sentencing practices for criminal convictions and the implementation of the death penalty.

We draw on two state surveys (one in 1999, and the other from 2007) by the Middle Tennessee State University (MTSU) Survey Group, which has conducted a biannual poll of state politics for two decades. We argue that polarization in Tennesseans' views about criminal justice policies, specifically along the lines of race, shifted in the twenty-first century. As the state legislature and advocates gave renewed attention to the death penalty, whites and nonwhites diverged in their attitudes toward this policy. The attention in 2007, compared to a decade earlier, made the death penalty a salient issue, and nonwhites in general (and African Americans in particular) were more concerned than their white neighbors that the death penalty lacked due process.

In this chapter, we provide a brief theoretical overview of racial polarization in support for criminal justice reform. We start by discussing several factors (racial polarization, devolution, advocacy initiatives, and party dynamics) affecting criminal justice policies in the South more generally. Then, we offer a historical and contextual summary of sentencing policy and the death penalty in Tennessee. Finally, drawing from the statewide surveys, we look more closely at racial attitudes toward the death penalty.

CRIMINAL JUSTICE AND TENNESSEE

Perhaps no other set of public policies has ignited racial divisions more forcefully than criminal justice reform. Criminal justice approaches in Tennessee were shaped by the devolution of federal power to state governments and the flexibility given to states to establish their own penalties for crimes. This was particularly the case in sentencing policy and the death penalty. As we demonstrate below, Tennessee and other states were given tremendous flexibility to establish sentencing guidelines and enhanced penalties at critical junctures of post–civil rights politics. Tennessee lawmakers had difficulty managing pressures from criminal justice advocates, many of whom understood the racial implications of punitive policies. Some lawmakers thus sought a compromise package of reforms that, at times, exacerbated crises in the criminal justice system. The late twentieth century experienced a bipartisan consensus of sorts in favor of zero-tolerance measures but also, at times, in favor of reforms. Republicans were usually more receptive to reforms when crises plagued the criminal justice system or when federal or state courts intervened with remedies. The aforementioned factors (racial polarization, devolution, advocacy initiatives, and partisanship) shaped Tennessee's approach to two major criminal justice arenas in the late twentieth and early twenty-first centuries: sentencing policies and the death penalty.

The end of the twentieth century and the beginning of the twenty-first was a transition period in criminal justice reform. For example, the state dissolved the Tennessee Sentencing Commission in 1995. The commission had been established in 1986 after widespread abuses and overcrowding plagued the state penal system. The commission's recommendations led to the passage of the Criminal Sentencing Reform Act of 1989, which created uniform sentencing guidelines and better oversight of state prisons.[10] With the dissolution of the commission in the mid-1990s, the state legislature eliminated parole for some capital offenses and enhanced sentencing for other crimes. By the early 2000s, the state's prison population had increased by 30 percent, far outpacing the overall population growth of 13 percent in the state.[11]

The twenty-first century also experienced a renewed debate over the death penalty. There were 2,000 first-degree murder cases in the state between 1977 and 2016, although only 193 led to death sentences.[12] Yet during the early twenty-first century, lawmakers and advocates debated several issues that extended beyond the morality of the death penalty. Procedural justice, lethal injection procedures, racial disparities in death sentences, and uneven sentencing consumed much of the attention of death penalty proponents and opponents. In the early 2000s, the American Bar Association and the Tennessee Bar Association both found major problems in how Tennessee handled the death penalty. This culminated in the state legislature creating a special committee in 2007 to study the administration of the death penalty.[13]

RACE, CRIMINAL JUSTICE REFORM, AND THE U.S. SOUTH

Criminal justice reform is among the most divisive of public policies. Historically, in the U.S. South, criminal justice policies were tied to the region's troubling racial history. Writing about the disenfranchising laws implemented by white southerners as a counter to Reconstruction, Pippa Holloway noted: "As they fought to preserve the social and political order, white southern political leaders soon realized that the rights of citizenship could still be denied to individuals deemed 'infamous' due to their conviction of certain criminal offenses."[14] New criminal penalties in the nineteenth century thus reinforced white racial domination and were used, according to Holloway, as "political interventions that would interrupt the revolutionary social changes facing the defeated Confederacy."[15] Southern states under the banner of states' rights regained control of the region not only due to racial terrorism, but also because of pro-segregation Supreme Court decisions (e.g., Civil Rights Cases, *Plessy v. Ferguson*, Slaughterhouse Cases, *United States v. Cruikshank*) and the imposition of Jim Crow laws, such as poll taxes, literacy and understanding tests, and the grandfather clause. Punitive and selective criminal justice policies also bolstered de jure segregation.

The South is where the starkest racial division exists in the United States. The death penalty's resurgence in the South occurred at the same time segregationists began to abandon the practice of racial lynching. This shift was because they, in part, believed that "the same degree of control and intimidation could still be exerted over blacks with capital punishment [as with lynching]."[16] Some criminologists have argued that the death penalty was used to control what were perceived as sexually aggressive black men in the South. Between the 1930s and 1970, 97 percent of the executions for rape occurred in the South, and in 400 out of 443 of these cases, the people executed were black men.[17]

The devolution of federal power to the states since the New Federalism and the law-and-order approach of President Richard Nixon placed an inordinate amount of pressure on Tennessee's criminal justice system in the twentieth century. As the crime and drug waves took hold in the United States, Tennessee responded with more zero-tolerance policies, which increased the prison population. In the early 1970s, the state legislature passed several laws enhancing prison sentences and reducing parole eligibility.[18] These were followed by the creation of a Class X felony category in 1979 that required mandatory minimum sentences for violent offenses, eliminated probation, and reduced parole, bail, and plea bargain agreements in some cases.[19] A few years later, the Tennessee General Assembly standardized prison sentences by shifting sentencing from juries to judges with the passage of the Criminal Sentencing Reform Act of 1982.[20]

The 1982 law did not improve conditions in the Tennessee prison system. In fact, conditions in Tennessee prisons worsened in the 1980s. Overcrowding and abuses led to prison riots, additional legislative oversight, and even federal court intervention mandating corrective action.[21] Governor Lamar Alexander called the legislature into a special session in 1985 to reduce overcrowding in the prisons. The resulting legislation, the Comprehensive Corrections Act, implemented several policies: it strengthened the "incentive credits" program, which allowed prisoners to get time off for good behavior; it reduced sentences for paying restitution and for participating in community rehabilitation programs; it expanded work-release programs while liberalizing parole eligibility requirements for violent offenders; and it poured more money into local jails instead of state prisons.[22]

One downfall of these reforms is that the legislation allowed for the privatization of two state prisons. In some respects, the reforms were considered an improvement on Tennessee's overcrowding crisis, but they opened the doors to the expansion of the private prison industry in the state. Corrections Corporation of America (now CoreCivic) was the direct beneficiary of this expansion. It was founded in 1983 in Nashville by Tom Beasley, a former chair of the Tennessee Republican Party.[23] It quickly became one of the world's most lucrative private prison companies.

The Criminal Sentencing Reform Act of 1989 added an additional layer of reforms for Tennessee. The Sentencing Commission established in 1986 had created a fairer and more uniform sentencing process.[24] Its closure a decade later disappointed many criminal justice reformers. David Raybin, a prominent sentencing reform advocate in the state, was quoted as saying, "We jumped off a cliff in 1995 [when we dissolved the commission], blindfolded. That's what happened. We took away our radar with the Sentencing Commission."[25] Although the commission dissolved due to a sunset clause, it had lost political support among zero-tolerance advocates and conservatives. Elizabeth Sykes, the executive director of the Sentencing Commission, stated, "I would say there would be some who felt the commission was not as tough on crime as they would have wanted."[26]

The federal Violent Crime Control and Law Enforcement Act of 1994 signaled the zero-tolerance approach during this time. The law encouraged states to increase prison populations by tying federal funds for prison construction to conviction rates and to sentencing for violent offenders.[27] It most likely harmed sentencing reform in Tennessee.

With the collapse of the Sentencing Commission, the prison population grew in Tennessee. Between 2000 and 2013, the percentage of incarcerated people grew by 30 percent.[28] The Tennessee Drug-Free School Zone Act of 1995 was one of the more controversial laws passed during this period. It created enhanced sentences for offenders caught distributing drugs within one thousand feet of a school zone. Black lawmakers and civil rights advocates later argued that the law discriminated against urban residents and particularly African Americans, who were most likely to live near a school in a population-dense community.[29] In 2016, 434 people in prison had received enhanced or stack-on sentences under this law; 300 (69 percent) of the recipients of these wrongfully inflated sentences were African American.[30]

The enhancements approach for some crimes has led to more punitive treatment of offenders in the state. Interestingly, the Supreme Court's *Blakely v. Washington* decision in 2004 attempted to curb judges who might increase sentences beyond the requisite amount established in law.[31] Yet still embedded in Tennessee's criminal code are enhancement factors that allow judges to stack on additional time for offenders who, as in the case of the Drug-Free School Zones Act, commit crimes in specific circumstances.

THE DEATH PENALTY IN TENNESSEE

The death penalty has been another area of attention in Tennessee's criminal justice arena. Certainly, the most troubling racial division in the criminal justice system is death penalty sentencing. The *McCleskey v. Kemp* (1987) case revealed that race matters most when blacks are alleged to have killed whites. This factor results in a disproportionate number of blacks on death row compared to whites.[32]

Interestingly, in the 1960s Tennessee was a hotbed of anti–death penalty advocacy. Governor Frank Clement, in fact, made a concerted attempt to abolish the death penalty in 1965. He believed that the state's political modernization—industrialization, economic growth, and urbanization—directly conflicted with regressive policies, such as capital punishment.

The civil rights movement and racial desegregation were equally important to Tennessee's political modernization, and both shaped Clement's views about the intersection of race and punishment. In the 1950s and 1960s, desegregation and black political integration were explicitly or implicitly linked to a broad range of policy debates in Tennessee involving labor standards, the minimum wage, municipal home rule, legislative reapportionment, and prison reform. The death penalty was included because of its disparate impact on southern blacks. Black people made up most of Tennessee's death row inmates and executions between 1915 and 1960—85 blacks (68 percent) were executed compared to 39 whites—and five blacks were scheduled for execution in 1965, when the legislature debated the death penalty.[33]

The intersection of Jim Crow policies—the South's penchant for state-sanctioned violence, the region's political modernization, and southern politics—has relevance for this discussion. Progressive views about the death penalty, at least as expressed by a governor, had the potential to inflame passions among white supremacists. Throughout the intense discussions in 1965, proponents and opponents of the death penalty repeal were mindful of the linkage between blacks and the death penalty and its connection to the ongoing civil rights struggle. During the legislative debate, one constituent told the governor (reproduced as written), "I would like to take this opportunity of protesting the abolition of the death penalty.... When the lynching law was outlawed the rapes in the entire U.S. has reached at least 100% to what it was when every man who raped a woman was killed by lynching."[34]

On the other side of the debate, the *Tennessean* editorial page, spearheaded by civil rights proponent John Seigenthaler, brought attention to the disparate impact of the death penalty: "By and large the shadow it [capital punishment] casts is only on the impoverished and on the Negro minority."[35] Septima Clark, a prominent civil rights activist associated with Myles Horton's Highlander Folk School and Dr. Martin Luther King Jr.'s Southern Christian Leadership Conference, wrote to Clement, commending him for his position:

> As an American Negro, I have always been extremely interested in the abolition of capital punishment. I never felt that it could help anyone to take the life for any crime committed.... [The death row inmates] were mostly those who had suffered from the most degrading experiences during their life time—like pains of hunger, inadequate or no schooling, and lop-sided shacks in designated ghettoes.[36]

This suggests that race and racial polarization were part of the subtext of the larger discussion of Tennessee's death penalty, and Clement understood the racial implications of his opposition to capital punishment. Even though he did not openly state that blacks were the disproportionate victims of the death penalty, he routinely said that the practice was wrong because of its unfair treatment of certain groups.

The most lasting impact on Clement's anti–death penalty advocacy was his experience interacting with death row inmates before they were executed. His second term in the late 1950s brought him face-to-face with eight prisoners scheduled for capital punishment, six of whom were executed. Clement chose to personally talk with each of the prisoners. James Edwards, the Tennessee State Prison's warden, observed these interactions. He said, "Clement agonized over every one of them [executions]," and "his emotions, sensitivity, and family upbringing put him in direct conflict with the state law on capital punishment."[37] In one instance, Clement met privately with the wife and children of Harry Kirkendall, a black inmate condemned to death.

By the end of his second term, the governor had publicly voiced his opposition to capital punishment. In his parting message in 1959, he had advised the General Assembly to reevaluate the state's death penalty law. When he was reelected in 1963, he indicated that some type of moratorium or repeal would be open for debate in his third term. The major question was how such a debate would occur. The governor was cautious about using his executive powers, either through a moratorium or commutations, to abolish the death penalty. Instead, he indicated in his State of the State address in January 1963 that he wanted the legislature's consent before deciding on the death penalty.[38]

Two years later, Clement made an aggressive push to end capital punishment in the state. In fact, he convened the House of Representatives on March 17, 1965, insisting that the members support his repeal of the death penalty. At the time, the Senate had already voted to abolish capital punishment with a few exceptions. In the House speech, Clement likened the death penalty to "legal murder" and said it was "unequally and inequitably administered."[39] Making matters more urgent were the impending executions of five death row inmates. Initially, three men were sentenced to die in the last month of the legislative session, but Clement delayed their execution dates until both chambers of the legislature had a chance to vote on the repeal law.

Despite the momentum behind the measure, both inside and outside the General Assembly, the repeal faced several obstacles. The most difficult set of barriers was the institutional constraints of the General Assembly: due to legislative logjams, legislators were forced to deliberate on many bills in a short amount of time. In March 1965, the last month of the session (Tennessee's state legislature only met for less than five months), the legislature had to consider more than four dozen bills. Death penalty opponents, consequently, had to deal with an overload of legislation that potentially threatened the success of the repeal. Pressure also mounted on Clement and his lobbyist team, who faced the difficult choices of prioritizing measures and deciding upon what parts of his agenda to expend their political capital.

Governor Clement and his legislative allies faced the additional burden of building a winning coalition in the House, which was complicated by the institution's size and diversity. The repeal proponents were further divided on the language of the Senate bill, specifically because it did not abolish the death penalty for all capital offenses: exemptions were made for offenders convicted of murdering on-duty police officers and prison guards. These exemptions were included as a compromise to curry favor with moderate and conservative lawmakers, who were reluctant to support the bill. There was some disagreement among the repeal coalition regarding whether these exemptions should be removed from the House bill.[40] These divisions and the stiff opposition from the bill's chief adversaries contributed to the defeat of death penalty repeal.

After the repeal failed, Clement used his executive powers to commute the death sentences of five prisoners. All five inmates were given the less harsh sentence of ninety-nine years with the possibility of parole after forty-eight years. After Clement left office, the state legislature passed the Post-Conviction Procedure Act of 1967. This law, reflecting the sentiments of Clement and anti–death penalty advocates, expanded the procedural and constitutional rights for death row inmates, giving them greater flexibility to challenge their convictions after sentencing.[41]

THE POLITICS OF THE DEATH PENALTY, 1970S-2000S

The 1970s were a watershed decade for the death penalty in Tennessee. The U.S. Supreme Court invalidated the death penalty in *Furman v. Georgia* (1972) but reinstated it a few years later with the *Gregg v. Georgia* (1976) decision. The state supreme court also upheld the death penalty initially in two cases from 1979–1981 and later in 1991.[42] In the late 1990s, Tennessee changed its method for execution from electrocution to lethal injection (for people convicted and given the death penalty after 1998).

After the Tennessee Supreme Court reversal, 194 people were given death sentences from 1977 to 2016. A study of Tennessee's death penalty by attorneys Bradley A. MacLean and H. E. Miller Jr. found widespread irregularities and inconsistencies, including ineffective counsel, uneven sentencing depending on the county of the conviction, and racial disparities in conviction rates since more blacks than whites were sentenced to death.[43]

Similar to the 1960s, there has been robust anti–death penalty activism in the state in the twenty-first century. Anti–death penalty advocates—known as "new abolitionists"[44]—have been instrumental in overturning wrongful convictions and sentences and exposing the problems with racial disparities in juror trials that led to convictions. They have also raised concerns about death penalty procedures, such as lethal injection.

Advocacy groups pressured lawmakers to establish the Special Committee to Study the Administration of the Death Penalty in 2007. The special committee was charged with assessing wrongful convictions, examining service provisions for victims' families and the families of capital defendants, and determining the fairness of the capital punishment process.[45] At the same time, the American Bar Association issued "Evaluating Fairness and Accuracy in State Death Penalty Systems: The Tennessee Death Penalty Assessment Report," which found problems with the death penalty, including the administration of lethal injection.[46] The report, combined with lobbying by anti–death penalty advocates, forced the governor to suspend the death penalty for ninety days until new protocols were established.

A CLOSER LOOK AT TENNESSEANS' ATTITUDES TOWARD THE DEATH PENALTY

Next, we delve into how Tennesseans viewed the death penalty. We draw from two surveys administered by the MTSU Survey Group. The 1999 survey ($N = 395$)

asked the respondents if they supported the death penalty or life without parole as an alternative to the death penalty. The responses to these questions (1 = approve, 0 = disapprove) serve as dependent variables. The 2007 survey ($N = 467$) asked three questions about the death penalty, which we measure as dependent variables: (1) whether they agreed with Governor Philip Bredesen's decision to suspend the death penalty for ninety days in 2007 (1 = approve, 0 = disapprove) after the state experienced problems with lethal injection; (2) whether the death penalty should be the maximum sentence for murder (1 = yes, 0 = no); and (3) whether life imprisonment should be the maximum sentence for murder (1 = yes, 0 = no). It is worth noting that the Bredesen item was asked only of a subset of respondents.

We controlled for identical sociodemographic and political variables in both polls. These were income, education, and religion (all are continuous variables); party identification (Democrat = 1, 0 = other; and Republican = 1, 0 = other); gender (1 = woman, 0 = man); race (1 = white, 0 = nonwhite); and metropolitan jurisdiction (1 = urban, 0 = rural). Because all of the dependent variables measuring criminal justice attitudes were dichotomous ("approve" versus "disapprove" or "yes" versus "no"), the findings presented below are based on logistic regression analyses.

RESULTS AND DISCUSSION

Table 8.1 displays the findings for the first regression model. The dependent variables in this table are the binary measures for respondents' opinions about the death penalty and life without parole as methods of punishing capital offenses. The theoretically central independent variable was the race of the respondent, and we controlled for the variables mentioned above that measure the impact of sociodemographic background. The estimates in table 8.1 tell us the impact of a particular independent variable on the log-odds of a person approving of one of the criminal justice policies, holding the impact of other variables constant.

The 1999 survey was conducted when Tennessee made the change from electrocution to lethal injection as the primary mode of capital punishment, and as expected, the results suggest that Tennesseans at this time were racially divided in their attitudes about this criminal justice practice. The regression estimates for the race of the respondent (1 = white, 0 = nonwhite) in the death penalty column of table 8.1 are positive and statistically significant. This means that the support for giving the death penalty to convicted murderers is greater among white respondents. Interestingly, the control variables for Republican and Democratic Party identification are negative and statistically significant. We interpret

TABLE 8.1 Exploring attitudes about the death penalty (regression tables), 1999

	Death penalty (SE)	Life without parole (SE)
Independent variables		
Race (1 = white, 0 = nonwhite)	0.85*	0.13
	(0.37)	(0.47)
Gender (1 = woman, 0 = man)	−0.32	−0.0023
	(0.22)	(0.30)
Attend religious services	−0.032	0.28
	(0.28)	(0.38)
MSA (1 = urban, 0 = rural)	−0.039	−0.030
	(0.22)	(0.30)
Party ID = Republican	−0.69*	−0.10
	(0.28)	(0.37)
Party ID = Democratic	−0.55*	−0.24
	(0.25)	(0.35)
Income	−0.24	−0.088
	(0.30)	(0.41)
Education	−0.41	−0.44
	(0.26)	(0.37)
Constant	−0.51	−1.85**
	(0.44)	(0.59)
Model fit	0.040	0.0083

Source: Fall 1999 wave of the MTSU poll.
Notes: * = $p < 0.05$; ** = $p < .01$; $N = 395$; MSA = Metropolitan Statistical Areas.

this set of findings as demonstrating that the likelihood of favoring the death penalty in 1999 was lower for Republicans (compared to independents, which is the omitted reference category). Likewise, support for the death penalty was lower among Democrats (again, when compared to independents). There are no statistically significant estimates in the life without parole column of table 8.1, which suggests, among other things, that white Tennesseans were not different from nonwhite residents when it came to attitudes about this criminal justice policy.

The 2007 survey provides more concrete results about shifting attitudes toward the death penalty. As already mentioned, due to pressure from the American Bar Association, concerns about potential constitutional violations with the lethal injection drug, and pressure from activists, Governor Bredesen had to suspend executions for three months. Further, the state formed a special committee to establish new protocols for evaluating the death penalty and its varied impact on victims' families and capital defendants. The results in table 8.2 add further context about the racial divide in attitudes about the death penalty. For example, the regression estimates for respondents' race are statistically significant in both columns of the table, but the effect of race on support for the death penalty is positive, while the effect of race on support for life without parole (in-

TABLE 8.2 Exploring attitudes about the death penalty (regression tables), 2007

	Death penalty (SE)	Life sentence (SE)
Independent variables		
Race (1 = white, 0 = nonwhite)	0.83**	−0.70*
	(0.32)	(0.31)
Gender (1 = woman, 0 = man)	−0.30	0.29
	(0.20)	(0.22)
Attend religious services	−0.48	0.65*
	(0.29)	(0.32)
MSA (1 = urban, 0 = rural)	−0.22	0.48
	(0.30)	(0.31)
Party ID = Republican	0.85***	−0.74**
	(0.25)	(0.27)
Party ID = Democratic	−0.13	0.0067
	(0.24)	(0.25)
Income	0.56†	−0.40
	(0.30)	(0.32)
Education	−0.44†	0.45†
	(0.23)	(0.25)
Constant	−0.086	−0.77†
	(0.43)	(0.45)
Pseudo R^2	0.068	0.059

Source: Spring 2007 wave of the MTSU poll.
Notes: † = $p < 0.10$; * = $p < 0.05$; ** = $p < .01$; *** = $p < .001$; $N = 467$; MSA = Metropolitan Statistical Areas.

stead of the death penalty) is negative. The findings suggest that white Tennessee residents preferred more punitive criminal justice policies than their nonwhite neighbors did.

There is a similar pattern for education: the results in the first and second columns of table 8.2 are negative and positive, respectively, and both results are statistically significant. This means that the log-odds of favoring the death penalty for convicted murderers declined as education increased, while support for giving them life sentences increases with education. The results are less stark for income: the likelihood of supporting death sentences for murderers increased with income levels (and this result is statistically significant), but there was no relationship between income and supporting life sentences.

The party measure for Republican identification also showed polarization. Republicans (compared to independents) were more apt to favor the death penalty, and the odds were lower that Republicans (compared to independents) supported life sentences. Moreover, there was an interesting religiosity effect in which the log-odds of supporting life sentences for convicted murderers got higher as a respondent's frequency of church attendance grew. Religiosity had no statistically significant impact on death penalty attitudes or Bredesen approval ratings.

DISCUSSION AND CONCLUSION

In this chapter we have examined criminal justice reforms in Tennessee by assessing debates over sentencing policies and the death penalty. Criminal justice reform has been an increasingly polarizing issue in Tennessee ever since. Race helped to fuel this polarization and the implementation of punitive crime laws.

Our findings suggest that race was the most defining variable in shaping attitudes toward the death penalty. The variable distinguishes between whites and nonwhites (with blacks making up the largest group of nonwhites). As we expected, whites supported the death penalty more than their nonwhite neighbors did. The most significant racial effect was found in 2007, as demonstrated by the racial divide regarding life without parole. Whites were more emphatically opposed to life sentences as punishment for convicted murderers.

The racial impact is not surprising. A wide body of research has demonstrated that blacks and whites view the criminal justice system through entirely different lenses.[47] For example, Jon Hurwitz and Mark Peffley found—and James Gibson and Michael Nelson confirmed—that blacks see the criminal justice system as unfair, while whites as an aggregate view it as fair. These views predispose the groups toward polarized interpretations of events, for example, adverse police-civilian interactions.[48]

In addition, a partisan divide was more apparent in 2007 than in 1999. Both Democrats and Republicans are more conservative in the South on issues such as the death penalty,[49] but independents were more supportive of the death penalty than were Democrats or Republicans. However, in 2007, Republican support for the death penalty was much more apparent than among Democrats and independents.

In general, we have provided some insight into criminal justice reform initiatives in Tennessee. By focusing on sentencing reform and the death penalty, we can see that polarization around critical criminal justice policies is shaped by devolution, partisan realignment, and race.

CONCLUSION

> I'm embarrassed about it. I think the Republicans that got in there did a sorry job. They beat the death out of the gun issue and two or three others, but they haven't done anything about controlling the size of the government or eliminating the waste that goes on. You're elected to govern, not to protest. It's hard for me to support Republicans who, when they get in there, all they do is raise Cain about no more taxes, no more governing.... I'm dismayed now. I used to tell people you don't win in Tennessee by being ultra-right. But my kind of Republican is a dying breed.
> —LEWIS DONELSON, SENIOR REPUBLICAN PARTY STRATEGIST (2012)

The inspiration for this book was a series of conversations in the mid-2000s when both authors were faculty members in the Department of Political Science at Middle Tennessee State University. At that time, we committed to exploring the complex relationship between racial polarization and black political influence, as well as multiracial coalitions, in the Volunteer State. Polarization, as we think of it, represents the racial differences in Tennesseans' political attitudes and actions. We sought to contribute to the polarization literature by studying the intersection of race and politics at the state and local levels (areas that are often overlooked compared to the appeal of national-level politics).

It turns out that our focus on state and local politics puts us in a strong position to weigh in on national trends, for Tennessee politics offer representations of U.S. politics on a smaller scale. We began this book with an epigraph exemplifying a commonly held belief about the 2006 Senate election: "the eyes of the nation are on Tennessee." This saying rings just as true today as it did in 2006, precisely because of the political trajectory the state is on. Before 2010, Tennessee had a reputation for being more racially moderate than other southern states. Although Tennessee is the birthplace of the Ku Klux Klan, it was also the first southern state to ratify the Fourteenth Amendment. For these and other reasons, Tennessee developed the reputation of being a swing state where the outcomes of elections were not guaranteed for either of the two dominant political parties.

Yet Tennessee's reputation as a swing state eroded in the twenty-first century.[1] Lewis Donelson, a longtime Republican Party leader, lamented the collapse of the state's two-party system. A few years before his death, while in his nineties, he criticized the dogmatism of the Republican Party and the hyperpolarization in the state. His voice was critical, given that he had helped to resuscitate the state's Republican Party, particularly the Memphis/Shelby County wing. Since 2010, Tennessee has become increasingly more conservative, and Republicans gained more seats in the state's legislature. This is partly due to party realignment: Democrats lost control of both the House of Representatives and the Senate in the Tennessee General Assembly. Democrats had solid majorities in both chambers in the year 2000, and they had control of the executive branch throughout much of the following decade. Yet by the end of 2010, they had lost two dozen seats in the state House of Representatives. In contrast, Republicans had gained a supermajority in both chambers for the first time since the nineteenth century.

With this realignment came a loss of African American political power in the state legislature. In the 105th General Assembly (2007–2008), blacks chaired more than one-fourth of the full committees and subcommittees in the House of Representatives. Four years later (after Republicans gained control of the House), no committees or subcommittees were chaired by black lawmakers. A similar decline of black political power occurred in the Senate. In 2009–2010, blacks chaired 13 percent of the committees and subcommittees. By 2012, no committees or subcommittees were chaired by African Americans. This loss of power contributed to an anti–racial egalitarianism shift in governmental priorities. It contributed to a retrenchment of social policies, civil rights, voting protections, social welfare, reproductive rights, and so on. It also contributed to the decreased representation of black interests more generally. Considering that African Americans are Tennessee's largest minority group (comprising nearly one-fifth of the state's population), such a shift calls into question the General Assembly's ability to represent the interests of a sizable portion of its constituents. These changes in power have widened the gap between blacks' and whites' political attitudes/actions, thus creating more racial polarization.

The 2018 U.S. Senate race in Tennessee provides a strong example of Tennessee's conversion from a center-right state to one of the most conservative states in the country. The race matched former Democratic governor Phil Bredesen against Republican representative Marsha Blackburn. Bredesen had governed as a fiscal conservative. His electoral victories in 2002 and 2006 were due largely to his reach in conservative rural counties, including in East Tennessee. Blackburn, on the other hand, is a pro–Donald Trump conservative, closely aligned with the Tea Party and with the far right of the Republican conference in Congress.[2]

By all accounts, Bredesen's political profile reflected the tradition of Democratic and Republican governors and senators in Tennessee—that is, center-right, pro-business, and fiscally conservative yet pragmatic and open to bipartisanship. However, he lost badly to Blackburn, 44 percent to 55 percent, even though preelection polls had the candidates nearly tied throughout most of the campaign. In fact, Bredesen performed worse than Harold Ford Jr. did in the 2006 Senate race. The former governor even won fewer white voters—only 36 percent, according to exit polling—than Ford did.[3]

This example underscores the central thesis of our book. Political polarization in Tennessee has become more pronounced in the twenty-first century, such that it is now embedded in the formal political institutions (the party system, the Tennessee General Assembly, and executive agencies) and reinforced by long-standing social, geographic, and cultural cleavages. Political polarization has had significant consequences for Tennessee's body politic. It has contributed to both a late-stage realignment and Republican Party resurgence. The conservative wing of the Republican Party has emerged as the dominant political force in state politics. Further, political polarization has inhibited social reform and racial justice, and led to the disintegration of a governing coalition that could advance ameliorative public policies.

As we have noted, racial polarization is not a new phenomenon in Tennessee politics. Polarization and its different manifestations (in race relations, in voting behavior, in partisan politics, in responses to issues) are enduring characteristics of Tennessee's political culture. And polarization is also shaped by tensions resulting from social movement pressures. In this book, we have explained how polarization in Tennessee contributes to anti-minority rhetoric among rank-and-file residents, to racially regressive policymaking among elites, to the rising difficulty that African American voters experience in electing politicians of their own race, and to the increasing number of barriers facing African Americans who are fortunate enough to win political office.

This book is our attempt to make sense of the recent and rapid change in Tennessee from Democratic control of state politics to Republican control, and we have considered what that shift means for African American politicians and for a racial equalitarian agenda. Using a diverse array of methodological approaches, we have found evidence of a racial polarization that is both one of the causes and one of the consequences of black Tennesseans' recent loss of political power. We examined this polarization during the early twenty-first century (2000–2012) with specific emphasis on state elections, political institutions, and public policy.

Our book expands on past and current debates about political polarization in the South. For much of the latter half of the twentieth century, southern politics were largely interpreted through two frameworks. Key's *Southern Politics* underscored the significance of racial divisions in the South.[4] However, some critics argued that class divisions have fueled polarized politics. To this point, Shafer and Johnston claimed that most enthusiasts of Key's work have misinterpreted his central arguments, which were that racial segregation *and* class divisions (or economic underdevelopment) define the character of southern society.[5] Our book has advanced a theory of polarization that looks at the intersectional impact of racial, class, geographic, and partisan divisions in Tennessee politics.

By exploring Tennessee's transition from a swing state to a solidly red one, we can gain insights into how (and why) similar changes are taking place elsewhere in the country. America's rightward shift may even intensify now that we are in the "age of Trump." We have witnessed President Trump's shocking defense of white nationalists and neo-Nazis marching in Charlottesville, Virginia, to protest the removal of statues of Confederate war heroes because he thought the neo-Nazis were "very fine people"; his recommendation that mostly black athletes "should be run off the field" for protesting police abuse during the national anthem at NFL games; the callous stance he took during the Supreme Court confirmation hearings of Brett Kavanaugh regarding sexual assault allegations and the #MeToo movement more broadly (a movement, it is important to note, that was founded in 2006 by New York City–based activist Tarana Burke to help underprivileged women of color affected by sexual abuse);[6] and his long history of disparaging remarks about women and people of color. All of this suggests that racially transcendent and nonracist judgments among whites will be less, not more, likely in the near term.

As the nation (including the state of Tennessee) learns to operate within the chaos of a Trump presidency, the lessons from this book will prove useful to anyone who is interested in understanding how whites' movement toward the racial extremes within the Republican Party is altering American politics. As evidenced by the rise of the Black Lives Matter and March for Our Lives movements protesting against police violence and for gun control, respectively, and by the groundswell of Democratic candidates (many of whom are women, people of color, and members of LGBTQ communities), Trump's rhetoric and political alliances are being met with resistance by social movements.

In addition to offering our unique theoretical perspective, our hope is that this book will inspire social scientists to refocus attention on southern politics.[7] *Losing Power* has shown that there is much to learn from the South, not just through covariation analyses of the region, but also through case studies of the states. Many topics can provide complicated portraits of contemporary southern politics: racial polarization; disputes over hot-button issues, such as budgetary politics, criminal justice reforms, health care, and immigration; electoral divisions and redistricting; the role of black legislators in advancing a racial equalitarian agenda while simultaneously building bipartisan relationships; and understanding how social movements and grassroots advocates shape state-level decisions.

Finally, *Losing Power* has underscored that the southern political landscape is not static, even though it has been shaped by long-standing grievances about race, class, and partisanship. We expect that Tennessee politics are likely to change in the coming decades. Perhaps the state will become more conservative; perhaps Democrats will experience a resurgence. Whatever change occurs, we understand that it will partly be shaped by shifting political contexts—national and regional—but also by the people who give voice to politics. This includes political elites and the media, as well as everyday people in the electorate who are central to the polarized debates that have and will continue to shape Tennessee politics in the twenty-first century.

NOTES

INTRODUCTION

The epigraph is from Hanes Walton, *Black Politics: A Theoretical and Structural Analysis* (Philadelphia, Pa.: Lippincott, 1972).

1. Robert C. Smith, *Conservatism and Racism and Why in America They Are the Same* (Albany: SUNY Press, 2010), 143–147.
2. As we explain in our historical overview of twentieth-century Tennessee (chapter 2), although most blacks were poor, the leadership infrastructure in the Volunteer State consisted of educators, business leaders, and others who were able to carve out some measure of economic independence. These "elites" were much more apt to privately negotiate concessions. Such strategies temper racial discord, often at the expense of substantive deliberations of public policy.
3. Clarissa Rile Hayward, "The Difference States Make: Democracy, Identity, and the American City," *American Political Science Review* 97, no. 4 (2003): 501–514; James M. Glaser, *The Hand of the Past in Contemporary Southern Politics* (New Haven, Conn.: Yale University Press, 2005), 7; Hana Brown, "Racialized Conflict and Policy Spillover Effects," *American Journal of Sociology* 119, no. 2 (2013): 394–443.
4. Paul Brace and Aubrey Jewett, "State of State Politics Research," *Political Research Quarterly* 48, no. 3 (1995): 646–681.
5. John Gerring, "What Is a Case Study and What Is It Good For?," *American Political Science Review* 98, no. 2 (2004): 341–354.
6. Jeffrey Stonecash, "The State Politics Literature: Moving beyond Covariation Studies and Pursuing Politics," *Polity* 28, no. 4 (1996): 567–570.
7. Rodney E. Hero, *Faces of Inequality: Social Diversity in American Politics* (New York: Oxford University Press, 1998).
8. Stonecash, "State Politics Literature."
9. Michael Dimock et al., *Political Polarization in the American Public: How Increasing Ideological Uniformity and Partisan Antipathy Affect Politics, Compromise and Everyday Life* (Washington, D.C.: Pew Research Center, 2014).
10. Hanes Walton, *Black Politics: A Theoretical and Structural Analysis* (Philadelphia, Pa.: Lippincott, 1972), 11.
11. George N. Redd, "Educational Desegregation in Tennessee—One Year Afterward," *Journal of Negro Education* 24, no. 3 (1955): 333–347, 339.

12. Sekou Franklin, "Frank G. Clement and the Death Penalty in Tennessee," in *The New Abolitionists*, ed. Amy L. Sayward and Margaret Vandiver (Knoxville: University of Tennessee Press, 2010), 40–60.

13. David J. Garrow, *Bearing the Cross: Martin Luther King Jr. and the Southern Christian Leadership Conference* (New York: Random House, 1986), 217.

14. Ibid., chap. 4.

15. Gerring, "What Is a Case Study?," 342–344.

16. Pearl Ford Dowe, ed., *African Americans in Georgia: A Reflection of Politics and Policy in the New South* (Macon, Ga.: Mercer University Press, 2010).

17. Sharon D. Wright Austin, *The Transformation of Plantation Politics: Black Politics, Concentrated Poverty, and Social Capital in the Mississippi Delta* (Albany: SUNY Press, 2006).

18. Christina Bejarano and Gary Seguro, "What Goes Around, Comes Around: Race, Blowback, the Louisiana Elections of 2002 and 2003," *Political Research Quarterly* 60, no. 2 (2007): 332.

19. Tom Sharp, "House Vote on Income Tax Could Come on Wednesday," Associated Press State and Local Wire, May 21, 2002.

20. Sekou Franklin, "Situational Deracialization, Harold Ford, and the 2006 Senate Race in Tennessee," in *Whose Black Politics? Cases in Post-Racial Black Leadership*, ed. Andra Gillespie (New York: Routledge, 2010), 214–240.

21. Delia Baldassari and Peter Bearman, "Dynamics of Political Polarization," *American Sociological Review* 72 (2007): 785.

22. Robert J. Antonio and Robert J. Brulle, "The Unbearable Lightness of Politics: Climate Change Denial and Political Polarization," *Sociological Quarterly* 52 (2011): 197–198.

23. Aaron M. McCright and Riley E. Dunlap, "The Polarization of Climate Change and Polarization in [the] American Public's Views of Global Warming, 2001–2010," *Sociological Quarterly* 52 (2011): 170.

24. Michael Henderson and D. Sunshine Hillygus, "The Dynamics of Health Care Opinion, 2008–2010: Partisanship, Self-Interest, and Racial Resentment," *Journal of Health Politics, Policy and Law* 36, no. 6 (2011): 953; Michael Tesler and David O. Sears, *Obama's Race: The 2008 Election and Dream of a Post-Racial America* (Chicago: University of Chicago Press, 2010), 156; Michael Tesler, "The Spillover of Racialization into Health Care: How President Obama Polarized Public Opinion by Racial Attitudes and Race," *American Journal of Political Science* 56, no. 3 (2012): 690–704.

25. The MTSU poll is a nonpartisan semiannual probability survey of Tennessee residents that is sponsored by Middle Tennessee State University's College of Mass Communication and School of Journalism. Details about the survey and its principal investigators (Ken Blake and Jason Reinke in the Office of Communication Research) can be found at http://mtsupoll.org. Any opinions, findings, conclusions, or recommendations expressed in this book are those of the authors and do not necessarily reflect the viewpoints of the survey organization or the university.

26. Kathleen M. Carley, "Dynamic Network Analysis," in *Dynamic Network Modeling*

and Analysis: Workshop Summary and Papers, ed. Ronald Breiger, Kathleen Carley, and Philippa Pattison (Washington, D.C.: National Academies Press, 2003), 133–145.

27. This book includes revised and updated versions of previous studies authored by Sekou M. Franklin, including "Frank G. Clement and the Death Penalty in Tennessee," in *Tennessee's New Abolitionists: The Fight to End the Death Penalty in the Volunteer State*, ed. Amy L. Sayward and Margaret Vandiver (Knoxville: University of Tennessee Press), copyright © 2010 by The University of Tennessee Press, reprinted by permission (chapter 2); "Situational Deracialization, Harold Ford, and the 2006 Senate Race in Tennessee," in *Whose Black Politics? Cases in Post-Racial Black Leadership*, ed. Andra Gillespie (New York: Routledge, 2010) (chapter 10); and "Black Political Development in Tennessee: From Reconstruction–2006," in *Blacks in Tennessee: Past and Present*, ed. Wornie Reed (Dubuque, Iowa: Kendall/Hunt, 2008) (chapter 4).

28. Paul Frymer, *Uneasy Alliances: Race and Party Competition in America* (Princeton, N.J.: Princeton University Press, 1999).

CHAPTER 1. RACE AND POLARIZATION

The epigraph is from Leon Alligood, "Race Put Eyes of the World on Us," *Tennessean*, November 8, 2006, A10.

1. Dan Balz, "In Tennessee, Consensus Politics Makes a Last Stand," *Washington Post*, July 29, 2014.

2. Richard T. Middleton IV and Sekou M. Franklin, "Southern Racial Etiquette and the 2006 Tennessee Senate Race: The Racialization of Harold Ford's Deracialized Campaign," *National Political Science Review* 12 (2009): 63–81.

3. Sekou Franklin, "Situational Deracialization, Harold Ford, and the 2006 Senate Race in Tennessee," in *Whose Black Politics? Cases in Post-Racial Black Leadership*, ed. Andra Gillespie (New York: Routledge, 2010), 219.

4. Ibid., 217.

5. Michele Wilson and John Lynxwiler, "The Federal Government and the Harassment of Black Leaders: A Case Study of Mayor Richard Arrington Jr. of Birmingham," *Journal of Black Studies* 28, no. 5 (1998): 540–560.

6. Middleton and Franklin, "Southern Racial Etiquette," 64, 68; Franklin, "Situational Deracialization," 215.

7. The majority of Memphis African Americans voted for Ford, although some analysts believe black voter turnout underperformed in the city. Leslie Collins, interview with A. J. Starling, executive assistant to the president of the AFL-CIO, March 30, 2012; Leslie Collins, interview with Ashford Hughes, a political activist and field organizer on the Harold Ford Jr. campaign, May 1, 2012.

8. Tali Mendelberg, *The Race Card: Campaign Strategy, Implicit Messages, and the Norm of Equality* (Princeton, N.J.: Princeton University Press, 2001).

9. Middleton and Franklin, "Southern Racial Etiquette."

10. Sekou Franklin, "Racially Polarized Voting, Redistricting, and Voting Rights in Tennessee," an expert witness report prepared for the National Commission on Voting Rights, regional hearing, Nashville, Tenn., May 8, 2014.

11. *United States v. Charleston County*, 318 F. Supp. 2d 302, 308 (D.S.C. 2002).

12. Dara R. Fisher, Joseph Waggle, and Philip Leifield, "Where Does Political Polarization Come From? Locating Polarization within the U.S. Climate Change Debate," *American Behavioral Scientist* 57, no. 1 (2013): 71.

13. Morris P. Fiorina and Samuel J. Abrams, "Political Polarization in the American Public," *Annual Review of Political Science* 11 (2008): 563–588.

14. Anthony Downs, *An Economic Theory of Democracy* (New York: Harper, 1957); Scott Ashworth, "Electoral Accountability: Recent Theoretical and Empirical Work," *Annual Review of Political Science* 15 (2012): 183–201.

15. Alan I. Abramowitz, *The Polarized Public? Why American Government Is So Dysfunctional* (Upper Saddle River, N.J.: Pearson Education, 2013); Pew Research Center, "Political Polarization in the American Public: How Increasing Ideological Uniformity and Partisan Antipathy Affect Politics, Compromise and Everyday Life," June 12, 2014, http://www.people-press.org/2014/06/12/political-polarization-in-the-american-public.

16. Ryan L. Claassen, "Political Awareness and Partisan Realignment: Are the Unaware Unevolved?," *Political Research Quarterly* 64, no. 4 (2011): 818–830; Paul Goren, Christopher M. Frederico, and Miki Claus Kittilson, "Source Cues, Partisan Identities, and Political Value Expression," *American Journal of Political Science* 53, no. 4 (2009): 805–820.

17. Stephen P. Nicholson, "Dominating Cues and the Limits of Influence," *Journal of Politics* 73, no. 4 (2011): 1174; Fiorina and Abrams, "Political Polarization," 575.

18. Jens Grosser and Thomas R. Palfrey, "Candidate Entry and Political Polarization: An Antimedian Voter Theorem," *American Journal of Political Science* 58, no. 1 (2014): 127–143; Kyle Saunders and Alan I. Abramowitz, "Ideological Realignment and Active Partisans in the American Electorate," *American Politics Research* 32, no. 3 (2004): 285–309.

19. Jonathan Knuckey, "The 'Palin Effect' in the 2008 Presidential Election," *Political Research Quarterly* 65, no. 2 (2012): 282–284.

20. John H. Evans, "Have Americans' Attitudes Become More Polarized?—An Update," *Social Science Quarterly* 84, no. 1 (2003): 71–90; Lilliana Mason, "The Rise of Uncivil Agreement: Issue versus Behavioral Polarization in the American Electorate," *American Behavioral Scientist* 57, no. 1 (2013): 140–159; Lilliana Mason, "A Cross-Cutting Calm: How Social Sorting Drives Affective Polarization," *Public Opinion Quarterly* 80, no. S1 (2018): 351–377.

21. Jonathan Knuckey, "Racial Resentment and the Changing Partisanship of Southern Politics," *Party Politics* 11, no. 1 (2005): 5–28.

22. V. O. Key Jr., *Southern Politics in State and Nation* (1949; repr., Knoxville: University of Tennessee Press, 1984).

23. Byron E. Shafer, "Foreword: The Master, the Acolytes, and the Study of American Politics," in *Unlocking V. O. Key Jr.: Southern Politics for the Twenty-First Century*, ed. Angie Maxwell and Todd Shields (Fayetteville: University of Arkansas Press, 2011), xiv–xvi; Avidit Acharya, Matthew Blackwell, and Maya Sen, *Deep Roots: How Slavery Still Shapes Southern Politics* (Princeton, N.J.: Princeton University Press, 2018).

24. Byron E. Shafer and Richard Johnston, *The End of Southern Exceptionalism: Class, Race, and Partisan Change in the Postwar South* (Cambridge, Mass.: Harvard University Press, 2006), 8–9; Shafer, "Foreword"; Jeffrey Stonecash and Mark D. Brewer, "Class, Race Issues and Political Change in the South," *Political Behavior* 23, no. 2 (2001): 131–156.

25. Nicholas A. Valentino and David O. Sears, "Old Times There Are Not Forgotten: Race and Partisan Realignment in the Contemporary South," *American Journal of Political Science* 49, no. 3 (2005): 672–688.

26. Shafer and Johnston, *End of Southern Exceptionalism*.

27. Jeffrey M. Stonecash, *Class and Party in American Politics* (Boulder, Colo.: Westview, 2000); Nolan M. McCarty, *Polarized America: The Dance of Ideology and Unequal Riches* (Cambridge, Mass.: MIT Press, 2006).

28. Christine H. Roch and Michael Rushton, "Racial Context and Voting over Taxes: Evidence from a Referendum in Alabama," *Public Finance Review* 36, no. 5 (2008): 614–634; Tetsuya Matsubayashi and Rene R. Roca, "Racial Diversity and Public Policy in States," *Political Research Quarterly* 65, no. 3 (2012): 600–614.

29. Ralph J. Bunche, *The Political Status of the Negro in the Age of FDR* (Chicago: University of Chicago Press, 1973), 33.

30. Mendelberg, *Race Card*.

31. Laura S. Hussey, "Polarized Politics and Citizen Disengagement: The Role of Belief Systems," *American Politics Research* 40, no. 1 (2012): 85–115.

32. Stephen Steinberg, "The Role of Race and Racism in the Devolution of the Left," June 20, 2011, Racism Review: Scholarship and Activism toward Racial Justice, http://www.racismreview.com/blog/2011/06/20/the-role-of-race-and-racism-in-the-devolution-of-the-left; Jon Michaels, "Deforming Welfare: How the Dominant Narratives of Devolution and Privatization Subverted Federal Welfare Reform," *Seton Hall Law Review* 34 (2004): 575–619.

33. Timothy J. Conlan and Paul L. Posner, "Inflection Point? Federalism and the Obama Administration," *Publius: The Journal of Federalism* 45, no. 1 (2014): 421–446.

34. Adam Nossiter, "Louisiana: A Test Case in Federal Aid," *New York Times*, April 5, 2009.

35. Ibid.

36. Jill Vickers, "Is Federalism Gendered? Incorporating Gender into Studies of Federalism," *Publius: The Journal of Federalism* 43, no. 1 (2012): 5.

37. Joe Soss, Richard C. Fording, and Sanford F. Schram, "The Color of Devolution: Race, Federalism, and the Politics of Social Control," *American Journal of Political Science* 52, no. 3 (2008): 540.

38. Ibid., 539 (emphasis added).

39. Doug McAdam and Karina Kloos, *Deeply Divided: Racial Politics and Social Movements in Postwar America* (New York: Oxford University Press, 2014), 24–25, 104–111; Ian Haney-Lopez, *Dog Whistle Politics: How Coded Racial Appeals Have Wrecked the Middle Class* (New York: Oxford University Press, 2014), 58–59.

40. Danny Hayes and Seth C. McKee, "Toward a One-Party South?," *American Politics Research* 36, no. 1 (2008): 10.

41. M. V. Hood, Quentin Kidd, and Irwin L. Morris, "The Reintroduction of the *Elephas maximus* to the Southern United States: The Rise of Republican State Parties, 1960 to 2000," *American Politics Research* 32, no. 1 (2004): 68–101, 73.

42. Carl Boggs, *The End of Politics: Corporate Power and the Decline of the Public Sphere* (New York: Guilford, 2000); Adolph Reed Jr., ed., *Without Justice for All: The New Liberalism and Our Retreat from Racial Equality* (Boulder, Colo.: Westview, 2001); Robert C. Smith, *We Have No Leaders: African Americans in the Post–Civil Rights Era* (Albany: SUNY Press, 1996), 255–276.

43. Paul Frymer, *Uneasy Alliances: Race and Party Competition in America* (Princeton, N.J.: Princeton University Press, 1999).

44. Ibid., 10.

45. Glen Browder with Artemesia Stanberry, *Stealth Reconstruction: An Untold Story of Racial Politics in Recent Southern History* (Montgomery, Ala.: New South Books, 2010), 20.

46. Rodney E. Hero and Christina Wolbrecht, "Introduction," in *The Politics of Democratic Inclusion*, ed. Christina Wolbrecht and Rodney E. Hero (Philadelphia, Pa.: Temple University Press, 2005), 2.

47. Frank Parker, *Black Votes Count: Political Empowerment in Mississippi after 1965* (Chapel Hill: University of North Carolina Press, 1990); Bernard Grofman, Lisa Handley, and Richard G. Niemi, *Minority Representation and the Quest for Voting Equality* (New York: Cambridge University Press, 1992); Richard H. Pildes, "Why the Center Does Not Hold: The Causes of Hyperpolarized Democracy in America," *California Law Review* 99, no. 2 (2011): 293–297.

48. Paul Frymer, "Debating the Causes of Party Polarization in America," *California Law Review* 99, no. 2 (2011): 345–346.

49. Reed, *Without Justice for All*, 10.

50. Dara Strolovitch, *Affirmative Advocacy: Race, Class, and Gender in Interest Groups* (Chicago: University of Chicago Press, 2007).

51. Mendelberg, *Race Card*, 10–25.

52. Ibid., 20.

53. Haney-Lopez, *Dog Whistle Politics*.

54. Gregory A. Huber and John S. Lapinski, "The 'Race Card' Revisited: Assessing Racial Priming in Policy Contests," *American Journal of Political Science* 50, no. 2 (2006): 421–440; Gregory A. Huber and John S. Lapinski, "Testing the Implicit-Explicit Model of Racialized Political Communication," *Perspectives on Politics* 6, no. 1 (2008): 125–134.

55. Tali Mendelberg, "Racial Priming Revived," *Perspectives on Politics* 6, no. 1 (2008): 109–123.

56. Ibid., 20.

57. Mendelberg, *Race Card*, 209–236.

58. Republicans, on the other hand, tend to win elections with lower turnouts because fewer minority voters make it to the ballot booth.

59. Daniel Q. Gillion, *Political Power in Protest: Minority Activism and Shifts in Public Policy* (Cambridge: Cambridge University Press, 2013).

60. McAdam and Kloos, *Deeply Divided*.

61. Rory McVeigh, David Cunningham, and Justin Farrell, "Political Polarization as a Social Movement Outcome: 1960s Klan Activism and Its Enduring Impact on Political Realignment in Southern Counties, 1960 to 2000," *American Sociological Review* 79, no. 6 (2014): 1146.

62. Ronald W. Walters, *Black Presidential Politics in America: A Strategic Approach* (Albany: SUNY Press, 1988), 110–183.

CHAPTER 2. BLACK POLITICS IN TENNESSEE FROM THE ANTEBELLUM PERIOD TO THE TWENTY-FIRST CENTURY

The epigraph is from "Mob Violence," a speech to the Tennessee General Assembly, February 23, 1887. This speech was also referred to as "An Ernest Appeal for Stronger Enactments against Judge Lynch."

1. *Report of the Select Committee on the Memphis Riots and Massacres, May 31, 1866* (Washington, D.C.: U.S. House of Representatives, 1866), 180.

2. Many violent confrontations between blacks and whites occurred in Tennessee during Reconstruction and immediately after the collapse of Reconstruction in places such as Shelbyville, Tullahoma, Athens, Decherd, Brentwood, Clarksville, Franklin, and Columbia. Rick Warwick, *Williamson County in Black and White* (Franklin, Tenn.: Williamson Historical Society, 2000), 72; and Alrutheus Ambush Taylor, *The Negro in Tennessee, 1865–1880* (Washington, D.C.: Associated Publishers, 1941), 79–89.

3. William Gillespie McBride, "Blacks and the Race Issue in Tennessee Politics, 1865–1876" (PhD diss., Vanderbilt University, 1989), 22.

4. Joseph Howard Cartwright, "Race Relations in Tennessee Politics in the Late 1880s: A Decade in Transition" (PhD diss., Vanderbilt University, 1973); Armstead Robinson, "'Plans Dat Comed from God': Institution Building and the Emergence of Black Leadership in Reconstruction Memphis," in *Toward a New South? Studies in Post–Civil War Southern Communities*, ed. Orville Vernon Burton and Robert C. McMath Jr. (Westport, Conn.: Greenwood, 1982), 79–90; John Cimprich, "The Beginning of the Black Suffrage Movement in Tennessee, 1864–1865," *Journal of Negro History* 65, no. 3 (1980): 185–195; Steven Hahn, *A Nation under Our Feet: Black Political Struggles in the Rural South from Slavery to Migration* (Cambridge, Mass.: Belknap, 2003), 71–76.

5. Richard Couto, *Lifting the Veil: A Political History of Struggles for Emancipation* (Knoxville: University of Tennessee Press, 1993), 7; Judy Bussell LeForge, "State Colored Conventions of Tennessee, 1865–1866," *Tennessee Historical Quarterly* 65, no. 3 (2006): 231.

6. Rogers Smith, *Civic Ideals: Conflicting Visions of Citizenship in U.S. History* (New Haven, Conn.: Yale University Press, 1997).

Notes to Chapter Two

7. Ibid., 22.

8. "Slave Laws of North Carolina and Tennessee, 1729–1806," box 14, s70, Tennessee Historical Society Miscellaneous (T100), Tennessee State Library and Archives, Nashville (hereafter TSLA). These laws detailed, among other things, the slave status of blacks, the appropriate designations for people of mixed-race heritage (e.g., "mulatto" or "mestizo"), and the codes of conduct governing interactions between whites and blacks.

9. Lewis L. Laska, "A History of Personal Income Taxation in Tennessee," *Tennessee Historical Quarterly* 60, no. 4 (2001): 220–243, 221.

10. For examples of how the cost of enslaved people varied by age, gender, and earning potential, see "Slave Records—Account Books," box 9, folder 46, and "Slave Records—Bills of Sale," box 9, folder 47, both in Erskine-Gordon-LeConte Papers, 1780–1940, TSLA. Dollar conversion from measuringworth.com using the calculation for the real price of a commodity.

11. James W. Patton, "The Progress of Emancipation in Tennessee, 1796–1860," *Journal of Negro History* 17, no. 1 (1932): 89.

12. Durwood Dunn, *An Abolitionist in the Appalachian South: Ezekiel Birdseye on Slavery, Capitalism, and Separate Statehood, 1841–1846* (Knoxville: University of Tennessee Press, 1997), 10–11.

13. Jonathan M. Atkins, "Party Politics and the Debate over the Tennessee Free Negro Bill, 1859–1860," *Journal of Southern History* 71, no. 2 (2005): 252.

14. Ibid.

15. For example, see petitions from Bedford, Blount, Jackson, McMinn, Maury, Sevier, Roane, and Rhea Counties, Petition Nos. 10, 16, 21, 23, 26, 30, 36, and 42, Legislative Petitions, 1799–1850, TSLA.

16. For example, see "Petition of the Tennessee State Colonization Society to the Tennessee General Assembly Asking That All Free Negroes Be Removed from the State of Tennessee to the New African Republic," 1833, Petition No. 203, Legislative Petitions, 1799–1850, TSLA.

17. Atkins, "Party Politics and the Debate," 248. For free blacks in Nashville, see Richard J. M. Blakett, "Montgomery Bell, William E. Kennedy, and Middle Tennessee and Liberian Colonization," *Tennessee Historical Quarterly* 69, no. 4 (2010): 293.

18. "Liberia Project—Sent Two Shiploads of Slaves to Liberia—1853 Slave Colonization," box 1, folder 8, Nannie Seawell Boyd Collection of Papers Relating to Montgomery Bell, 1853–1939, TSLA.

19. Ibid.

20. Blakett, "Montgomery Bell, William E. Kennedy, and Middle Tennessee," 295.

21. Ibid., 311–312.

22. Atkins, "Party Politics and the Debate," 252–258.

23. Arthur F. Howington, "'Not in the Condition of a Horse or an Ox': *Ford v. Ford*, the Law of Testamentary Manumission, and the Tennessee Courts' Recognition of Slave Humanity," *Tennessee Historical Quarterly* 34, no. 3 (1975): 260–263.

24. Theodore Brown Jr., "The Formative Period in the History of the Supreme Court of Tennessee, 1796–1835," in *A History of the Tennessee Supreme Court*, ed. James W. Ely and Theodore Brown Jr. (Knoxville: University of Tennessee Press, 2002), 27.

25. Ibid., 29.

26. Howington, "Not in the Condition of a Horse or an Ox," 260–263.

27. Ibid., 251–252.

28. Ibid., 260–263.

29. The franchise was only granted to African American men at this time. Black women did not secure the right to vote until 1920, with the ratification of the Nineteenth Amendment to the U.S. Constitution.

30. The Redeemers were a coalition of ultraconservative southern Democrats who sought to push Radical Republicans from the North out of the South during Reconstruction. Most of them were wealthy landowners and businessmen. Their movement gained momentum until the Compromise of 1877, which ended the Reconstruction period.

31. Mingo Scott, *The Negro in Tennessee Politics and Governmental Affairs, 1865–1965: "The Hundred Years Story"* (Nashville, Tenn.: Rich Printing, 1964), 15.

32. It is important to point out that a large number of Confederates were excluded from voting in this election due to Reconstruction era voting restrictions.

33. Walter J. Fraser Jr., "Black Reconstructionists in Tennessee," *Tennessee Historical Quarterly* 34, no. 4 (1975): 364–365; Taylor, *Negro in Tennessee*, 46–49.

34. May Ridley, "The Black Community of Nashville and Davidson County" (PhD diss., University of Pittsburgh, 1982), 96; James Welch Patton, *Unionism and Reconstruction in Tennessee, 1860–1869* (Chapel Hill: University of North Carolina Press, 1934); Richard Lowe, "The Freedmen's Bureau and Local Black Leadership," *Journal of American History* 80, no. 3 (1993): 989–998.

35. Phillip Langsdon, *Tennessee: A Political History* (Franklin, Tenn.: Hillsboro Press, 2000), 183.

36. Ibid., 184.

37. James B. Jones, *Knoxville's African American Community, 1860–1920* (Nashville: Tennessee Historical Commission, 1989), 38–44.

38. Bobby Lovett, ed., *From Winter to Winter: The Afro-American History of Nashville, Tennessee, 1870–1930: Elites and Dilemmas* (Nashville: Tennessee State University Press, 1981), 166–170.

39. Frank B. Williams Jr., "The Poll Tax as a Suffrage Requirement in the South, 1870–1901," *Journal of Southern History* 18, no. 4 (1952): 471. Williams stated that the poll tax was not heavily enforced in the period 1870–1873.

40. Margaret Endsley Holloway, "The Reaction in Tennessee to the Federal Elections Bill of 1890" (MA thesis, University of Tennessee, 1972), 99; Roberta Church and Ronald Walter, *Nineteenth Century Memphis Families of Color, 1850–1900* (Memphis, Tenn.: N.p., 1987), 84.

41. J. Morgan Kousser, "Post-Reconstruction Suffrage Restrictions in Tennessee: A New Look at the V. O. Key Thesis," *Political Science Quarterly* 88, no. 4 (1973): 681–683.

42. Cartwright, "Race Relations in Tennessee Politics," 195; Couto, *Lifting the Veil*, 53–57.

43. Alex Lichtenstein, *Twice the Work of Free Labor: The Political Economy of Convict Labor in the New South* (New York: Verso, 1996); Matthew J. Mancini, *"One Dies, Get Another": Convict Leasing in the American South, 1866–1928* (Columbia: University of South Carolina Press, 1966).

44. W. A. Reed and Alex Bontemps, "Brave Tennessean Forgotten by History," *Tennessean*, February 13, 1971, 6; Couto, *Lifting the Veil*, 58; Dorothy Granberry, "Black Community Leadership in a Rural Tennessee County, 1865–1903," *Journal of Negro History* 83, no. 4 (1998): 255; and Paul H. Bergeron, Stephen V. Ash, and Jeanette Keith, *Tennesseans and Their History* (Knoxville: University of Tennessee Press, 1990), 196.

45. Cartwright, "Race Relations in Tennessee Politics," 352–373.

46. Kousser, "Post-Reconstruction Suffrage Restrictions," 655–681.

47. Ibid., 674.

48. Patricia A. Schechter, *Ida B. Wells Barnett and American Reform, 1880–1930* (Chapel Hill: University of North Carolina Press, 2001), 71.

49. Washington Butler Jr., "Blacks in Tennessee Politics: A Potent Force since 1865," in *The Black Tennessean*, ed. Patricia Bell-Scott et al. (N.p.: n.p., 1976), 60–61.

50. Frank Parker, *Black Votes Count: Political Empowerment in Mississippi after 1965* (Chapel Hill: University of North Carolina Press, 1990), 160.

51. Lester C. Lamon, *Blacks in Tennessee, 1791–1970* (Knoxville: University of Tennessee Press, 1981), 41.

52. Don H. Doyle, "Hilary Howse," in *The Tennessee Encyclopedia of History and Culture* 3.0, http://tennesseeencyclopedia.net/entry.php?rec=665.

53. Lovett, *From Winter to Winter*, 166–170.

54. Cartwright, "Race Relations in Tennessee Politics," 147; McBride, "Blacks and the Race Issue," 340; Taylor, *Negro in Tennessee*, 247–255.

55. Yollette Trigg Jones, "The Black Community, Politics, and Race Relations in the 'Iris City': Nashville, Tennessee, 1870–1954" (PhD diss., Duke University, 1985); and Faye Wellborn Robbins, "A World-within-a-World: Black Nashville, 1880–1915" (PhD diss., University of Arkansas, 1980).

56. Jones, "Black Community," 106.

57. Rayford W. Logan and Michael R. Winston, eds., *Dictionary of American Negro Biography* (New York: Norton, 1982), s.v. "Napier, James Carroll"; http://www.blackpast.org/aah/napier-james-carroll-1845-1940#sthash.TA8ZN7EE.dpuf.

58. Booker T. Washington, "The Atlanta Exposition Address," in *Up from Slavery: An Autobiography* (New York: Avon, 1965), 145–157.

59. Schechter, *Ida B. Wells Barnett*; Bergeron, Ash, and Keith, *Tennesseans and Their History*, 197.

60. Mary Church Terrell, *A Colored Woman in a White World* (New York: Arno, 1980); Cynthia Neverdon-Morton, "Mary Church Terrell," in *African American Lives*, ed. Henry Louis Gates Jr. and Evelyn Brooks Higginbotham (New York: Oxford University Press, 2004).

61. Cartwright, "Race Relations in Tennessee Politics," 377–378.
62. Lovett, *From Winter to Winter*, 166–170.
63. David Tucker, *Memphis since Crump: Bossism, Blacks, and Civic Reformers, 1948–1968* (Knoxville: University of Tennessee Press, 1980), 18–19.
64. Linda T. Wynn and Bobby Lovett, *Profiles of African Americans in Tennessee* (Nashville, Tenn.: Annual Local Conference on Afro-American Culture and History, 1996), 33.
65. Sharon D. Wright, *Race, Power, and Political Emergence in Memphis* (New York: Garland, 2000), 37.
66. Tucker, *Memphis since Crump*, 18–19.
67. Ronald W. Walters, *Black Presidential Politics in America: A Strategic Approach* (Albany: SUNY Press, 1988), 160.
68. Wynn and Lovett, *Profiles of African Americans in Tennessee*, 34.
69. Cookie Lommell, *Robert Church, Entrepreneur* (Los Angeles, Calif.: Melrose Square, 1995).
70. G. Michael McCarthy, "Smith vs. Hoover—The Politics of Race in West Tennessee," *Phylon* 39, no. 2 (1978): 160–167.
71. Moses Freeman, interview with Clarence B. Robinson, Oral History Project, April 1983, Chattanooga–Hamilton County Bicentennial Public Library, Chattanooga, Tenn.
72. Nancy Grant, *TVA and Black Americans: Planning for the Status Quo* (Philadelphia, Pa.: Temple University Press, 1990), 130; Roger Biles, *Memphis in the Great Depression* (Knoxville: University of Tennessee Press, 1986).
73. G. Wayne Dowdy, "'We Engaged in a Hard Campaign': Primary Sources Related to the 1940 and 1944 Presidential Election[s] in Shelby County, Tennessee," unpublished monograph, n.d., Memphis–Shelby County Public Library and Information Center, Memphis, Tenn.
74. Lamon, *Blacks in Tennessee*, 68–70; Lovett, *From Winter to Winter*, 187.
75. J. Morgan Kousser, "Tennessee Politics and the Negro: 1948–1964" (senior thesis, Princeton University, 1965), 3.
76. Biles, *Memphis in the Great Depression*, 40.
77. Robert Guy Spinney, *World War II in Nashville: Transformation of the Homefront* (Knoxville: University of Tennessee Press, 1998), 55.
78. "Negro Controversy" (1940), box 83, folder 3, Governor Prentice Cooper Papers, 1939–1945, TSLA.
79. Ibid., James C. Dickerson, "Cooper Makes a Political Blunder," *Memphis Sentinel*, clipping, box 83, folder 31, Governor Prentice Cooper Papers, 1939–1945, TSLA.
80. Dickerson, "Cooper Makes a Political Blunder"; "Negro Controversy."
81. "Negro Controversy."
82. J. F. Pierce, City Federation of Colored Women's Clubs, to Governor Prentice Cooper, February 29, 1940, box 84, folder 17, Governor Prentice Cooper Papers, 1939–1945, TSLA.
83. Young Democratic Clubs of Tennessee to Governor Prentice Cooper, box 84,

folder 16: Poll Tax Abolishment, 1939, Governor Prentice Cooper Papers, 1939–1945, TSLA.

84. Letters from labor unions and workers associations on the poll tax in box 84, folders 16 and 17: Poll Tax Abolishment, 1939, Governor Prentice Cooper Papers, 1939–1945, TSLA.

85. Theron P. Wilson, "The Voting Population of Tennessee," box 223, folder 12: Poll Tax Abolishment, 1939–1940, Governor Prentice Cooper Papers, 1939–1945, TSLA. We made this monetary conversion using https://www.measuringworth.com.

86. "Poll Tax Law Repeal in State Is Held Invalid," *Bedford County Times* (Shelbyville, Tenn.), July 8, 1943, clipping, box 223, folder 15, Governor Prentice Cooper Papers, 1939–1945, TSLA.

87. Jones, "Black Community," 167.

88. "Poll Tax Legislation, 1942–1943," box 223, folder 17, Governor Prentice Cooper Papers, 1939–1945, TSLA.

89. Marcus Pohlmann, *Racial Politics at the Crossroads: Memphis Elects Dr. W. W. Herenton* (Knoxville: University of Tennessee Press, 1996), 14.

90. William D. Miller, *Mr. Crump of Memphis* (Baton Rouge: Louisiana State University Press, 1964), 204–205.

91. Wright, *Race, Power, and Political Emergence*, 31.

92. Ibid., 40–45.

93. "The Declaration of Constitutional Principles: The Southern Manifesto," in *Debating the Civil Rights Movement, 1945–1968*, ed. Steven F. Lawson and Charles Payne (Lanham, Md.: Rowman and Littlefield, 1998), 57. The Southern Manifesto was signed by nineteen members of the U.S. Senate and eighty-two members of the House of Representatives. Walter F. George, a senator from Georgia, and Howard Smith, a Virginia congressman, introduced the manifesto in their respective chambers. See also Joseph Bruce Gorman, *Kefauver: A Political Biography* (New York: Oxford University Press, 1971).

94. Earl Black, *Southern Governors and Civil Rights: Racial Segregation as a Campaign Issue in the Second Reconstruction* (Cambridge, Mass.: Harvard University Press, 1976).

95. Frank G. Clement, "The South and Its Future," April 15, 1953, box 76, folder 44, Frank Goad Clement Papers, 1920–1969, TSLA.

96. George N. Redd, "Educational Desegregation in Tennessee—One Year Afterward," *Journal of Negro Education* 24, no. 3 (1955): 333–347. Local economic interests, including the Atomic Energy Commission, pushed for school desegregation immediately after the *Brown* decision.

97. Jack Bass and Walter De Vries, *The Transformation of Southern Politics: Social Change and Political Consequence since 1945* (1976; repr., Athens: University of Georgia Press, 1995), 292–295.

98. David Halberstam, "End of a Populist," *Harper's* 242 (January 1971): 37–43.

99. Hugh Davis Graham, *Civil Rights and the Presidency: Race and Gender in American Politics, 1960–1972* (Oxford: Oxford University Press, 1992).

100. Kyle Longley, *Senator Albert Gore Sr.: Tennessee Maverick* (Baton Rouge: Louisiana State University Press, 2004), 186–187.

101. "Proposed Governor's Code of Fair Practices and Commission on Human Rights for the State of Tennessee," January–May 1963, box 25, folder 1, Frank Goad Clement Papers, 1963–1967, TSLA.

102. John Bowman, *The Cambridge Dictionary of American Biography* (Cambridge: Cambridge University Press 1995), s.v. "Clement, Frank (Goad)."

103. Elizabeth Gritter, "Black Memphians and New Frontiers: The Shelby County Democratic Club, the Kennedy Administration, and the Quest for Black Political Power, 1959–1964," in *An Unseen Light: Black Struggles for Freedom in Memphis, Tennessee*, ed. Aram Goudsouzian and Charles W. McKinney (Lexington: University Press of Kentucky, 2018), 194.

104. Ibid.

105. Kousser, "Tennessee Politics and the Negro," 85–86. It is important to note that Clement ended up winning the Democratic primary, but he lost the Senate race to Republican Howard Baker.

106. Myles Horton, *Long Haul: An Autobiography* (New York: Teachers College Press, 1998); C. Alvin Hughes, "A New Agenda for the South: The Role and Influence of the Highlander Folk School, 1953–1961," *Phylon* 46, no. 3 (1985): 242–250; Arthur C. Hill, "The History of Black People in Franklin County, Tennessee" (PhD diss., University of Minnesota, 1982).

107. Washington Butler speech, August 6, 1962, tape 55, Highlander Folk School Audio Collection, TSLA. Due to government repression, Highlander was forced to reorganize and is now called the Highlander Research and Education Center.

108. Clayborne Carson, *In Struggle: SNCC and the Black Awakening of the 1960s* (1981; repr., Cambridge, Mass.: Harvard University Press, 2000), 21–22; Peter Ackerman and Jack DuVall, *A Force More Powerful: A Century of Nonviolent Conflict* (New York: St. Martin's, 2000), 305–333.

109. Ronald C. White Jr. and C. Howard Hopkins, *The Social Gospel: Religion and Reform in Changing America* (Philadelphia, Pa.: Temple University Press, 1976).

110. Bernard Lafayette, interview, January 17, 2003, Nashville Oral History Project, Nashville Public Library, http://digital.library.nashville.org/cdm/ref/collection/nr/id/1557.

111. Joan Turner Beifuss, *At the River I Stand: Memphis, the 1968 Strike, and Martin Luther King* (Memphis, Tenn.: B&W Books, 1985).

112. J. Edwin Stanfield, *In Memphis: Mirror to America?* (Atlanta, Ga.: Southern Regional Council, 1968), 21.

113. Michael K. Honey, *Black Workers Remember* (Berkeley: University of California Press, 1999), 309.

114. AFL-CIO Industrial Union Department, *Tent City: "Home of the Brave"* (Washington, D.C.: AFL-CIO, 1961); Robert Hamburger, *Our Portion of Hell, Fayette County, Tennessee: An Oral History of the Struggle for Civil Rights* (New York: Links Books, 1973).

115. James Forman, *The Making of Black Revolutionaries* (1955; repr., Seattle: University of Washington Press, 1995).

116. "October 1960: The Untold Story of Jackson's Civil Rights Movement," *Jackson Sun*, October 2000, http://orig.jacksonsun.com/civilrights.

117. Forman, *Making of Black Revolutionaries*, 126.

118. Septima Clark (director of education, Highlander Folk School), Highlander Folk School Training Workshop, August 6, 1961, tape 54b, Highlander Folk School Audio Collection, TSLA.

119. Couto, *Lifting the Veil*, 201.

120. James Smith to Governor Clement, June 25, 1965, box 25, folder 8: Civil Rights—Somerville, Frank Goad Clement Papers, 1963–1967, TSLA.

121. Box 25, folder 8: Civil Rights—Somerville, Frank Goad Clement Papers, 1963–1967, TSLA.

122. *Fear Runs Deep: A Report by the Tennessee State Advisory Committee to the U.S. Commission on Civil Rights Open Meeting, March 17–18, 1971, Somerville, Tennessee* (N.p.: Tennessee State Advisory Committee, 1971), 23.

123. Vernon Francis et al., *Preserving a Fundamental Right: Reauthorization of the Voting Rights Act* (Washington D.C.: Lawyers' Committee for Civil Rights under Law, 2003), 4.

124. Ibid.

125. Robert B. McKay, "Racial Discrimination in the Electoral Process," *Annals of the American Academy of Political and Social Science* 407 (May 1973): 113.

126. Numan V. Bartley and Hugh D. Graham, *Southern Elections: County and Precinct Data, 1950–1972* (Baton Rouge: Louisiana State University Press, 1978), 217. The number of white voter registrants also increased during this period.

127. By the 1960s and 1970s, the locus of black political power had been solidified in West Tennessee, particularly in Memphis/Shelby County. The black population in West Tennessee grew from 191,000 in 1890 to almost 373,000 in 1970. Lamon, *Blacks in Tennessee*, appendix. The white population, however, grew almost twice as fast as the black population. Bureau of the Census, *1970 Census of Population*, vol. 1: *Characteristics of the Population, Part 44 (Tennessee)* (Washington, D.C.: Government Printing Office, 1970), 40.

128. Tom Ingram, "Blacks Urged to Think Radically, Act Militantly," *Tennessean*, April 6, 1971, 2; Tom Ingram, "Davidson County Black Legislators Call forBCC Support, Unity," *Tennessean*, May 25, 1971, 9.

129. Robert C. Smith, *We Have No Leaders: African Americans in the Post–Civil Rights Era* (Albany: SUNY Press, 1996), 21.

130. Wright, *Race, Power, and Political Emergence*, 40.

131. David M. Tucker, *Black Pastors and Leaders: Memphis, 1819–1972* (Memphis, Tenn.: Memphis State University Press, 1975), 129–130.

132. Bell-Scott et al., *The Black Tennessean*.

133. "Negroes Are Filling Important Positions," *Nashville Commentator*, April 18, 1964, 1.

134. Washington Butler Jr., "Blacks in Tennessee Politics: A Potent Force since 1865," in Bell-Scott et al., *The Black Tennessean*, 60–61.

135. David Campbell and Joe R. Fagin, "Black Electoral Victories in the South," *Phylon* 45, no. 4 (1984): 332.

136. Tucker, *Black Pastors and Leaders*, 129–130; Stanfield, *In Memphis*, 3; and Wright, *Race, Power, and Political Emergence*, 107.

137. Max-El Saffold, "Shelby County Elects First African American Mayor," *Urban Journal*, August 7, 2002, 6; Sam Latham, "Howard Gentry Wins Vice-Mayoral Post," *Urban Journal*, September 4, 2002, 1.

138. Terry Tomziac and Mario Perez-Riley, "Effects of *Baker v. Carr* on the Distribution of Influence in the Tennessee General Assembly: An Application of Linkage Policy," in *The Volunteer State: Readings in Tennessee Politics*, ed. Dorothy F. Olshfki and T. Simpson III (Knoxville: Tennessee Political Science Association, 1985), 95–113.

139. Tucker, *Black Pastors and Leaders*, 129–130; J. W. Stanfield, *In Memphis: Mirror to America?* (Atlanta, Ga.: Southern Regional Council, 1968); Sharon D. Wright, *Race, Power, and Political Emergence in Memphis* (New York: Garland, 2000), 3, 62.

140. Jeannine Hunter, "Robert Booker Played Role in Integration Fight," *Knoxville News Sentinel*, February 19, 2003.

141. Wynn and Lovett, *Profiles of African Americans in Tennessee*, 145.

142. Bracey Campbell, "9 Black Assembly Members May Bargain for Offices," *Nashville Banner*, December 18, 1972, 1; Michael Willard, "'Black Caucus' Increases Power," *Nashville Banner*, December 26, 1972, 17.

143. "More Black Legislators Given Posts," *Nashville Banner*, January 18, 1973, 9.

144. Walters, *Black Presidential Politics*.

145. Tennessee Black Caucus of State Legislators, *Report on Findings at the Annual Legislative Retreat* (Nashville: Tennessee General Assembly Office of Minority Affairs, 1980).

146. Richard Locker, "Rep. DeBerry Has Left Mark on House—And It on Her," *Commercial Appeal*, March 8, 2004, B1.

147. Wright, *Race, Power, and Political Emergence*, 14.

148. Daniel Elazar, *American Federalism: A View from the States* (New York: Crowell, 1966).

149. Bonna de la Cruz, "The Fords of Memphis: Service and Scandal Define a Dynasty," *Tennessean*, July 31, 2005, A1.

150. Dwight Lewis and Doug Hall, "State's First Black Elected to Congress," *Tennessean*, November 6, 1974.

151. "Redrawn 8th Again Elects Kuykendall," *Tennessean*, November 8, 1972, 12.

152. Wright, *Race, Power, and Political Emergence*, 88.

153. A. J. Starling (AFL-CIO political affairs director), "Campaigns and Lobbying," AFL-CIO handout to the NAACP Labor Committee, spring 2005, Nashville, Tenn., in authors' possession.

154. Jon F. Hale, "The Making of New Democrats," *Political Science Quarterly* 110, no. 2 (1995): 207–232. For unsympathetic views of Ford, see Margaret Kimberley, "Har-

old Ford Jr.: Don't Know Much about History," *Black Commentator*, February 26, 2004, http://www.blackcommentator.com/79/79_fr_ford.html; "Why We Can't Trust Harold Ford Jr.," *Black Commentator*, March 17, 2005, http://www.blackcommentator.com/130/130_cover_ford.html; "Black Point Man for the Right: Rep. Harold Ford Jr.," *Black Commentator*, January 6, 2005, http://www.blackcommentator.com/120/120_cover_harold_ford.html; Flyer Staff, "Harold Ford Jr. for Senate?," *Memphis Flyer*, August 26, 2005, http://www.memphisflyer.com/memphis/harold-ford-jr-for-senate/Content?oid=1122464.

155. Roger Abramson, "Prince Harold: The Sky Could Be the Limit for Harold Ford Jr., Conventional Wisdom Be Damned," *Nashville Scene*, March 18, 2004, 26; Jack E. White, "Harold Ford Jr. Reaches for the Stars," *Time*, December 10, 2002, http://www.time.com/time/nation/article/0,8599,397281,00.html.

156. This point is discussed in several studies on black political history in the South. See Tera Hunter, *To 'Joy My Freedom: Southern Black Lives and Labor after the Civil War* (1997; repr., Cambridge, Mass.: Harvard University Press, 1998); Eric Foner, *Forever Free: The Story of Emancipation and Reconstruction* (New York: Knopf, 2005); and Robin D. G. Kelley, *Hammer and Hoe: Alabama Communists during the Great Depression* (Chapel Hill: University of North Carolina Press, 1990).

CHAPTER 3. RACE, ELECTORAL REALIGNMENT, AND POLARIZATION

The epigraph is from Michael Riley and Kimberly S. Johnson, "Obama and the Southern Vote," *Denver Post*, January 20, 2008, A1.

1. V. O. Key Jr., *Southern Politics in State and Nation* (1949; repr., Knoxville: University of Tennessee Press, 1984).

2. Earl Black and Merle Black, *The Rise of Southern Republicans* (Cambridge, Mass.: Harvard University Press, 2002), 256–263; Andrew Gelman, *Red State, Blue State, Rich State, Poor State: Why Americans Vote the Way They Do* (Princeton, N.J.: Princeton University Press, 2008).

3. Byron E. Shafer and Richard Johnston, *The End of Southern Exceptionalism: Class, Race, and Partisan Change in the Postwar South* (Cambridge, Mass.: Harvard University Press, 2006), 8–9. See also Jeffrey Stonecash and Mark D. Brewer, "Class, Race Issues and Political Change in the South," *Political Behavior* 23, no. 2 (2001): 131–156.

4. Hanes Walton, *Black Politics: A Theoretical and Structural Analysis* (Philadelphia, Pa.: Lippincott, 1972), 11–12.

5. James C. Cobb, *Away Down South: A History of Southern Identity* (New York: Oxford University Press, 2006), 296–303.

6. David Tucker, *Memphis since Crump: Bossism, Blacks, and Civic Reformers, 1948–1968* (Knoxville: University of Tennessee Press, 1980); G. Michael McCarthy, "Smith vs. Hoover—The Politics of Race in West Tennessee," *Phylon* 39, no. 2 (1978): 160–167; William Majors, *Change and Continuity in the South* (Macon, Ga.: Mercer University Press, 1986), 56.

7. Tony Badger, "The Rise and Fall of Biracial Politics in the South," in *The Southern*

State of Mind, ed. Jan Nordby Gretlund (Columbia: University of South Carolina Press, 1999), 23–33, 24.

8. Rodney Hero, *Faces of Inequality: Social Diversity in American Politics* (New York: Oxford University Press, 1998), 145.

9. A conservative magazine identified Williamson County as America's most "conservative-friendly county." Aleksandra Kulczuga, "America's Most Conservative-Friendly County Is Williamson County: Horse Farms, Guitar-Shaped Pools and Low Taxes," *Daily Caller*, March 19, 2010, http://dailycaller.com/2010/03/19/americas-most-conservative-friendly-county-is-williamson-county-horse-farms-guitar-shaped-pools-and-low-taxes.

10. Tom Humphrey, "Stimulus to Add Jobs in 'Poorest' ET County," *Knoxville News Sentinel*, January 6, 2010.

11. Tennessee Secretary of State, Division of Elections, https://sos.tn.gov/products/elections/election-results.

12. Dave Flessner, "Metro Jobless Rate Hits '84 Level," *Chattanooga Times Free Press*, March 27, 2009, A1.

13. Badger, "Rise and Fall of Biracial Politics," 30.

14. Thomas D. Ungs and Frank Essex, "The Institutionalization of the Tennessee Legislature, 1968–1997," in *Tennessee Government and Politics: Democracy in the Volunteer State*, ed. John R. Vile and Mark Byrnes (Nashville, Tenn.: Vanderbilt University Press, 1998), 25–54, 26.

15. James Glaser, *Race, Campaign Politics, and the Realignment in the South* (New Haven, Conn.: Yale University Press, 1996).

16. Sekou Franklin, "Situational Deracialization, Harold Ford, and the 2006 Senate Race in Tennessee," in *Whose Black Politics? Cases in Post-Racial Black Leadership*, ed. Andra Gillespie (New York: Routledge, 2010), 214–240.

17. M. V. Hood, Quentin Kidd, and Irwin L. Morris, "The Reintroduction of the *Elephas maximus* to the Southern United States: The Rise of Republican State Parties, 1960 to 2000," *American Politics Research* 32, no. 1 (2004): 68–101.

18. David Lublin, *The Republican South: Democratization and Partisan Change* (Princeton, N.J.: Princeton University Press, 2004).

19. Leslie Collins, interview with A. J. Starling (executive assistant to the president of the AFL-CIO), March 30, 2012. The interview was conducted on behalf of the authors of this book.

20. Kenneth T. Andrews, "Social Movements and Policy Implementation: The Mississippi Civil Rights Movement and the War on Poverty, 1965 to 1971," *American Sociological Review* 66, no. 1 (2001): 78; Christine Rocha and Michael Rushton, "Racial Context and Voting over Taxes: Evidence from a Referendum in Alabama," *Public Finance Review* 36, no. 5 (2008): 623.

21. Regina P. Bratton and Bradford S. Jones, "Reexamining Racial Attitudes: The Conditional Relationship between Diversity and Socioeconomic Environment," *American Journal of Political Science* 49, no. 2 (2005): 359–372.

22. David A. Kanervo, "Local Government and Politics," in Vile and Byrnes, *Tennessee Government and Politics*, 76–114.

23. Ibid., 77.

24. EI is a commonly used statistical technique developed by political scientist Gary King to remedy the problem associated with estimating individual-level patterns from aggregate data. Gary King, *A Solution to the Ecological Inference Problem: Reconstructing Individual Behavior from Aggregate Data* (Princeton, N.J.: Princeton University Press, 1997).

25. David Krackhardt, "Predicting with Networks: Nonparametric Multiple Regression Analysis of Dyadic Data," *Social Networks* 10 (1988): 359–378, 362.

26. Kathleen M. Carley et al., *ORA User's Guide 2009*, CMU-ISR-09–115, CASOS (Pittsburgh, Pa.: Carnegie Mellon University), 394.

27. Shayla C. Nunnally, *Trust in Black America: Race, Discrimination, and Politics* (New York: NYU Press, 2012), 235–238.

28. The difference is statistically significant: $p < .10$.

29. Samuel Popkin, *The Candidate: What It Takes to Win and Hold the White House* (New York: Oxford University Press), chap. 8.

30. Franklin, "Situational Deracialization."

31. Starling, interview.

32. Balz, "In Tennessee, Consensus Politics."

CHAPTER 4. THE LEGISLATIVE BEHAVIOR OF TENNESSEE'S BLACK LAWMAKERS

The epigraph is from Barbara Cooper, interview with Sekou Franklin, April 4, 2012.

1. Rebekah Gleaves, "Nobody's Children," *Memphis Flyer*, https://www.memphisflyer.com/memphis/nobodys-children/Content?oid=1105619, February 28, 2001; Andy Shookhoff et al., *Lessons Learned from Class Action Litigation: A Case Study of Tennessee's Reform* (Washington, D.C.: Center for the Study of Social Policy, 2019), 5–19.

2. Catherine Lee, "Race Categorization and the Regulation of Business and Science," *Law and Society Review* 44, nos. 3–4 (2010): 636.

3. Representative Kathryn Bowers, Resolution 03 11: Quality of Patient Medical Care, 32–33; Senator Roscoe Dixon, Resolution 03 21: Proposed Protection of Medicaid Beneficiaries' Access to Pharmaceuticals, 36, both in Resolutions Ratified in Plenary Sessions, National Black Caucus of State Legislators, December 13, 2002, Indianapolis, Ind., https://nbcsl.org/public-policy/docs/category/39-1998-2015-ratified-policy-resolutions.html.

4. Tennessee Black Caucus of State Legislators, *Report of the Findings at the Annual Legislative Retreat* (Nashville: Tennessee General Assembly Office of Minority Affairs, 1977, 1980–1995).

5. Mary E. Hawkesworth, "Congressional Enactments of Race-Gender: Toward a Theory of Raced-Gendered Institutions," *American Political Science Review* 97 (2003): 529–555.

6. Nils Ringe, Jennifer Nicoll Victor, and Wendy Tam Cho, "Legislative Networks,"

in *Oxford Handbooks Online* (2015), http://www.oxfordhandbooks.com/view/10.1093/oxfordhb/9780190228217.001.0001/oxfordhb-9780190228217-e-19.

7. James H. Fowler, "Connecting the Congress: A Study of Cosponsorship Networks," *Political Analysis* 14 (2006): 458–459. Also see Robert Huckfeldt, "Interdependence, Density Dependence, and Networks in Politics," *American Politics Research* 37, no. 5 (2009): 921–950.

8. Fowler, "Connecting the Congress."

9. Kerry L. Haynie, *African American Legislators in the American States* (New York: Columbia University Press), 103.

10. Michael S. Rocca and Gabriel Sanchez, "The Effect of Race and Ethnicity on Bill Sponsorship and Cosponsorship in Congress," *American Politics Research* 36, no. 1 (2008): 130–152.

11. Charles E. Menifield and Stephen D. Shaffer, eds., *Politics in the New South: Representation of African Americans in Southern State Legislatures* (Albany: SUNY Press, 2005); Haynie, *African American Legislators*.

12. Robert R. Preuhs, "The Conditional Effects of Minority Descriptive Representation: Black Legislators and Policy Influence in the American States," *Journal of Politics* 68, no. 3 (2006): 585–599.

13. Haynie, *African American Legislators*.

14. Glen Browder, *The South's New Racial Politics: Inside the Race Game of Southern History* (Montgomery, Ala.: New South Books, 2009), 46.

15. Kathleen A. Bratton and Kerry L. Haynie, "Agenda Setting and Legislative Success in State Legislatures: The Effects of Gender and Race," *Journal of Politics* 61 (1999): 658–679.

16. William D. Anderson, Janet M. Box-Steffensmeier, and Valerie Sinclair Chapman, "The Keys to Legislative Success in the U.S. House of Representatives," *Legislative Studies Quarterly* 28, no. 3 (2003): 357–386; Michelle G. Briscoe, "Cohesiveness and Diversity among Black Members of the Texas State Legislature," in Menifield and Shaffer, *Politics in the New South*, 131–156.

17. Willie M. Legette, "The South Carolina Legislative Black Caucus, 1970 to 1988," *Journal of Black Studies* 30, no. 6 (2000): 850–852.

18. Alan Rosenthal, "Legislative Behavior and Legislative Oversight," *Legislative Studies Quarterly* 6 (1981): 115–131.

19. Jane Mansbridge, "Should Blacks Represent Blacks and Women Represent Women? A Contingent Yes," *Journal of Politics* 61, no. 3 (1999): 628–657; Suzanne Dovi, "Preferable Descriptive Representatives: Will Just Any Woman, Black or Latino Do?," *American Political Science Review* 94, no. 4 (2002): 745–754.

20. Johnnie Turner, interview with Sekou Franklin, December 18, 2013.

21. Cooper, interview.

22. Brenda Gilmore, interview with Sekou Franklin, December 28, 2011.

23. Chas Sisk, "Day of Union Protests Ends with 7 Arrested," *Tennessean*, March 16, 2011.

24. Kevin Lessmiller, "Students Claim Tenn. Voter ID Law Is Unfair," March 5, 2015, *Courthouse News Service*, https://www.courthousenews.com/Students-Claim-Tenn.-Voter-ID-Law-Is-Unfair.

25. Keesha Gaskins and Sundeep Iyer, *The Challenge of Obtaining Voter Identification* (New York: Brennan Center for Justice, New York University School of Law, 2012); *Issues Related to State Voter Identification Laws* (Washington, D.C.: GAO, 2014).

26. These findings are based on ecological inference analyses using 2000 Census data.

27. Tyson King-Meadows and Thomas F. Schaller, *Devolution and Black State Legislators: Challenges and Choices in the Twenty-First Century* (Albany: SUNY Press, 2006), 30–31.

28. Nicholas O. Stephanopoulos, "The South after Shelby County," *Supreme Court Review* 2014, no. 1 (2014): 82.

29. An earlier version of this analysis of the Tennessee Black Caucus of State Legislators appeared in Sekou M. Franklin, "Black Political Development in Tennessee: From Reconstruction–2006," in *Blacks in Tennessee: Past and Present*, ed. Wornie Reed (Dubuque, Iowa: Kendall/Hunt, 2008), 123–172.

30. Terry Tomziac and Mario Perez-Riley, "Effects of *Baker v. Carr* on the Distribution of Influence in the Tennessee General Assembly: An Application of Linkage Policy," in *The Volunteer State: Readings in Tennessee Politics*, ed. Dorothy F. Olshfski and T. Simpson III (Knoxville: Tennessee Political Science Association, 1985), 95–113.

31. Sharon D. Wright, "The Tennessee Black Caucus of State Legislators," *Journal of Black Studies* 31, no. 1 (2000): 3–19.

32. Executive Order by the Governor, No. 8, October 15, 1979, box 896, folder 3: Black Caucus and Legislation, 1981–1983; also see box 717, folder 2: Black Caucus, 1979–1986, Governor Lamar Alexander Papers, 1979–1987, Tennessee State Library and Archives, Nashville (hereafter TSLA).

33. Francis S. Guess (assistant commissioner for human resource development, Department of Personnel), "Prospecting for Employment Opportunities in the '80s: An Approach to the Public Sector," presentation at the Fifth Annual Legislation Retreat of the Black Caucus of the Tennessee General Assembly, Henry Horton State Park, Chapel Hill, Tenn., September 27–29, 1979, box 896, folder 3: Black Caucus and Legislation, 1981–1983; also see box 717, folder 2: Black Caucus, 1979–1986, Governor Lamar Alexander Papers, 1979–1987, TSLA.

34. Francis S. Guess, "Summary of Governor Alexander's Administration," memorandum to the Black Caucus of the Tennessee General Assembly, Participants, Seventh Annual Legislative Retreat, October 23, 1981, box 896, folder 3: Black Caucus and Legislation, 1981–1983, Governor Lamar Alexander Papers, 1979–1987, TSLA.

35. "Excerpts from the Address of Governor Lamar Alexander to the Seventh Annual Tennessee Black Caucus Legislative Retreat, Paris Landing State Park, Buchanan, Tennessee" (translated by Francis S. Guess), box 896, folder 3: Black Caucus and Legislation, 1981–1983, Governor Lamar Alexander Papers, 1979–1987, TSLA.

36. Wright, "Tennessee Black Caucus."

37. Ibid., 13.

38. Richard Locker, "Assembly: New Faces, Possible New Leaders," *Commercial Appeal*, November 7, 2002, A8.

39. *Rural West Tennessee African American Affairs Council Inc. v. McWherter*, 836 F. Supp. 453 (W.D. Tenn. 1993), vacated and remanded, 512 U.S. 1248 (1994) (mem).

40. Nate Hobbs, "Activist Lifts Voice for Rural Blacks in W. Tenn.," *Commercial Appeal*, January 17, 1994, A1.

41. Richard Carelli, "W. Tenn. Majority-Black Vote Dist. OK'd," *Commercial Appeal*, April 5, 2000, A16. For more information about the legal battles, see *Rural West Tennessee African American Affairs Council Inc. v. McWherter*, 836 F. Supp. 453 (W.D. Tenn. 1993), vacated and remanded, 512 U.S. 1248 (1994) (mem); *Rural West Tennessee African American Affairs Council Inc. v. McWherter*, 877 F. Supp. 1096 (W.D. Tenn. 1994); *Rural West Tennessee African American Affairs Council Inc. v. Sundquist*, 116 S. Ct. 42 (1995) (mem); *Langsdon v. Darnell*, 9 F. Supp. 2d 880 (W.D. Tenn. 1998); *Rural West Tennessee African American Affairs Council v. Sundquist*, 29 F. Supp. 2d 448 (W.D. Tenn. 1998), affirmed 209 F.3d 835 (6th Cir. 2000).

42. Lois DeBerry, interview with Sekou Franklin, September 26, 2012.

43. Richard Locker, "Black Lawmakers Back Push for Execution Moratorium," *Commercial Appeal*, March 29, 2001, B1; Sam Latham, "Black Caucus Asks to Commute Abdur Rahman Death Sentence," *Urban Journal*, January 23, 2002, 1.

44. This information is based on my brief involvement in the restoration campaign and discussions with advocates and supporters of the restoration bill.

45. Tennessee Black Caucus of State Legislators, *Report of the Findings*.

46. Haynie, *African American Legislators*, 10, 27.

47. For example, at the January 29 and February 15, 2008, meetings, the black caucus discussed sign-on slips and how they would support each other's legislation. See Minutes and Agenda, Tennessee Black Caucus, 2008, in author's possession.

48. Gover L. Porter, "Ethical Scandals Rock State Governments," *Strategic Finance* 88, no. 3 (2006): 11–12.

49. Commercial Appeal Archives, "Tennessee Waltz Archive: Key Players in the Tennessee Waltz Legislation Influence Case," May 24, 2018 (originally published May 27, 2005), *Commercial Appeal*, https://www.commercialappeal.com/story/news/2018/05/24/tennessee-waltz-john-ford-kathryn-bowers-roscoe-dixon/641617002.

50. Some political observers believe that there has been a long-term bias against Memphis by state lawmakers, which may be related to race. Mary Freeman, a former chief lobbyist for Governor Phil Bredesen who previously worked for Representative Lois DeBerry, stated that "it was always a fight to make sure Memphis was included." Mary Freeman, interview with Sekou Franklin, May 24, 2012.

51. Andy Sher, "Tennessee: Minority Democrats Elect Republican Williams House Speaker," *Times Free Press*, January 14, 2009, http://www.timesfreepress.com/news/local/story/2009/jan/14/tennessee-minority-democrats-elect-republican-will/203499.

52. Turner, interview.

53. DNA integrates social network and link analyses, as well as multimodal and

time-series approaches not commonly associated with traditional network procedures. DNA and the companion software called ORA were developed by Carnegie Mellon's Center for Computational Analysis of Social and Organizational Systems (CASOS). Kathleen M. Carley, "Dynamic Network Analysis," in *Dynamic Social Network Modeling and Analysis: Workshop Summary and Proceedings*, ed. Ron Breiger, Kathleen M. Carley, and Philippa Pattison (Washington, D.C.: National Research Council, 2003), 133–145.

54. A resolution can be passed by one chamber without the other chamber's consent, or there can be joint resolutions. In Tennessee, resolutions usually recognize a resident, an institution (e.g., a high school), or a celebrity for their achievements. Legislation, on the other hand, deals with policy: it requires a fiscal evaluation and must be passed by both chambers.

55. Wright, "Tennessee Black Caucus."

56. Michael S. Rocca, "Nonlegislative Debate in the U.S. House of Representatives," *American Politics Research* 35 (2007): 490; Gregory Koger, "Position Taking and Cosponsorship in the U.S. House," *Legislative Studies Quarterly* 28 (2003): 225–246.

57. Jeffery C. Talbert and Matthew Potoski, "Setting the Legislative Agenda: The Dimensional Structure of Bill Cosponsoring and Floor Voting," *Journal of Politics* 64 (2002): 864–891, 866; J. E. Campbell, "Cosponsoring Legislation in the U.S. Congress," *Legislative Studies Quarterly* 7 (1982): 415–422.

58. Kathleen M. Carley et al., *ORA's User Guide 2009*, CMU-ISR-09-115, CASOS (Pittsburgh, Pa.: Carnegie Mellon University, 2009), 52.

59. Ibid., 384. The algorithm is $1/(1 + \exp(10 \times (0.5 - d[i]))$.

60. Charles E. Menifield, Stephen D. Shaffer, and Brandi J. Brassell, "An Overview of African American Representation in Other Southern States," in Menifield and Shaffer, *Politics in the New South*, 172.

61. TBCSL meeting minutes, 2008, in author's possession.

62. Representative Joe Armstrong, H.B. 847; Representative Joe Armstrong, H.B. 550; and Public Chapter 630, all in 103rd General Assembly.

63. Turner, interview.

CHAPTER 5. THE RACIAL POLITICS OF TAX AND SPENDING POLICIES

The epigraph is from Paula Wade, "Ford Says Revised Plan Guards Lawmakers' Jobs," *Commercial Appeal*, June 20, 2001, B5.

1. The court cases are *Evans v. McCabe* (1932) and *Cole v. MacFarland* (1960). See Lewis L. Laska, "A History of Personal Income Taxation in Tennessee," *Tennessee Historical Quarterly* 60, no. 4 (2001): 220–243.

2. Richard Locker, "Riot Police Block Tax Protestors Threatening Lawmakers at Capitol," *Commercial Appeal*, July 13, 2001, A1.

3. Rebecca Ferrar, "Tight Rules Will Greet Capitol Protestors: Anti-Tax Anger Expected," *Commercial Appeal*, August 4, 2001, B1 (originally reported in the *Knoxville News Sentinel*).

4. Wade, "Ford Says Revised Plan Guards," B5.

5. Robert C. Smith and Richard Seltzer, *Race, Class, and Culture: A Study in Afro-American Mass Opinion* (Albany: SUNY Press, 1992); Robert C. Smith and Richard Seltzer, *Contemporary Controversies and the American Racial Divide* (Lanham, Md.: Rowman and Littlefield, 2000).

6. Christopher Faricy and Christopher Ellis, "Public Attitudes toward Social Spending in the United States: The Differences between Direct Spending and Tax Expenditures," *Political Behavior* 36, no. 1 (2014): 53–76.

7. See Andrew Kohut, "Debt and Deficit: A Public Opinion Dilemma," Pew Research Center, June 14, 2012, http://www.people-press.org/2012/06/14/debt-and-deficit-a-public-opinion-dilemma.

8. Andrea Louise Campbell, "What Americans Think of Taxes," in *The New Fiscal Sociology: Taxation in Comparative and Historical Perspective*, ed. Isaac William Martin, Ajay K. Mehrotra, and Monica Prasad (Cambridge: Cambridge University Press, 2009).

9. Marc J. Hetherington and John D. Nugent, "Explaining Public Support for Devolution: The Role of Political Trust," in *What Is It about Government That Americans Dislike?*, ed. John R. Hibbing and Elizabeth Theiss-Morse (Cambridge: Cambridge University Press, 2001).

10. Christine H. Roch and Michael Rushton, "Racial Context and Voting over Taxes: Evidence from a Referendum in Alabama," *Public Finance Review* 36, no. 5 (2008): 614–634, 619–620.

11. Ibid., 625, 629.

12. John M. Foster, "Voter Ideology, Economic Factors, and State and Local Tax Progressivity," *Public Finance Review* 41, no. 2 (2013): 191–195.

13. Alberto Alesina, Reza Baqir, and William Easterly, "Public Goods and Ethnic Divisions," *Quarterly Journal of Economics* 114, no. 4 (1999): 1243–1284; Daniel J. Hopkins, "The Diversity Discount: When Increasing Ethnic and Racial Diversity Prevents Tax Increases," *Journal of Politics* 71, no. 1 (2009): 160–177; Patrick Mason, "Immigration and African American Wages and Employment: Critically Appraising the Empirical Evidence," *Review of Black Political Economy* 41 (April 2014): 271–297.

14. Fay L. Cook and Edith J. Barrett, *Support for the American Welfare State: The Views of Congress and the Public* (New York: Columbia University Press, 1992); William G. Jacoby, "Public Attitudes toward Government Spending," *American Journal of Political Science* 38, no. 2 (1994): 336–361; William G. Jacoby, "Issue Framing and Public Opinion on Government Spending," *American Journal of Political Science* 44, no. 4 (2000): 750–767; Thomas J. Rudolph and Jillian Evans, "Political Trust, Ideology, and Public Support for Government Spending," *American Journal of Political Science* 49, no. 3 (2005): 660–671; Stuart N. Soroka and Christopher C. Wlezien, *Degrees of Democracy: Politics, Public Opinion, and Policy* (Cambridge: Cambridge University Press, 2010); James Stimson, *Tides of Consent: How Public Opinion Shapes American Politics* (Cambridge: Cambridge University Press, 2004); Christopher C. Wlezien, "The Public as Thermostat: Dynamics of Preferences for Spending," *American Journal of Political*

Science 39, no. 4 (1995): 981–1000; Christopher C. Wlezien, "Patterns of Representation: Dynamics of Public Preferences and Policy," *Journal of Politics* 66, no. 1 (2004): 1–24.

15. Laska, "History of Personal Income Taxation," 224.
16. Ibid., 225–226.
17. Ibid., 227–228.
18. Ibid., 229.
19. Rebecca Ferrar, "Slowing Economy Hurts State Revenues," *Commercial Appeal*, December 15, 2000, A18 (originally reported in the *Knoxville News Sentinel*).
20. Stephen Moore and Richard Vedder, "The Case against a Tennessee Income Tax," November 1, 1999, Cato Institute, http://www.cato.org/publications/briefing-paper/case-against-tennessee-income-tax.
21. David Firestone, "Tennessee's Fiscal Troubles Grow after Futile Push for Income Tax," *New York Times*, August 23, 2001, A1.
22. Paula Wade, "Sundquist, Legislators Trim Options to 7 Tax Plans," *Commercial Appeal*, February 7, 2002, B1; Tom Sharp, "House Vote on Income Tax Could Come on Wednesday," Associated Press State and Local Wire, May 21, 2002; Associated Press, "Anti-Tax Protestors Expected at Capitol on Wednesday," Associated Press State and Local Wire, May 22, 2002.
23. Wade, "Ford Says Revised Plan Guards," B5.
24. Sara Kyle et al., "Tennessee Regulatory Authority," *Tennessee Blue Book*, 313, https://sharetngov.tnsosfiles.com/sos/bluebook/11-12/WholeBBook.pdf.
25. Associated Press, "Black Caucus Tries to Leverage Tax Reform Support into TRA Seat," Associated Press State and Local Wire, May 10, 2002.
26. Richard Locker, "Interest Groups Push Tax Reform in Day at Capitol," *Commercial Appeal*, March 21, 2002, B1.
27. G. Michael Yopp, "Tennessee," *State and Local Tax Lawyer* 8 (2003): 535.
28. Tom Humphrey, "Deal Struck: Legislature OKs Sales Tax Boost," *Knoxville News Sentinel*, July 4, 2002, A1.
29. A difference of proportions test confirms this racial gap in attitudes about the Volunteer State implementing an income tax: $z = -2.06$, $p = .04$.
30. Difference of proportions test: $z = 15.27$, $p < .05$.
31. Chi-squared difference test: $\chi^2 = 0.308$, $p = .58$.
32. Equality of proportions test: $z = 7.53$, $p < .05$.
33. Chi-squared difference test: $\chi^2 = 3.53$, $p = .06$.
34. The percentage change is determined by $\frac{.583 - .197}{.197} \times 100 \approx 195.94$.
35. The percentage change is determined by $\frac{.583 - .388}{.388} \times 100 \approx 50.257$.
36. Difference of proportions test: $z = 9.00$, $p < .05$.
37. Chi-squared difference test: $\chi^2 = 4.48$, $p = .03$.
38. In both cases, the difference of proportions tests demonstrate that we cannot reject the null hypothesis of no racial difference in "don't know" responses ($z = 1.57$, $p = .11$) and in attitudes about the graduated tax ($z = 1.718$, $p = .09$).
39. Herbert Hiram Hyman and Paul B. Sheatsley, *The Current Status of American Public Opinion* (N.p.: N.p., 1950).

40. Opposition to the plain ($z = -0.633$, $p = .52$), sales-tax-lowering ($z = -0.95$, $p = .34$), and education-benefiting ($z = -0.17$, $p = .86$) income tax polling items changed only slightly depending on whether these respondents received questions about the flat tax or graduated tax first. None of these changes, however, are statistically significant.

41. Difference of proportions test for lower sales tax: $z = -0.61$, $p = .54$; for funding education: $z = -0.78$, $p = .44$.

42. Difference of proportions test: $z = -1.78$, $p = .04$.

43. David O. Sears, "Self-Interest vs. Symbolic Politics in Policy Attitudes and Presidential Voting," *American Political Science Review* 74 (September 1980): 670–684.

44. Paul Allen Beck and Thomas Dye, "Sources of Public Opinion on Taxes: The Florida Case," *Journal of Politics* 44, no. 1 (1982): 172–182.

45. Kent L. Tedin, Richard E. Matland, and Gregory R. Weiher, "Age, Race, Self-Interest, and Financing Public Schools through Referenda," *Journal of Politics* 63 (February 2001): 270–294.

46. Our primary concern is examining the effect of race on attitudes about income taxes, so we focus our interpretations there. Nevertheless, it is worth mentioning briefly the other statistically significant independent variables in table 5.1. For example, one of the dummy variables for party identification in the flat-tax-first model is both positive and significant (logit estimate = .62, standard error = .29, $p < .05$), which suggests that compared to political independents, Republicans express more opposition to an income tax. Furthermore, the regular and squared age variables are consistently significant. In both models, the coefficient estimate is positive and greater than 0 for the non-squared age term and virtually 0 for the squared term. This means that regardless of question order, opposition to an income tax increases initially with age and then eventually flattens out. The plateau points are ages forty-eight and fifty-two for the flat-tax-first and graduated-tax-first models, respectively.

47. Logit estimate = .61, standard error = .36, $p > .05$.

48. These debates have little to do with whether a taxation–government spending relationship exists. There is a relative consensus on that point. Rather, the debates focus more on the causal structure of that relationship. See William Andersen, Myles Wallace, and John T. Warner, "Government Spending and Taxation: What Causes What?," *Southern Economic Journal* 52, no. 3 (1986): 630–639.

49. In each case, the racial differences are statistically significant: $p < .05$.

50. $p < .05$.

51. Difference of proportions test: $z = -1.54$, $p = 0.06$.

52. For the state spending index: Cronbach's alpha (α) = .71; for the federal spending index, $\alpha = .76$.

53. Two-sample mean difference test: $t = -1.88$, $p < .03$.

54. Mean difference test: $t = -2.24$, $p = 0.01$.

55. Mean difference test: $t = -0.97$, $p = 0.17$.

56. Andrew Hacker, *Two Nations: Black and White, Separate, Hostile, Unequal* (New York: Simon and Schuster 1993).

CHAPTER 6. THE RISE AND FALL OF TENNCARE

The epigraph is from Patricia Barron to Phil Bredesen, 2005, box 118, folder 6: Correspondence 2003–2010, Phil Bredesen Papers, Tennessee State Library and Archives, Nashville (hereafter TSLA).

1. Governor's Communications Office, "State Moves toward Medicaid: 'Persistent Lawsuits' Block TennCare Reform Effort" (news release), November 10, 2004, https://tnjustice.org/wp-content/uploads/2011/01/Bredesen-release-re-consent-decrees.pdf.

2. Christina Bennett, *TennCare: One State's Experiment with Medicaid Expansion* (Nashville, Tenn.: Vanderbilt University Press, 2014).

3. Carole R. Myers, "Failed Promises: The Demise of the Original TennCare Vision," *Managed Care Interface* 20, no. 2 (2007): 24–30.

4. The stakeholders included TennCare enrollees, the state's General Assembly, the Tennessee Medical Association, the Tennessee Hospital Association, the Tennessee Pharmacists Association, and the Children's Hospital Alliance of Tennessee. The advocates included the attorneys representing TennCare enrollees in legal disputes, the civil rights leaders pushing for fairer access to quality health care, and the members of public organizations like the TennCare Advocacy Program and the Tennessee Community Services Agency.

5. Cyril F. Chang and Stephanie C. Steinberg, "TennCare Timeline: Major Events and Milestones from 1992 to 2016," Methodist Le Bonheur Center for Healthcare Economics, University of Memphis, September 2016, http://www.memphis.edu/mlche/pdfs/tenncare/tenncare_bulleted_timeline.pdf.

6. "Resolution Urging Governor and General Assembly to Explore TennCare Solutions That Would Not Require Disenrollment of TennCare Recipients," Resolution 04092705, October 13, 2005, box 776, folder 1: Department Files—TennCare, 2005, Phil Bredesen Papers, TSLA.

7. Ceci Connolly, "Tennessee's Retreat on Medicaid Points to Struggle: Planned Cuts May Signal National Trend," *Washington Post*, January 18, 2005, A3.

8. William M. Welch and Julie Appleby, "States Watching Tennessee's Health Care Plan for the Poor: Proposal Limits Visits to Doctors, Prescriptions," *USA Today*, July 6, 2004, http://usatoday30.usatoday.com/educate/college/healthscience/articles/20040711.htm.

9. Bob Herbert, "Curing Health Costs: Let the Sick Suffer," *New York Times*, September 1, 2005.

10. Phil Bredesen, "Medicaid 2.0," report presented at North Carolina Emerging Issues Forum, February 8, 2005, TennCare Saves Lives Coalition Files, in author's possession.

11. Alan I Abramowitz., *The Polarized Public? Why American Government Is So Dysfunctional* (Upper Saddle River, N.J.: Pearson Education, 2013).

12. Sekou Franklin worked closely with several organizations that tried to rescue the program, including the TennCare Saves Lives Coalition. Its records were obtained after a federal court ordered the governor to submit them to health-care advocates and the

Tennessean, Nashville's daily newspaper, during the legal battles over TennCare. These records and other documents obtained from health-care advocates are referred to in the notes as the TennCare Saves Lives Coalition Files.

13. Douglas Blanks Hindman, "Knowledge Gaps, Belief Gaps, and Public Opinion about Health Care Reform," *Journalism and Mass Communication Quarterly* 89, no. 4 (2012): 585–605.

14. Jonathan Engel, *Poor People's Medicine: Medicaid and American Charity Care since 1965* (Durham, N.C.: Duke University Press, 2006), 55–59.

15. Michael Tesler, "The Spillover of Racialization of Health Care: How President Obama Polarized Public Opinion by Racial Attitudes and Race," *American Journal of Political Science* 56, no. 3 (2012): 690–704.

16. Michael Henderson and D. Sunshine Hillygus, "The Dynamics of Health Care Opinion, 2008–2010: Partisanship, Self-Interest, and Racial Resentment," *Journal of Health Politics, Policy and Law* 36 (December 2011): 945–960; see also Hindman, "Knowledge Gaps, Belief Gaps," 597.

17. Paul Frymer, *Uneasy Alliances: Race and Party Competition in America* (Princeton, N.J.: Princeton University Press, 1999).

18. David G. Smith and Judith D. Moore, *Medicaid Politics and Policy, 1965–2007* (New Brunswick, N.J.: Transaction, 2008), 64.

19. Ibid., 332.

20. Mark D. Daniels, ed., *Medicaid Reform and the American States: Case Studies of Managed Care* (Westport, Conn.: Auburn House, 1998), 59.

21. Polly Elliot, "McWherter Presses Clinton for Waiver to Approve TennCare," States News Service, June 16, 1993.

22. Stephen M. Davidson and Stephen A. Somers, eds., *Remaking Medicaid: Managed Care for the Public Good* (San Francisco, Calif.: Jossey-Bass, 1998); Smith and Moore, *Medicaid Politics and Policy*, 336.

23. Daniels, *Medicaid Reform and the American States*.

24. Taylor Brown, "TennCare and the Clinton Presidency: Health Care Policy in State and Nation," 2, unpublished paper in possession of author.

25. Robert Dallek, *Lyndon B. Johnson: Portrait of a President* (Oxford: Oxford University Press, 1991).

26. Engel, *Poor People's Medicine*, 59.

27. Ibid., 55–57.

28. Ibid., 61.

29. Marian Lief Palley, "Intergovernmentalization of Health Care Reform: The Limits of the Devolution Revolution," *Journal of Politics* 59, no. 3 (1997): 657–679.

30. Robert C. Saunders and Craig Anne Heflinger, "Effects of Managed Care on Southern Youths' Behavioral Services Use," *Health Care Financing Review* 26, no. 1 (2004): 23–41.

31. Christopher J. Conover and Hester H. Davies, *The Role of TennCare in Health Policy for Low-Income People in Tennessee* (Washington, D.C.: Urban Institute, 2000).

32. J. E. Bailey et al., "Impact of a Statewide Medicaid Managed Care System on Healthcare Utilization and Outcomes for People Living with HIV," *American Journal of the Medical Sciences* 328, no. 6 (2004): 305–314; D. E. Jess, "Prenatal Psychosocial Needs: Differences between a TennCare Group and a Privately Insured Group in Appalachia," *Journal of Health Care for the Poor and Underserved* 14, no. 4 (2003): 535–549; and R. J. Womeodu et al., "Diabetic Patient Experiences in a Medicaid Managed Care System," *Tennessee Medicine: Journal of the Tennessee Medical Association* 96, no. 10 (2003): 465–469. See also L. Moreno and S. D. Hoag, "Covering the Uninsured through TennCare: Does It Make a Difference?," *Mathematica Policy Research* 20, no. 1 (2001): 231–239; C. J. Conover, P. J. Rankin, and F. A. Sloan, "Effects of Tennessee Medicaid Managed Care on Obstetrical Care and Birth Outcomes," *Journal of Health Politics, Policy and Law* 26, no. 6 (2001): 1291.

33. Alan Sager and Deborah Socolar, "Poorer, Sicker States Face Heavier Drug Cost Burdens: Rising Burdens Mean Pressure for Action Likely to Grow," Boston University School of Public Health, Health Reform Program, July 14, 2004, http://www.bu.edu/sph/files/2015/05/Poorer_Sicker_States_Face_Heavier_Drug_Cost_Burdens_14_July_2004.pdf.

34. Sidney Watson, "Medicaid Physician Participation: Patients, Poverty, and Physician Self-Interest," *American Journal of Law and Medicine* 21, nos. 2–3 (1995): 191–220.

35. Chang and Steinberg, "TennCare Timeline."

36. Ibid.

37. Paula Wade, "Access's Lawsuit Says Racial Bias Fed the Drive to Push It to Failure: Doctors Protest to Sundquist," *Commercial Appeal*, January 6, 2001, B1; Paula Wade, "State Files Action to Take over Access," *Commercial Appeal*, January 5, 2001, A1.

38. McKinsey and Company, "Achieving a Critical Mission in Difficult Times—TennCare's Financial Viability," December 11, 2003; McKinsey and Company, "Achieving a Critical Mission in Difficult Times—Illustrative Strategic Options for TennCare," February 11, 2004, both in TennCare Saves Lives Coalition Files, in author's possession.

39. In some respects, the study reinforced concerns some experts had expressed about the long-term solvency of TennCare even before Bredesen came into office. In 1998, the Sundquist administration had contracted with William M. Mercer, Inc., a consulting group, for a study designed to determine the best strategy for balancing existing funds (and, if necessary, generating new funding) to support its health-care program. The report concluded that the program's enrollment growth could create insurmountable costs for the state. One reason for the upsurge in TennCare beneficiaries was the fact that commercial insurance companies were dumping high-risk individuals from their rolls. These were individuals with chronic illnesses who were expensive to maintain or who were referred to as "uninsurable." These people were being absorbed into the TennCare program. The study recommended that the state cut benefits and make changes to the eligibility requirements in order to curtail enrollment. William M. Mercer, Inc., "Evaluation of Critical Issues Facing the TennCare Program: Report," 2, State Department of Health, March 1999, box 585, folder 6: Committee and Department Files, TennCare, 1998–1999, Don Sundquist Papers, TSLA.

40. McKinsey and Company, "Achieving a Critical Mission in Difficult Times—TennCare's Financial Viability."

41. Bonna de La Cruz, "Governor Taking No Guff from TennCare Plan Critics," *Tennessean*, February 21, 2004, B1.

42. Myers, "Failed Promises."

43. Governor's TennCare Tour, 2/17–2/26, box 826, folder 20: TennCare Tour—TennCare Roll Out, February 2004, Phil Bredesen Papers, TSLA.

44. Ibid.

45. Black Caucus points (email from Michelle Mowery Johnson, director of communications at the YWCA—"Possible Black Caucus/GOP Positions"), box 826, folder 20: TennCare Tour—TennCare Roll Out, February 2004, Phil Bredesen Papers, TSLA.

46. GOP reaction (email from Johnson), ibid.

47. For a general discussion of these and related ideas, see Jay Haycock, "A Ground-Up Look at the Medicaid Managed-Care Reforms Debate," *Med City News*, April 28, 2015.

48. John Commins, "TennCare Plan under Review," *Chattanooga Times Free Press*, April 14, 2004, B1.

49. See also Duren Cheek, "TennCare Plan Likely to Fly, but Questions Remain," *Tennessean*, April 25, 2004, A21.

50. Ashley M. Heher and John Commins, "State House Overwhelmingly Approves TennCare Reform Package," *Chattanooga Times Free Press*, May 6, 2004, A1.

51. John Commins, "Senate Sends TennCare Bill to Governor," *Chattanooga Times Free Press*, May 7, 2004, A1.

52. House Journal of the One Hundred Third General Assembly, 1:3796–3801.

53. Alice G. Gosfield, "Medical Necessity in Medicare and Medicaid: The Implications of Professional Standards Review Organizations," *Temple Law Quarterly* 51 (1978): 229–280.

54. Bennett, *TennCare*, 80–81.

55. Tennessee Code 71-5-144: Medically Necessary Items and Services, ch. 673, § 22, *LawServer*, https://www.lawserver.com/law/state/tennessee/tn-code/tennessee_code_71-5-144.

56. House Journal of the One Hundred Third General Assembly, 1:3821.

57. Andy Schneider, "Tennessee's New 'Medically Necessary' Standard: Uncovering the Insured?," Kaiser Commission on Medicaid and the Uninsured, July 2004, https://kaiserfamilyfoundation.files.wordpress.com/2013/01/tennessee-s-new-medically-necessary-standard-uncovering-the-insured-policy-brief.pdf.

58. Ibid.

59. Tom Humphrey, "Bredesen TennCare Reforms Criticized," *Knoxville News Sentinel*, April 27, 2004, B1. See also Marian Wright Edelman to Dr. Mark B. McClellan, March 30, 2005, and Theodore M. Shaw (president and director-counsel of the NAACP Legal Defense and Educational Fund) to Phil Bredesen, September 15, 2004, both in TennCare Saves Lives Coalition Files, in author's possession.

60. Shaw to Bredesen, September 15, 2004.

61. "Bredesen Doesn't Want TennCare to Be a Pawn in National Battle," *Southern Standard*, July 2, 2004.

62. House Journal of the One Hundred Third General Assembly, 1:3796.

63. Welch and Appleby, "States Watching Tennessee's Health Care Plan."

64. University of Memphis, "TennCare Timeline," https://www.memphis.edu/mlche/pdfs/tenncare/tenncare_bulleted_timeline.pdf.

65. Robert E. Hurley, "TennCare—A Failure of Politics, Not Policy: A Conversation with Gordon Bonnyman," Health Affairs 25 (2006): 217–225.

66. Testimony of Honorable M. D. Goetz Jr., U.S. House of Representatives Judiciary Committee's Subcommittee on Courts, the Internet, and Intellectual Property, Regarding H.R. 1229, June 21, 2005, 7, TennCare Saves Lives Coalition Files, in author's possession.

67. "Framing the TennCare Contingency Plan," October 15, 2004, box 49, folder 1: Communications Office, Correspondence, TennCare, 2004, Phil Bredesen Papers, TSLA.

68. Ibid.

69. Maria Burnham, "Hopes Rise for Cure for Troubled Tennessee Medicaid Program TennCare," *Commercial Appeal*, November 16, 2004; "TennCare Advocates Back Off Court Wins in Effort to Save Program," *Obesity, Fitness and Wellness Week*, December 11, 2004, 704.

70. Roy Moore, "Back to Plan A: Bredesen Moves to Dissolve TennCare," *Nashville Business Journal*, November 12, 2004.

71. Governor Phil Bredesen, "Back to Medicaid Kick-Off," November 22, 2004, 4, 12, TennCare Saves Lives Coalition Files, in author's possession.

72. Carole R. Myers, "A Critical Case Study of Program Fidelity in TennCare" (PhD diss., University of Tennessee, Knoxville, 2006), 215.

73. Anita Wadhwani, "Savings Potential of TennCare Cuts Argued," *Tennessean*, July 15, 2005, B1.

74. Trudy Lieberman, "Mismanaged Care," *Nation*, December 12, 2015, https://www.thenation.com/article/mismanaged-care.

75. Anita Wadhwani, "TennCare Not Giving Appeals," *Tennessean*, January 12, 2006, B1. For example, Tene Franklin, the co-chair of the Nashville NAACP Health Committee, organized a session with two dozen TennCare disenrollees to help them appeal their disenrollments. She found enormous problems with the appeals process. Tene Hamilton Franklin, "Health Committee Report: Focus on TennCare Fallout," Nashville Branch of the NAACP, May 26, 2005, TennCare Saves Lives Coalition Files, in author's possession.

76. Wadhwani, "TennCare Not Giving Appeals."

77. Franklin, "Health Committee Report," 2005.

78. NAACP Tennessee State Conference, resolution: "Expressing Concerns about Governor Bredesen's TennCare Reform Proposal," October 2, 2004, TennCare Saves Lives Coalition Files, in author's possession.

79. Edelman to McClellan, March 30, 2005; Shaw to Bredesen, September 15, 2004.

80. Richard Locker, "Clergy Oppose TennCare Cuts: Black Leaders Lobby Lawmakers about Plan," *Commercial Appeal*, March 2, 2005, B3.

81. Rev. Victor Michael Singletary to Representative Johnny Shaw, March 3, 2005, TennCare Saves Lives Coalition Files, in author's possession. Sekou Franklin attended this meeting.

82. Terri L. Carter, "Marchers Raise 'Moral Issue' of Protecting Enrollees," *Tennessean*, April 9, 2005, B1.

83. Mary Powers, "Black Caucus Rep: Poor Face Health Cuts," *Commercial Appeal*, November 5, 2005, B3.

84. Phil Bredesen to Representative Gary Odom, September 25, 2005, box 776, folder 2: Department Files—TennCare—Special Sessions Requests, 2005, Phil Bredesen Papers, TSLA.

85. TennCare Special Session Poll (September 23, 2005) by Becky Gregory (assistant to the senior advisor for legislation and policy), September 15, 2005, box 776, folder 1: Department Files—TennCare—Special Sessions Requests, 2005, Phil Bredesen Papers, TSLA.

86. Governor Phil Bredesen, "Administration's 'Outreach' to Local Government," memorandum, August 1, 2005, TennCare Saves Lives Coalition Files, in author's possession.

87. The state refused to provide data in response to several Open Records requests we made.

88. Sekou Franklin, "The Politics of Race, Administrative Appeals, and Medicaid Disenrollment in Tennessee," *Social Sciences* 6, no. 3 (2017): 1–15.

89. Richard Locker, "Clergy Oppose TennCare Cuts: Black Leaders Lobby about Plan," *Commercial Appeal*, March 2, 2005, B3; Shaw to Bredesen, September 15, 2004; Pamela Perkins, "Connecting King's Dream," *Commercial Appeal*, January 15, 2006, B1; Ashley M. Heher, "TennCare Oversight Panel Members Worried about Impact on Hospitals," *Chattanooga Times Free Press*, A1; Bartholomew Sullivan, "State's TennCare Cuts Are 'Terrorism Incognito,' SCLC Leader Tells Congressional Black Caucus," *Commercial Appeal*, September 24, 2005, B1.

90. Anita Wadhwani, "Protests Resume against Proposed TennCare Cuts," *Tennessean*, December 16, 2004, B1.

91. Tom Catron and Veronica Gunn, "Improving Birth Outcomes in Tennessee," *Advocate: A Newsletter on Children's Issues* 16, no. 2 (2006): 5–6.

92. Kenneth S. Robinson (commissioner of health), Governor's Task Force on the Health Care Safety Net, General Guidance for Working Groups, February 2005, box 939, item 30, Interrogating Intervenor nos. 9 and 10, Phil Bredesen Papers, TSLA.

93. Bonna de la Cruz, "State Moves to Add Docs to TennCare Safety Net," *Tennessean*, May 25, 2005.

94. Sekou Franklin, "Racial Hierarchy, Second-Order Devolution, and Medicaid Reform before Obamacare," paper presented at the annual meeting of the National Conference of Black Political Scientists, November 14, 2014, Wilmington, Del.

95. Sheila Wissner, "Bredesen Cool to Special Session Idea," *Tennessean*, August 9,

2005, B1; Claudia Pinto, "TennCare Advocates Rally for Reversal of Cuts," *Tennessean*, August 28, 2005, B1; Bonna de la Cruz, "Lawmakers Request TennCare Session," *Tennessean*, August 6, 20005, B1.

96. Andy Sher, "Preschool Hinges on TennCare," *Chattanooga Times Free Press*, November 19, 2004, B1.

97. Phil Bredesen to Lt. Governor John S. Wilder and Jimmy Naifeh, March 9, 2005, TennCare Saves Lives Coalition Files, in author's possession.

98. Matt Gouras, "House Meets over Holiday after Budget Fight Erupts," Associated Press State and Local Wire, May 28, 2005.

99. Trent Seibert, "$26B Budget a Victory for Bredesen," *Tennessean*, May 29, 2005, A12.

100. Stefanie Cousins, "Governor's Office of Children's Care Coordination: A Clear History, an Uncertain Future" (MA thesis, University of North Carolina, Chapel Hill, 2009), 7–10.

101. Thomas Byrne Edsall and Mary Edsall, *Chain Reaction: The Impact of Race, Rights, and Taxes on American Politics* (New York: Norton, 1991); Ronald Walters, *White Nationalism, Black Interests: Conservative Public Policy and the Black Community* (Detroit, Mich.: Wayne State University Press, 2003).

102. McKinsey and Company, "Achieving a Critical Mission in Difficult Times—TennCare's Financial Viability."

103. Matthew Gabel and Kenneth Scheve, "Estimating the Effect of Elite Communication on [the] Public Using Instrumental Variables," *American Journal of Political Science* 51, no. 4 (2007): 1013.

104. We give specific information about the variables used in our analyses in appendix 6.2.

105. "TennCare Once Was Model for Public Health Care, but Now Is Cautionary Tale," *AIDS Alert* 21, no. 1 (2006): 4–5.

106. Ibid.

107. Amy Ritchart, "TennCare Cuts, Gas Costs Send More to Food Banks," *Leaf Chronicle*, February 25, 2006.

108. Duren Cheek, "Pastor: Cuts Would Hurt Black Enrollees," *Tennessean*, September 9, 2004, B3.

109. African Americans comprised 7.5 percent of the respondents in the spring 2006 MTSU poll. Whites made up approximately 67 percent of the sample.

110. Michael O'Grady and Gooloo Wunderlich, eds., *Medical Care Economic Risk: Measuring Financial Vulnerability from Spending on Medical Care* (Washington, D.C.: National Research Council and Institute of Medicine, 2012).

111. The index has a Cronbach's alpha of .71, which means that it is adequately reliable. See Jum Nunally, *Psychometric Theory* (New York: McGraw-Hill, 1978).

112. A chi-squared goodness-of-fit test confirms that we cannot reject the null hypothesis that the actual distribution of subjects across conditions is similar to the expected distribution ($\chi 2 = .14$, $p = .998$). In this case, 20 percent, or 120 subjects, should

Notes to Chapter Six 233

have ended up in each treatment, and the number of subjects in each condition is close to that benchmark—so close that we can rest assured that random assignment was executed properly in our field experiment.

113. We confirmed this racial group difference using a one-way analysis of variance that compared blacks' and whites' average approval levels of Bredesen's TennCare policies ($F = 31.03, p < .01$).

114. For whites: $F = .83, p = .56$; for blacks: $F = .75, p = .52$.

115. $F = 7.60, p < .01$.

116. $F = 3.76, p < .10$.

117. $F = 1.36, p = .25$.

118. For all but the two exceptions mentioned above, these differences in economic disadvantage are statistically significant at the .05 level.

119. $F = 31.03, p < .01$.

120. For whites: $F = .83, p < .56$; for blacks: $F = .75, p < .52$.

121. $F = 7.60, p < .01$.

122. $F = 1.36, p = .25$.

123. "Tenncare Enrollees and Advocates Say Tennesseans Will Die if State's Health Insurance Program Is Eliminated," *Independent Media Center*, January 13, 2005, https://indymedia.org/en/2005/01/817184.shtml. Our discussion of Bredesen as out of touch draws on the analysis in Bennett, *TennCare*.

124. Ceci Connolly, "Tennessee's Retreat on Medicaid Points to Struggle: Planned Cuts May Signal National Trend," *Washington Post*, January 18, 2005, A3; Alan Weil, "Next Steps for Tennessee: A Conversation with Governor Phil Bredesen," *Health Affairs* 26, no. 4 (2007): w456–w462.

125. "Companies in the U.S. That Still Offer Defined Benefit Pension Plans," *Pension-Retirement*, 2013, http://pensionretirement.com/companies-in-the-us-that-still-offer-defined-benefit-pension-plans.

126. William J. Wiatrowski, "The Last Private Industry Pension Plans: A Visual Essay," *Monthly Labor Review* (December 2012): 3, http://www.bls.gov/opub/mlr/2012/12/art-1full.pdf.

127. Roger Lowenstein, "The End of Pensions," *New York Times*, October 30, 2005.

128. Center for Business and Economic Research, University of Tennessee, "The State of Employer-Sponsored Health Insurance in Tennessee," May 2005, http://cber.haslam.utk.edu/pubs/covertn1.pdf, 16.

129. R. E. Hurley, "TennCare—A Failure of Politics, Not Policy: A Conversation with Gordon Bonnyman," *Health Affairs* 25, no. 3 (2006), http://content.healthaffairs.org/content/25/3/w217.full. See also Bennett, *TennCare*, 126.

130. Hurley, "TennCare—A Failure of Politics."

131. Ibid.

132. "Bredesen Reflects on TennCare Cuts," *TimesNews* (Kingsport, Tenn.), December 18, 2010, http://www.timesnews.net/News/2010/12/18/Bredesen-reflects-on-TennCare-cuts.

133. Ibid.

134. Andy Sher, "Bredesen Cites Education, Jobs as Legacy, Rues TennCare," *Times Free Press*, December 19, 2010, http://www.timesfreepress.com/news/news/story/2010/dec/19/bredesen-education-jobs-legacy/37348.

135. Julie Rovner, "Tennessee Health-Care Cuts Roil Poor Community," NPR, June 19, 2006, http://www.npr.org/templates/story/story.php?storyId=5491337; Sher, "Bredesen Cites Education, Jobs as Legacy."

136. Teresa M. Waters, "The Impact of Reducing TennCare Enrollment on Mortality Rates," Center for Health Services Research, University of Tennessee, 2010, https://tnjustice.org/wp-content/uploads/2010/12/UT-Ctr-for-Hlth-Svc.Res_.-Bulletin-3-02.pdf.

CHAPTER 7. IMMIGRATION AND THE NEW TENNESSEANS

The epigraph is from Alex Seitz-Wald, "Tennessee GOP Lawmaker Warns Undocumented Immigrants Will 'Multiply' Like 'Rats,'" *Think Progress*, November 11, 2010, http://www.thinkprogress.org/2010/11/11/tennessee-immigrants-rats.

1. Michael J. Wishnie, "Laboratories of Bigotry? Devolution of the Immigration Power, Equal Protection, and Federalism," 2001, Faculty Scholarship Series, Paper 933, http://digitalcommons.law.yale.edu/fss_papers/933; Roger C. Hartley, "Congressional Devolution of Immigration Policymaking: A Separation of Powers Critique," *Duke Journal of Constitutional Law and Public Policy* 2 (2007): 93–158, http://scholarship.law.duke.edu/djclpp/vol2/iss1/2.

2. See the full text of the Arizona immigration bill (S.B. 1070), http://www.azleg.gov/legtext/49leg/2r/bills/sb1070s.pdf.

3. Mariana van Zeller and Janell Ross, "Despite Supreme Court SB 1070 Ruling, Climate of Fear Persists in Arizona," *Huffington Post*, June 25, 2012, http://www.huffingtonpost.com/2012/06/25/supreme-court-sb-1070-ruling-arizona_n_1624708.html.

4. *Arizona Republic*, July 2010.

5. Michael Coleman, "The 'Local' Migration State: The Site-Specific Devolution of Immigration Enforcement in the U.S. South," *Law and Policy* 34 (April 2012): 159–190.

6. Lola Alapo, "Tennessee Wrestles with Immigration Problem," *Knoxville News Sentinel*, July 10, 2010, http://archive.knoxnews.com/news/local/tennessee-wrestles-with-immigration-problem-ep-408098472-358639221.html.

7. M. Augoustinos and C. J. Quinn, "Social Categorization and Attitudinal Evaluations: Illegal Immigrants, Refugees, or Asylum Seekers?," *New Review of Social Psychology* 2 (2003): 29–37; Ted Brader, Nicholas Valentino, and Elizabeth Suhay, "What Triggers Public Opposition to Immigration? Anxiety, Group Cues, and Immigration Threat," *American Journal of Political Science* 52 (2008): 959–978; Benjamin Knoll, David Redlawsk, and Howard Sanborn, "Framing Labels and Immigration Policy Attitudes in the Iowa Caucuses: Trying to Out-Tancredo Tancredo," *Political Behavior* 33, no. 3 (2011); Erin McAdams, Sarah, Sokhey, and Herbert Weisberg, "Group Labels, Group Affect and Immigration: What's in a Name?" Paper prepared for the annual meet-

ing of the Midwest Political Science Association, April 3–5, 2008, Chicago, Ill.; Maykel Verkuyten, "Immigration Discourses and Their Impact on Multiculturalism: A Discursive and Experimental Study," *British Journal of Social Psychology* 44, no. 201 (2005): 223–240.

8. CNN Newswire Staff, "Tennessee Lawmaker Calls Some Illegal Immigrants 'Rats,'" November 12, 2010, http://www.cnn.com/2010/US/11/12/tennessee.lawmaker.remark/index.html.

9. Seitz-Wald, "Tennessee GOP Lawmaker."

10. Thomas J. Espenshade, Jessica L. Baraka, and Gregory A. Huber, "Immigration Reform, Welfare Reform, and Future Patterns of U.S. Immigration," *In Defense of the Alien* 21 (1998): 26–48; Austin T. Fragomen Jr., "The Illegal Immigration Reform and Immigrant Responsibility Act of 1996," *International Migration Review* 31, no. 2 (1997): 438–460.

11. Kevin R. Johnson and Bernard Trujillo, *Immigration Law and the U.S.–Mexico Border: ¿Sí Se Puede?* (Tucson: University of Arizona Press, 2011), 242.

12. Lisa M. Martinez, "Flowers from the Same Soil: Latino Solidarity in the Wake of the 2006 Immigrant Mobilizations," *American Behavioral Scientist* 52, no. 4 (2008): 557–579.

13. Adrian D. Pantoja, Cecilia Menjívar, and Lisa Magaña, "The Spring Marches of 2006: Latinos, Immigration, and Political Mobilization in the 21st Century," *American Behavioral Scientist* 52 (December 2008): 499–506; Johnson and Trujillo, *Immigration Law and the U.S.–Mexico Border*.

14. David L. Leal et al., "Immigration and the 2006 Midterm Elections," *PS: Political Science and Politics* 41, no. 2 (2008): 309.

15. Ibid., 315.

16. Katherine Tate, *What's Going On? Political Incorporation and the Transformation of Black Public Opinion* (Washington, D.C.: Georgetown University Press, 2010), 115.

17. Marisa Abrajano and Zoltan L. Hajnal, *White Backlash: Immigration, Race, and American Politics* (Princeton, N.J.: Princeton University Press, 2015).

18. Gyung-Ho Jeong et al., "Cracks in the Opposition: Immigration as a Wedge Issue for the Reagan Coalition," *American Journal of Political Science* 55, no. 3 (2011): 511–525.

19. Zoltan Hajnal and Michael U. Rivera, "Immigration, Latinos, and White Partisan Politics: The New Democratic Defection," *American Journal of Political Science* 58, no. 4 (2014): 773–789.

20. Jeong et al. "Cracks in the Opposition," 519.

21. Julia Albarracin, *At the Core and in the Margins: Incorporation of Mexican Immigrants in Two Rural Midwestern Communities* (Lansing: Michigan State University Press, 2016), 17.

22. A. Elena Lacayo, "The Impact of 287(g) of the Immigration and Nationality Act on the Latino Community," National Council of La Raza, 2010, Issue Brief No. 21, http://publications.nclr.org/bitstream/handle/123456789/1067/287g_issuebrief_pubstore.pdf?sequence=1.

23. Letter, Neil M. Corwin (U.S. Department of Justice) to Omar Jadwat (aclu), July 22, 2005, http://www.fairus.org/DocServer/OLC_Opinion_2002.pdf.

24. Graeme Boushey and Adam Luedtke, "Immigrants across the U.S. Federal Laboratory: Explaining State-Level Innovation in Immigration Policy," *State Politics and Policy Quarterly* 11, no. 4 (2011):390–414.

25. Albarracin, *At the Core and in the Margins*, 17.

26. Johnson and Trujillo, *Immigration Law and the U.S.–Mexico Border*.

27. "NAACP Policy Handbook: Resolutions Approved by the National Board of Directors," https://www.naacp.org/wp-content/uploads/2018/07/Policy_Handbook_5_9_07-1.pdf, 189.

28. National Black Caucus of State Legislators, "2011 Ratified Policy Resolutions," https://nbcsl.org/public-policy/docs/category/39-1998-2015-ratified-policy-resolutions.html.

29. Tate, *What's Going On?*, 119–121.

30. Robert C. Smith, "African Americans and Immigration: The Economic, Political, and Strategic Implications," in *Race and Human Rights*, ed. Curtis Stokes (Lansing: Michigan State University Press, 2009).

31. Ibid., 187.

32. Dennis Chong and James N. Druckman, "Framing Theory," *Annual Review of Political Science* 10 (June 2007): 103–126.

33. For example, Nota Cate Schaeffer and Stanley Presser, "The Science of Asking Questions," *Annual Review of Sociology* 29 (2003): 65–88; Shanto Iyengar and Donald Kinder, *News That Matters: Television and American Opinion* (Chicago: University of Chicago Press, 1987); Thomas Nelson, Rosalee Clawson, and Zoe Oxley, "Media Framing of a Civil Liberties Conflict and Its Effect on Tolerance," *American Political Science Review* 91 (1997): 567–583; and Daniel Kahneman and Amos Tversky, "Prospect Theory: An Analysis of Decision under Risk," *Econometrica* 47, no. 2 (1979): 263–292.

34. Hana E. Brown, "Race, Legality, and the Social Policy Consequences of Anti-Immigration Mobilization," *American Sociological Review* 78, no. 2 (2013): 290–314.

35. Brader, Valentino, and Suhay, "What Triggers Public Opposition"; Knoll, Redlawsk, and Sanborn, "Framing Labels and Immigration Policy Attitudes"; Jennifer Merolla, S. Karthick Ramakrishnan, and Chris Haynes, "'Illegal,' 'Undocumented,' or 'Unauthorized': Equivalency Frames, Issue Frames, and Public Opinion on Immigration," *Perspectives on Politics* 11, no. 3 (2013): 789–807; Tom Head, "What Is the Proper Term: Illegal or Undocumented Immigrant?," Thought.co, June 21, 2018, http://civilliberty.about.com/od/immigrantsrights/qt/illegal_undoc.htm; Edward Sifuentes, "'Illegal versus Undocumented': When Language Defines the Debate," *San Diego Union-Tribune*, March 21, 2004, https://www.sandiegouniontribune.com/sdut-illegal-vs-undocumented-when-language-defines-the-2004mar21-story.html.

36. George Lakoff and Sam Ferguson, "The Framing of Immigration," Rockridge Institute, University of California, Berkeley, 2006, https://escholarship.org/uc/item/0j89f85g.

37. Robert L. Young, "Race, Conceptions of Crime and Justice, and Support for the Death Penalty," *Social Psychology Quarterly* 54 (1991): 67–75; Jeremy Blumenthal, "Perceptions of Crime: A Multidimensional Analysis with Implications for Law and Psychology," *McGeorge Law Review* (2007): 629–651; Ronald Weitzer, "Citizens' Perceptions of Police Misconduct: Race and Neighborhood Context," *Justice Quarterly* 16 (1999): 819–846; Ronald Weitzer and Steven Tuch, "Race, Class, and Perceptions of Discrimination by the Police," *Crime and Delinquency* 45 (1999): 494–507.

38. Jorge Ramos, *The Other Face of America: Chronicles of the Immigrants Shaping Our Future* (New York: HarperCollins, 2000); Raúl Hinojosa-Ojeda, "Raising the Floor for American Workers: The Economic Benefits of Comprehensive Immigration Reform," Center for American Progress, January 2010, https://www.americanimmigration council.org/sites/default/files/research/Hinojosa_-_Raising_the_Floor_for_American _Workers_010710.pdf.

39. Dominique Apollon et al., *Moving the Race Conversation Forward: Racial Discourse Change in Practice*, part 2 (January 2014), https://www.raceforward.org/research /reports/moving-race-conversation-forward.

40. Ibid., 10.

41. Mariuce Mangum and Ray Block Jr., "Social Identity Theory and Public Opinion towards Immigration," *Social Sciences* 7, no. 3 (2018), https://www.mdpi.com/2076 -0760/7/3/41.

42. Spring Miller, "Latino Immigrants in Tennessee: A Survey of Demographic and Social Science Research," June 2004, http://webprod.law.utk.edu/library/teachinglearn ing/permanent/LU/LUimg/TNdemograp.pdf; University of Tennessee Agricultural Extension Service, "PB1762—The Growing Hispanic Population in Tennessee—A Potential Market Opportunity for Farmers and Value-Added Entrepreneurs," June 2006, http:// trace.tennessee.edu/utk_agexmkt/24.

43. National Conference of State Legislatures, "2006 State Legislation Related to I mmigration: Enacted and Vetoed," October 31, 2006, http://www.ncsl.org/research /immigration/immigrant-policy-2006-state-legislation-related-t.aspx.

44. Katherine J. Bogle, "The Intersection of Policy and Perception: Scapegoat Narrative Theory in Middle Tennessee" (thesis, Honors College, Middle Tennessee State University, 2012).

45. Chas Sisk, "Illegal Immigrants Get Blame and Sympathy in Tennessee Poll," *Tennessean*, February 9, 2011.

46. Lacayo, "Impact of 287(g)," 8.

47. Michael Cass, "African-American Leaders Lash Out at English-Only Plan," *Tennessean*, January 10, 2009.

48. Ibid.

49. We are comfortable in our belief that the sample of respondents in the MTSU poll represented a proper cross section of adult Tennessee residents.

50. If the random assignment procedure were perfect, each version of the experimental manipulation would have received one-third of the respondents ($\frac{1}{3}(549) = 183$). How-

ever, as noted above, the subsamples for the "immigrants in general," "illegal" immigrants, and "undocumented" immigrants conditions were 156, 210, and 183, respectively. The discrepancies between the observed and expected numbers of respondents were large enough that we had to reject the null hypothesis of similar subsample sizes across the experimental conditions ($\chi 2 = 7.96$, $p = .02$).

51. There were no significant differences between experimental conditions on age ($F = .85$, $p = .42$), gender ($F = 1.55$, $p = .21$), political ideology ($F = .58$, $p = .56$), party identification ($F = 1.01$, $p = .36$), education level ($F = .29$, $p = 0.74$), or the race/ethnicity of the respondent ($F = .59$, $p = .55$).

52. In this case, the theoretically central variables of interest are race and the dichotomized versions of the experimental manipulations in which respondents who were assigned to a particular issue-framing condition received a score of 1 and all other respondents got a score of 0. We created separate variables for each manipulation and, as is common in regression analyses of experimental data, we included only two of the three dichotomous variables for the framing conditions, leaving the third ("immigrants in general") as the reference category to which all other framing results were compared.

53. Estimate = .21, $p < .05$.

54. Victoria M. Esses, Lynne M. Jackson, and Tamara L. Armstrong, "Intergroup Competition and Attitudes toward Immigrants and Immigration: An Instrumental Model of Group Conflict," *Journal of Social Issues* 54 (Winter 2010): 699–742.

55. Estimate = .71, $p < .01$. As we saw in figure 7.5, the average AIAI score for the full sample was .83 for the "immigrants in general" control group. We compared its mean to that of the "illegal" immigrant frame (average AIAI score = 1.54). Some quick math confirms that, all things being equal, moving from the control group to the "illegal" condition resulted in an increase of .71 (1.54 − .83 = .71) in respondents' anti-immigration attitudes. Again, this change in the mean AIAI score across experimental conditions is too large to be happenstance, and this finding lends some credence to our direct effects hypothesis.

56. The constant (estimate = .46, $p < .01$) gives us the average value of the dependent variable when all other independent variables are set to a value of 0. In this case, this amounts to examining the mean AIAI score of nonwhite respondents (i.e., when race = 0) who received the "immigrants in general" manipulation: if the "illegal" and "undocumented" frame conditions are set to 0, then logically speaking, the omitted reference category (the control group) is activated.

57. Estimate = .44, $p < .01$.

58. Estimate = .76, $p < .01$. Moving from the control group to the "illegal" condition produced a change in average AIAI scores of .46 + .76, or 1.22. As we saw in figure 7.5, the value of 1.22 is the mean anti-immigration score for nonwhites who were exposed to rhetoric about "illegal" immigrants.

59. The increase is from .46 to 1.09 if one adds the estimate for the constant (.46) to the "illegal" coefficient (.63).

60. $p < .05$.

61. $p > .05$.

CHAPTER 8. CONTROVERSIES AND CONFLICTS OVER SENTENCING POLICIES AND THE DEATH PENALTY

The epigraph is from Tennessee Black Caucus of State Legislators, "Criminal Justice Questions," submitted to Governor Ray Blanton after the annual legislative retreat in 1976.

1. Joel Ebert, "Black Caucus Finds Crime Bill Support," *Tennessean*, March 7, 2016, A11.
2. Michelle Alexander, *The New Jim Crow: Mass Incarceration in the Age of Colorblindness* (New York: New Press, 2012).
3. Michael McRay, "It's Time to Stop Killing: A Former Tennessee Prison Chaplain on Capital Punishment," *Red Letter Christians*, July 8, 2014, https://www.redletter christians.org/time-stop-killing-former-tennessee-prison-chaplain-capital-punishment; Barry Friedman, *Unwarranted: Policing without Permission* (New York: Farrar, Straus and Giroux, 2017).
4. Amy Ritchart, "Forum to Help Felons See Their Second Chance at Voting," *Leaf Chronicle*, August 31, 2006, A1.
5. Details about how tapd operates can be found on its website: http://out.easycounter.com/external/tennesseedeathpenalty.org.
6. The quote is from Justin Owen, the organization's president and CEO: http://www.beacontn.org/our-story.
7. For example, the Sentencing Project submitted comments to a Tennessee panel studying how the state might bring more of its citizens into the electoral process rather than excluding them through felony disenfranchisement (http://www.sentencingproject.org/publications/letter-in-support-of-felony-disenfranchisement-reform-in-tennessee). See also Molly Mulroy, "How Tennessee Laws Keep Ex-Offenders from Getting Good Jobs," MLK50, October 5, 2017, https://mlk50.com/state-licensing-restrictions-keep-convicted-tennesseans-from-obtaining-jobs-a26e28242b38.
8. W. Dale Young to Lewis Donelson, "Capsule Report: Accomplishments of the Dunn Administration for Blacks," box 92, folder 22: Blacks—Dunn Accomplishments, Governor Bryant Winfield Culberson Dunn Papers, 1971–1975, Tennessee State Library and Archives, Nashville (hereafter TSLA).
9. Charles M. Traughber to Ed Sisk (legal counsel to the governor), memorandum, Legislative Retreat—November 18–19, 1976, criminal justice questionnaire; and reports on executive clemency, November 12, 1976, both in box 138, folder 3, Governor (Leonard) Ray Blanton Papers, 1975–1979, TSLA.
10. Brian Haas, "State's Prisons Spill Over Again," *Tennessean*, February 23, 2013, 2.
11. Ibid.
12. Stacey Barchenger, "Cruel, Unusual and Unfair?," *Tennessean*, October 2, 2016, A18.
13. Gilbert Merritt, "Perhaps, New Study Will Prove Valuable," *Tennessean*, October 15, 2007.
14. Pippa Holloway, *Living in Infamy: Felon Disenfranchisement and the History of American Citizenship* (New York: Oxford University Press), 2.
15. Ibid.

16. James W. Clarke, "Without Fear or Shame: Lynching, Capital Punishment, and the Subculture of Violence in the American South," *British Journal of Political Science* 28, no. 2 (1998): 285.

17. Raymond Paternoster, *Capital Punishment in America* (New York: Lexington, 1991), 14–16.

18. David L. Raybin, "Tennessee Sentencing Practices, 1790–1999," https://www.nashvilletnlaw.com/articles/tennessee-sentencing-practices-1790-1999.

19. Ibid.

20. Stanton P. Fjeld and Roger D. Thompson, "Prison Overcrowding: The Experience in Tennessee," *American Journal of Criminal Justice* 11, no. 1 (1986): 95–102.

21. In *Grubbs v. Bradley* (1982), for example, a special master was appointed to oversee reforms in Tennessee's prisons from 1982 to 1992. https://www.clearinghouse.net/detail.php?id=952.

22. Tom Humphrey, "Tennessee Set to Begin Prison Reform," *Christian Science Monitor*, December 11, 1985, https://www.csmonitor.com/1985/1211/atenn.html.

23. Lauren-Brooke Eisen, *Inside Private Prisons: An American Dilemma in the Age of Mass Incarceration* (New York: Columbia University Press, 2018), 234–235.

24. Richard S. Frase, "Sentencing Guidelines in the States: Lessons for State and Federal Reformers," *Federal Sentencing Reporter* 10, no. 1 (1997): 46–50.

25. Haas, "State's Prisons Spill Over Again," A2.

26. Quoted in Lisa Stansky, "Breaking Up Prison Gridlock: The Federal Sentencing Commission Is Looking to the States for Reform Guidance Even as Their Policies Are Being Bent by Political and Fiscal Pressures," *ABA Journal* 82, no. 5 (1996): 70–75.

27. Michael Tonry, "Sentencing in America, 1975–2025," *Crime and Justice* 42, no. 1 (2013): 141–198.

28. Haas, "State's Prisons Spill Over Again."

29. Lee Harris, "Drug-Free School Zones Law Needs Review," *Times Free Press*, August 8, 2016, http://www.timesfreepress.com/news/opinion/times-commentary/story/2016/aug/08/harris-drug-free-school-zones-law-needs-revie/380046.

30. These data were compiled by Senator Lee Harris (D-Memphis).

31. Jon Wool and Don Stemen, "Aggravated Sentencing: *Blakely v. Washington*: Practical Implications for State Sentencing Systems," *Federal Sentencing Reporter* 17, no. 1 (2004): 60–61.

32. David Cole, "What's Criminology Got to Do," *Stanford Law Review* 48, no. 6 (1996): 1605–1606.

33. Lee S. Greene, *Lead Me On: Frank Goad Clement and Tennessee Politics* (Knoxville: University of Tennessee Press, 1982), 170.

34. Letter to the governor, March 5, 1965, box 23, folder 12: Capital Punishment—Against the Repeal, February–March 1965, Frank Goad Clement Papers 1963–1967, TSLA.

35. "Where Was the Governor's Courage?," *Tennessean*, March 11, 1965, 14.

36. Septima Clark (supervisor of teacher training for the Citizenship Education Pro-

gram of the SCLC), letter to the governor, April 13, 1965, box 24, folder 8: Capital Punishment—For the Repeal, April–June 1965, Frank Goad Clement Papers, 1963–1967, TSLA.

37. Jay Warner, *Just Walkin' in the Rain* (Los Angeles, Calif.: Renaissance Books, 2001), 139.

38. Governor Frank G. Clement, "Address of Frank G. Clement to the 83rd General Assembly of Tennessee," January 22, 1963, box 78, folder 2, Frank Goad Clement Papers, 1920–1967, TSLA.

39. Governor Frank G. Clement, "Address of Frank G. Clement to the 84th General Assembly of Tennessee," March 17, 1965, box 81, folder 10, Frank Goad Clement Papers, 1920–1967, TSLA.

40. Bill Kovach and Larry Daughtrey, "House Rejects Death Bill," *Tennessean*, March 11, 1965, 2.

41. John G. Morgan, Comptroller of the Treasury, State of Tennessee, "Tennessee's Death Penalty: Costs and Consequences," July 2004, https://deathpenaltyinfo.org/documents/deathpenalty.pdf.

42. Tennessee Department of Correction, "Capital Punishment Chronology," https://www.tn.gov/content/dam/tn/correction/documents/chronology.pdf.

43. Bradley A. MacLean and H. E. Miller Jr., "Tennessee's Death Penalty Lottery," *Tennessee Journal of Law and Policy* 13, no. 1 (2018): 84–256. See also Barchenger, "Cruel, Unusual and Unfair?," A18; David Reutter, "Tennessee's Death Penalty on Hold," *Prison Legal News*, December 22, 2017, https://www.prisonlegalnews.org/news/2017/dec/22/tennessees-death-penalty-hold.

44. Amy L. Sayward and Margaret Vandiver, eds., *Tennessee's New Abolitionists: The Fight to End the Death Penalty in the Volunteer State* (Knoxville: University of Tennessee Press, 2010).

45. Tennessee General Assembly, Public Chapter No. 549 (2007), https://publications.tnsosfiles.com/acts/105/pub/pc0549.pdf.

46. American Bar Association, "Evaluating Fairness and Accuracy in State Death Penalty Systems: The Tennessee Death Penalty Assessment Report," March 2007, https://www.americanbar.org/content/dam/aba/migrated/moratorium/assessmentproject/tennessee/finalreport.authcheckdam.pdf.

47. Scot Wortley, John Hagan, and Ross Macmillan, "Just Des(s)erts? The Racial Polarization of Perceptions of Criminal Injustice," *Law and Society Review* 31, no. 4 (1997): 637–676.

48. Jon Hurwitz and Mark Peffley, "Explaining the Great Racial Divide: Perceptions of Fairness in the U.S. Criminal Justice System," *Journal of Politics* 67, no. 3 (2005): 762–783; James L. Gibson and Michael J. Nelson, *Black and Blue: African Americans and Legal Legitimacy* (New York: Oxford University Press, 2018).

49. Barbara A. Patrick et al., "Mass-Elite Linkages and Partisan Change in the South," in *Southern Political Party Activists: Patterns of Conflict and Change*, ed. John A. Clark and Charles L. Prysby (Lexington: University Press of Kentucky, 2004), 115.

CONCLUSION

The epigraph is from Jackson Baker, "A Man for All Seasons," *Memphis: The City Magazine*, July 1, 2012, http://memphismagazine.com/features/a-man-for-all-seasons.

1. Michael Nelson, "Tennessee: Once a Bluish State, Now a Reddish One," *Tennessee Historical Quarterly* 65, no. 2 (2006): 162–183.
2. Michael Warren, "Can Phil Bredesen Pull Off the Upset in Tennessee?," *Weekly Standard*, October 19, 2018, https://www.weeklystandard.com/michael-warren/tennessee-senate-race-can-phil-bredesen-upset-marsha-blackburn.
3. CNN, "Exit Polls," https://www.cnn.com/election/2018/exit-polls/tennessee/senate.
4. V. O. Key Jr., *Southern Politics in State and Nation* (1949; repr., Knoxville: University of Tennessee Press, 1984).
5. Byron E. Shafer and Richard Johnston, *The End of Southern Exceptionalism: Class, Race, and Partisan Change in the Postwar South* (Cambridge, Mass.: Harvard University Press, 2006), 8–9; Jeffrey Stonecash and Mark D. Brewer, "Class, Race Issues and Political Change in the South," *Political Behavior* 23, no. 2 (2001): 131–156.
6. Najja Parker, "Who Is Tarana Burke? Meet the Woman Who Started the MeToo Movement a Decade Ago," AJC News, December 6, 2017, https://www.ajc.com/news/world/who-tarana-burke-meet-the-woman-who-started-the-too-movement-decade-ago/i8NEiuFHKaIvBh9ucukidK.
7. Our book has been informed by important contemporary texts, such as Melynda J. Price's *At the Cross: Race, Religion, and Citizenship in the Politics of the Death Penalty* (New York: Oxford University Press, 2015); Ravi K. Perry and D. LaRouth Perry's *The Little Rock Crisis: What Desegregation Politics Says about Us* (New York: Palgrave Macmillan, 2015); and Sharon D. Wright's *Race, Power, and Political Emergence in Memphis* (New York: Garland, 2000).

INDEX

Abramowitz, Alan, 19, 126
Access MedPlus (insurance company), 131
accommodationist philosophy, 42, 43
activism/activists: anti-death penalty, 189; black political, 38, 139; civic, 3–4; conservative, 7, 80; progressive, 16, 28–29; racial justice, 169, 178. *See also* civil rights movement; TennCare Saves Lives Coalition
African Americans. *See* blacks
Alabama, income tax hikes in, 107–108
Alapo, Lola, 164
Alexander, Lamar, 86–87, 136, 184–185
Alexander, Michelle, 180
animus, racial, 7, 17, 21–23, 66, 164, 169. *See also* racial polarization
Appleby, Julie, 125
Armstrong, Joe, 94, 95, 98, 111
Austin, Sharon D. Wright, 7, 60, 87, 91

Badger, Tony, 69
Bain, George C., 36
Baker v. Carr (1962), 57, 59, 69, 86. *See also* Supreme Court (U.S.), decisions
Baldassari, Delia, 8
Balz, Dan, 15
Banner, Maye Guyer, 56
Bass, Ross, 51
Bearman, Peter, 8
Beasley, Tom, 185
Bell, Montgomery, 36
bipartisanship, 20, 23–24. *See also* coalitions: bipartisan
Black, Diane, 12
Blackburn, Marsha, 197
Black Community Conference, 55
black lawmakers, 80–101; influence of, 39, 57–59, 81, 86–89, 94; sponsorship networks of, 9, 82–86, 89–99. *See also* Tennessee Black Caucus of State Legislators

black politics, 1, 4, 32–62; antebellum, 34–38; civil rights movement and, 46–55, 61–62; Ford dynasty, 59–61; instability of, 48–49; institutionalization of, 55–57, 62; legislative, 57–59, 81, 82, 84–86, 98, 181; partisan/political realignment and, 44–46, 87, 95, 99; political bounds thesis, 82–86, 98–99; trajectory of, 33–34. *See also* Jim Crow era; racial equalitarianism/equity; racial politics; Reconstruction

blacks, 27, 29, 42, 66, 172, 201n2, 207n2; in antebellum Tennessee, 34–38; criminal justice reform views, 192, 193; disproportionate number receiving death sentences, 184, 186, 189; free, 36–38; immigration reform views, 167–168; impact of TennCare cuts on, 127–129, 139, 140–143, 148–149, 151–152, 156; loss of political power, 2, 3, 18–19, 78, 89, 95, 182, 196–198; political comity with whites, 27, 28, 29; political experiences of, 1–2, 26, 30–31, 34, 39–40, 214n127; racial polarization and, 4, 20, 21–23, 50–51, 195; in Republican Party, 26, 31, 38–42, 44, 45

Blake, Ken, 202n5
Blakett, Richard, 36
Blanton, Ray, 109
Blaze, Henry, 142
Blue Dog Coalition, 25, 60
Bogle, Katherine J., 170
Bommer, Minnie, 87
Bonnyman, Gordon, 154, 155
Booker, Robert, 58
Bowden, J. Willard, 51, 56

Bowers, Kathryn, 80, 90, 111, 133; protesting TennCare reforms, 133, 135, 143
Bredesen, Phil: approval rating for, 149–156, 233n113; gubernatorial election, 70, 74, 75, 77, 111; suspension of death penalty, 190, 191, 192; TennCare reform measures, 7, 125–126, 127, 131–145, 145–153
Bredesen-Blackburn U.S. Senate race, 196–197
Broke, J. Michael, 56
Browder, Glen, 26–27
Brown, Dorothy, 58–59
Brown, Hana, 168
Brown, Theodore, Jr., 37
Brown, Tommie, 80
Brownlow, William, 38, 39
Bryson, Jim, 143
budget issues, 107–108, 128, 131
Burchett, Tim, 98
Burke, Tarana, 198
Bush, George W., 65, 163, 166
Butler, John Washington, Jr., 56

California Proposition 187, 165, 167
capability measures, 91–92, 94, 97, 98
capital punishment. *See* death penalty
Carr, Benjamin, 44
Cebrun, Anthony, 131
Chattanooga/Hamilton County, 67–68, 84–85; black candidates / elected officials, 39, 41, 58
Children's Defense Fund, 134, 139
Chong, Dennis, 168
Christensen, Donna, 139
Church, Robert Reed, Jr., 44, 45, 61
Civic Ideals (Rogers Smith), 33–34
civil rights movement, 30, 38, 40; democratizing impact of, 69–70; immigration reform and, 165, 166, 167–168; legislation regarding, 50–51, 54, 56, 62; modern era of, 5–6, 28, 46–55, 61–62; in 1960s, 26–27, 49, 186–187; popular mobilization and, 51–55; rollback of policies, 23, 25; white backlash against, 41, 50, 67, 68. *See also* justice, racial; racial equalitarianism/equity
Clabough, Bill, 98
Clark, Septima, 187
class, 4, 31, 115; division over TennCare reforms by, 140, 146–148, 156; nexus with race and geography, 21–23, 67–68, 198; partisan realignment and, 22, 72. *See also* hierarchy, racial
Clement, Frank: attempts to abolish death penalty, 49–50, 186–189; desegregation by, 5–6, 51
Clinton, Bill: attack on welfare, 26; county voting patterns for, 62, 74, 75, 77; health-care debate and, 8, 128
coalitions, 61, 75, 91; bipartisan, 15, 78, 91, 95, 143–144, 199; biracial, 27, 29, 69, 84–85; Blue Dog Coalition, 25, 60; building, 9, 94, 167, 188; cross-racial, 68, 99; Democratic Leadership Council, 25, 60, 126; electoral, 21–22, 107; multiracial, 2, 33, 45, 195; political, 27, 67–68, 168; Rainbow Coalition, 30. *See also* TennCare Saves Lives Coalition; Tennessee Black Caucus of State Legislators
coattails effect, 74–75, 77
coding, racial, 22, 28
Cohen, Stephen, 98
colonization movement, 35–36
comity, political, 95, 110, 127; black-white, 27, 28, 29; polarization and, 107, 141–147
Community Census and Redistricting Institute, 1
Compromise of 1877, 40, 209n30. *See also* Reconstruction
Confederates, former, 32, 38, 39, 40, 48, 209n32
Connolly, Ceci, 125
conservatives/conservatism, 20, 23–24, 61, 77, 168; activist, 7, 80; in legislatures, 85, 89; racial, 50, 65, 76, 166–167; Redeemers, 38, 48, 209n30; in Republican Party, 66–68, 143; in Tennessee, 94, 196–197, 199, 217n9. *See also* Democratic Party / Democrats: conservatives in; Republican Party / Republicans
Constitution, U.S., amendments, 38, 39, 43, 51, 59, 196
Cooper, Barbara, 80, 81, 83
Cooper, Prentice, 46–47, 48
Corker-Ford U.S. Senate race, 1, 9, 15–18, 28, 61, 170–171, 197
Corrections Corporation of America (CoreCivic), 185
cosponsorship/sponsorship networks, 81, 82–86, 89–99
counties, voting patterns in, 9, 72–76, 79. *See also specific counties*

covariation method, 4–6
criminal justice reform, 180–193; race and, 183–186; racial polarization over, 12, 181, 182–183, 193. *See also* death penalty; sentencing policies
cross pressures, 22–23
Crump, Edward Hull, political machine, 44, 45, 48–49, 55
Crutcher, W. T., 58
Crutchfield, Ward, 90, 98

death penalty, 12, 50, 182, 186–193. *See also* criminal justice reform
DeBerry, Lois, 2, 59, 88, 90, 95, 98
Democratic Leadership Council, 25, 60, 126
Democratic Party / Democrats, 21, 25, 38; blacks in, 26, 45–46, 82–83; conservatives in, 2, 15–16, 39, 40–41, 62, 78, 90; death penalty views, 191, 193; fragmentation of, 66, 67, 69–70, 70–76, 77; Latinos in, 166; lose majority in Tennessee General Assembly, 2–3, 25, 78, 85, 89, 127, 196, 197–198; New Deal, 25, 45–46, 68; progressive wing of, 1, 168; whites in, 22, 27–28, 31, 69
desegregation, 5–6, 49–50, 51, 58, 186, 188
DesJarlais, Scott, 12
devolution, 87, 123, 128; of federal power to state governments, 18, 182–183, 184; of immigration policies, 163, 164, 166–167, 173, 179; polarization and, 106, 107; racial polarization and, 23–25, 119
Dixon, Roscoe, 80, 89, 90, 97, 98; tax reform proposals, 110, 111, 133
Doar, John, 53–54
dog whistle politics, 28–29. *See also* politics
Donelson, Lewis, 195, 196
Dowe, Pearl Ford, 7
Downs, Anthony, 19
Drew, Charles "Pete," 87
Druckman, James, 168
Dunn, Winfield, 109, 181
Dyer, Leonidas, 45
dynamic network analysis (DNA), 9, 72, 221–222n53

Eaton, John and Lucien, 39
ecological inference (EI) analysis, 9, 72, 218n24, 220n26

Economic Disadvantage Index, 150–152, 156, 232n111
Economic Theory of Democracy, An (Downs), 19
Edelman, Marian Wright, 139
education, raising taxes to fund, 11, 51, 106, 108, 112–113, 115
Edwards, James, 187
Elazar, Daniel, 59
elections: Bredesen-Blackburn U.S. Senate race, 196–197; county, 9, 72–76, 79; U.S., 19–20. *See also* Corker-Ford U.S. Senate race
electoral capture concept, 9, 25–30, 127
elites, 21, 68, 127; black, 28, 43–44, 201n2; issue framing by, 168, 169, 178–179; party, 8, 18, 19–20, 25; political, 3, 9, 11, 28, 30–31, 36, 164–165, 171. *See also* hierarchy, racial
Ellis, Christopher, 106–107
Engel, Jonathan, 129
ethnic congruence model, 108
Evans, John, 20

Families USA, 135
Faricy, Christopher, 106–107
Farmer, Don, 65, 66, 78
Fayette County, black voting rights struggle in, 53–54
federalism, 23–25, 27, 59; New Federalism, 23, 25, 184
Fifteenth Amendment, U.S. Constitution, 38, 39
Ford, Harold, Jr., 60–61, 203n7; county voting patterns for, 74–75, 77. *See also* Corker-Ford U.S. Senate race
Ford, Harold, Sr., 17, 59–60
Ford, John, 16, 57, 60, 66, 90, 97, 98; tax reform proposals, 105, 106, 110, 111, 133
Ford, Lloyd, Sr., 37–38
Ford family, political dynasty of, 59–61
Fording, Richard, 24
Forman, James, 53
Forrest, Nathan Bedford, 39
Fourteenth Amendment, U.S. Constitution, 38, 51, 196
Fowler, James, 81
Franklin, Sekou, work to rescue TennCare, 11, 226–227n12
Freedmen's Bureau, U.S., 39
Freeman, Mary, 221n50

Frymer, Paul: electoral capture concept, 9, 127; on zero-sum game of party politics, 26, 27–28

Gabel, Matthew, 145
Gadson, Sandra, 139
Gailor, Frank, 48
Gentry, Howard, 57
geography: nexus with race and class, 21–23, 67–68, 198; politics and, 69, 84–85; racial polarization and, 4, 66; voter distribution by, 9, 24, 31, 72–79. *See also specific cities, counties, and states*
George, Walter F., 212n93
Georgia, racial politics in, 6–7
Gibson, James, 193
Gilmore, Brenda, 83–84, 172
Glaser, James, 69
Goetz, David, 132, 136
Goldwater, Barry, 30
Gore, Albert J., Jr., 65; county voting patterns for, 72, 75, 77, 79
Gore, Albert J., Sr., 5–6, 49, 50, 68
Governor's Advisory Committee on Equal Employment Opportunity, 86–87
Green, Nathan, 37–38
Guess, Francis, 86

Hacker, Andrew, 123
Hackett, Dick, 57
Hale, John Henry, 44
Haney-Lopez, Ian, 28–29
Hardeman County, black candidates / elected officials, 57
Harper, Thelma, 59, 89, 97, 98, 111, 133
Harris, Solomon Parker, 41
Harwell, Beth, 133
Hawkesworth, Mary, 81
Haynie, Kerry L., 82, 89
Haywood County, black voting rights struggle in, 53–54
Head, Timmy, 110, 111
Henderson, Ash-Lee Woodard, 84
Henderson, Michael, 127
Hensley, Joey, 143
Herbert, Bob, 125
Herenton, Willie, 57, 132
Hero, Rodney, 4, 68

hierarchy, racial, 2, 61; assessing, 34, 46; class-based, 22, 43; resistance to, 33, 56. *See also* class; elites
Higgs, Otis, 57
Highlander Folk School (Highlander Research and Education Center, Monteagle), 52, 53, 84, 213n107
Hilleary, Van, 74, 111
Hillygus, D. Sunshine, 127
Hindman, Douglas Banks, 126
Holloway, Pippa, 183–184
Honey, Michael, 53
Hooks, Benjamin, 49, 56
Hooper, Ben, 44
Hoover, Herbert, 45
Horton, Henry, 108
Howington, Arthur, 37
Howse, Hilary Ewing, 41
Huber, Gregory, 28–29
Hurwitz, John, 193
Hyman, Herbert, 114

immigration, 163–179; Anti-Immigration Attitudes Index (AIAI), 174–178, 179, 238nn55–56, 238n58; devolution of policies regarding, 163, 164, 166–167, 173; issue framing on, 164, 165, 168–169, 172–179, 237–238n50, 238nn55–56; laws regarding, 163–164, 165, 166–167, 171, 172; polarization over, 10, 78–79, 164, 165–168; politics of, 164, 165–172, 178–179; progressive reform proposals, 187–188; racial polarization over, 11–12, 164, 170, 171, 172–179
income tax, state: conservative views on, 117, 124; debate over, 105–106, 108–112; racial polarization over, 11, 80, 107–108, 112–122, 224n29, 225n46; Sundquist's proposal for, 7, 80, 105, 107, 109–110. *See also* tax and spending policies
Independent Workers Association, 52
industrialization, 49, 57, 72, 86
influence districts, 92, 98, 99
issue framing, on immigration. *See* immigration: issue framing on

Jackson, Doug, 133
James, Robert E., 58
Jeong, Gyung-Ho, 166
Jim Crow era, 31, 33, 51–52, 78, 180, 186. *See*

also lynchings; racism/racists; segregation/segregationists
Jindal, Piyush "Bobby," 7, 24
Johnson, Lyndon, 49, 129
Johnston, Richard, 67, 198
Jones, Justin, 84
Jones, T. O., 52
Jones, Ulysses, 90
justice, racial, 2, 26–28, 30–31, 169, 178, 197. *See also* civil rights movement; racial equalitarianism/equity

Kavanaugh, Brett, 198
Keeble, Sampson, 40
Kefauver, Estes, 49, 51, 68
Kernell, Mike, 98
Kerry, John, 65, 72, 75, 76, 79
Key, V. O., Jr., 21; *Southern Politics*, 66–67, 198
King, Gary, 218n24
King, Martin Luther, Jr., 52, 53
King-Meadows, Tyson, 85
Kloos, Karina, 29–30
Knoxville / Knox County, 58, 85, 94; black candidates / elected officials, 39–40, 56
Knuckey, Jonathan, 20
Ku Klux Klan, 30, 39, 196. *See also* white supremacists / white supremacy
Kuykendall, Dan, 60
Kyle, John, 98

Lafayette, Bernard, 52
Langsdon, Philip R., 87
Langster, Edith, 111
Lapinski, John, 28–29
Laska, Lewis, 109
Latinos, 165, 167, 170, 177, 179; political power of, 163–164, 166; racial profiling of, 163, 171
Lawson, James, 52
Legislative Political Network Profile (LPNP), 9
Levin, Nell, 139
Lewis, Barbour, 39
Liberia, 35, 36
Lieberman, Trudy, 138
Lincoln League, 44–45
Loeb, Henry, 53
Long, Huey, 20
Looby, Z. Alexander, 56
Love, Harold, 56

Lovett, Bobby, 44, 45
Lublin, David, 70
lynchings, 46, 184, 187; crusades against, 40, 43, 45, 61. *See also* Ku Klux Klan; terrorism, racial; white supremacists / white supremacy

MacLean, Bradley A., 189
Making of Black Revolutionaries, The (Forman), 53
Malone, Eva, 56
managed-care programs, 129–130, 132–133. *See also* Medicaid; TennCare/Medicaid program
Marrero, Beverly, 98
Mason, Lilliana, 20
Maupin, John, Jr., 138
McAdam, Doug, 29–30
McCain, John, 20
McCarthy, Joseph, 20
McElwee, Samuel, 32, 33, 39; anti-lynching campaign, 40, 61
McKinsey Report, 131–132, 145, 228n39
McWherter, Ned, 88; introduces TennCare, 127, 128, 130
media, 8, 164, 169
Medicaid, 124, 126–127, 128, 129, 148–149. *See also* TennCare/Medicaid program
medical necessity, TennCare's definition of, 133–134
Memphis/Shelby County, 141, 221n50; black candidates / elected officials, 49, 56, 57, 59, 84; corruption scandals in, 1, 17, 90; locus of black political power in, 46, 214n127; political machines in, 39, 67–68; race riot in 1866, 32–33; sanitation workers' strike of 1967–1968, 10, 52–53. *See also* Crump, Edward Hull, political machine
Mendelberg, Tali, 22, 28–29
Middle Tennessee State University (MTSU) poll, 8, 202n25, 232n109; on criminal justice reform, 182; on death penalty attitudes, 189–192; on income taxes, 11; on TennCare reforms, 126, 149, 159
Miller, H. E., 189
Mississippi Freedom Democratic Party (MFDP), 30
Mitchell, Arthur, 47
Mitchell, Edwin, 55

moderates: black, 42, 43; white, 17, 20, 50, 67
Montgomery, Dwight, 142
multiple regression quadratic assignment procedure (MRQAP), 73
Murfreesboro, 12, 56. See also Middle Tennessee State University (MTSU) poll
Myers, Carol, 124–125

Naifeh, James "Jimmy" (legislator), 2, 110, 111, 143
Napier, James Carroll, 42, 43
Nashville Christian Leadership Conference, 52
Nashville/Davidson County: black candidates / elected officials, 40, 41, 42, 56, 57; boycott of 1905, 42, 56, 61; English-only referendum, 172; political machine in, 67–68; 287(g) program in, 164, 166–167, 171
National Association of Colored Women, 43
National Equal Rights League, 33
National Medical Association, 139
nativism/nativists, 166, 168
Nelson, Michael, 193
New Deal programs, 25, 45–46, 68
New Federalism, 23, 25, 184
New Jim Crow, The (M. Alexander), 180. See also Jim Crow era
Nineteenth Amendment, U.S. Constitution, 43
Nixon, John, 138
Nixon, Richard, 23, 25, 30, 184
Nunnally, Shayla C., 76

Obama, Barack, 65, 66, 76, 78; county voting patterns for, 72, 75, 77; legislative initiatives, 8, 23–24
O'Grady, Michael, 150
Operation Tennessee Waltz (bribery scandal), 1, 16–17, 90

Palin, Sarah, 20
Parks, Rosa, 52
partisanship, 164, 168, 186, 198; bipartisanship, 20, 23–24; partisan politics, 5, 82. See also realignment, partisan/political
Patterson, John O., 57, 58, 60
Patton, James W., 35
Peffley, Mark, 193
Perry County, unemployment rate in, 68

Pew Research Center for the People and the Press study of political polarization, 5
polarization, 19, 192, 198; over budget issues, 107–108; over immigration, 10, 78–79, 164, 165–168; partisan/political realignment and, 21–23, 26, 89, 164; political, 2–5, 12, 27, 28, 33, 197, 198; surplus politics and, 68–72; over TennCare reforms, 11, 126–128, 140, 144, 145–149, 156; in Tennessee, 3–4, 7, 33, 197; use of term, 8, 18. See also racial polarization
political bounds thesis, 82–86
politics, 16, 34, 52, 56, 115, 186, 189; coalition, 27, 67–68, 168; dog whistle, 28–29; of electoral capture, 9, 25–30, 127; geography and, 69, 84–85; immigration, 164, 165–172, 178–179; machine, 44, 45, 48, 49, 55; New Deal-style, 25, 45–46, 68; partisan, 5, 82; party, 21, 45; polarization in, 2–5, 12, 27, 28, 33, 197, 198; political bounds thesis, 82–86; segregation in, 21, 41, 45, 50, 69; southern, 6, 7, 21, 30, 69, 199; stealth reconstruction model of, 26–27; surplus politics concept, 10, 66, 68–72; in Tennessee, 4–8, 15, 31, 45, 199; zero-sum game of, 20, 26. See also black politics; comity, political; polarization: political; racial politics; realignment, partisan/political
Pollack, Ron, 135
poll taxes, 47–48, 49, 209n39. See also tax and spending policies
pragmatism, 15, 62, 78
Pritchett, Laurie, 6
privileges, tax on. See income tax, state
Progressive Era, 41–44
progressives/progressivism, 25, 27, 45, 60, 127, 141; activist, 28–29; racial, 95, 99

race, 24, 76, 85; criminal justice reform and, 183–186; death penalty views and, 186, 187, 190, 193; division over TennCare reforms by, 148–149, 150–153, 156; electoral capture and, 25–30; nexus with class and geography, 21–23, 67–68, 198; partisan realignment and, 21–23, 72; tax reform and, 107–108, 225n46
racial bounds thesis, 82–86, 98–99
racial equalitarianism/equity, 2, 196; agenda of, 7, 107, 123, 127, 198, 199; barriers to, 18–19; policies of, 25–26, 29, 31, 42. See also civil rights movement; justice, racial

racial polarization, 8, 15–31, 65–79, 156; antidote to, 29–30; black political influence related to, 195, 198; over criminal justice reform, 12, 181, 182–183, 193; over death penalty, 182, 183, 186–193; devolution's effects on, 23–25, 119; electoral capture politics and, 25–30; geography and, 4, 66; over immigration, 11–12, 164, 170, 171, 172–179; over income tax, 11, 80, 106, 107, 224n29, 225n46; increases in, 26, 90, 196; issue framing causing, 172–179; loss of black power due to, 18–19; partisan/political realignment and, 10, 66, 78–80; over sentencing policy, 182–186; in South, 66–68, 69; surplus politics and, 68–72; in Tennessee, 9, 61, 82–83, 90, 123; theories of, 19–20. *See also* animus, racial; polarization

racial politics, 22, 66, 88; equalitarian, 25–26; in Georgia, 6–7; polarization in, 4, 30–31, 69; in South, 1–2, 6, 69, 76, 85, 183–186; of tax and spending policies, 105–123; of TennCare reform, 127, 156; in Tennessee, 6, 33, 78; inside Tennessee General Assembly, 82–83. *See also* black lawmakers; black politics; politics

racial priming, 17–18, 22, 28–29

racism/racists, 7, 28, 29, 42, 44. *See also* segregation/segregationists; white supremacists / white supremacy

Rainbow Coalition, 30

Randolph, A. Philip, 45

Raybin, David, 185

Reagan, Ronald, 30, 128; approach to federalism, 23, 25, 27; welfare cuts by, 144–145

realignment, partisan/political, 30, 65–79, 81, 166; black politics and, 44–46, 87, 95, 99; electoral, 25, 74; factors contributing to, 3, 18, 75, 78–79; polarization's impact on, 21–23, 26, 89, 164; racial polarization and, 10, 66, 78–80; in South, 66–68; surplus politics and, 68–72; in Tennessee, 1, 31, 69. *See also* Tennessee General Assembly: partisan/political realignment in

reapportionment, legislative. *See* redistricting, legislative

Reconstruction, 38–44, 66, 72, 207n2; disenfranchising laws passed during, 183–184, 209n32

Redeemers, the, 38, 48, 209n30. *See also* conservatives/conservatism

redistricting, legislative, 1, 57, 59–60, 69, 86–88

Reed, Adolph, Jr., 28

Reinke, Jason, 202n25

Republican Party / Republicans, 15, 30, 45, 67, 94, 166, 225n46; ascent in South, 21, 25, 50, 65–66, 70–72, 77; blacks in, 26, 31, 38–42, 44, 45; conservatives in, 66–68, 143; death penalty views, 191, 192, 193; racial polarization in, 69; supermajority in Tennessee General Assembly, 1, 3, 62, 66, 78, 81, 85, 89, 182, 196–198; whites in, 22, 73–74

Riley, Bob, 107–108

Robinson, Clarence, 45, 58

Robinson, Kenneth, 141, 142, 148

Rocca, Michael S., 82

Rochelle, Robert, 110, 111

Romney, Mitt, 65

Roosevelt, Franklin D., 45–46

Ross, Janell, 163

Rove, Karl, 166

Rowe, Gary, 90

safety-net programs, 125, 126, 142, 143–144, 145–152, 156

sales taxes, state, 89, 109, 111; lowering, 11, 110, 112–113, 115, 123. *See also* tax and spending policies

Sanchez, Gabriel, 82

Sanders, Ed, 111

Scales, Robert, 56

Schaller, Thomas F., 85

Scheve, Kenneth, 145

Schram, Sanford, 24

Sears, David, 21, 115

segregation/segregationists, 22, 67; abolition of de jure, 2, 56; attack on black suffrage rights, 1, 6, 46–48; polarization and, 107–108; in politics, 21, 41, 45, 50, 69; of public accommodations, 40, 42, 52. *See also* Jim Crow era; lynchings; racism/racists; white supremacists / white supremacy

Seigenthaler, John, 187

Seltzer, Richard, 106

Sen, Rinku, 169

Sensenbrenner, Jim, 165

sentencing policies, 12, 179, 181, 182–186, 189, 193

Shafer, Byron E., 67, 198

Shaw, Edward, 39, 40
Shaw, Johnny, 87, 139
Shaw, Theodore, 134–135, 139
Sheatsley, Paul, 114
Shelbyville, black elected officials, 57
Shuttlesworth, Fred L., 54
single case study method, 6–7
Singletary, Victor, 139
slavery/slaves, 34–38, 208n8. *See also* Jim Crow era; Reconstruction
Smith, Al, 45
Smith, Howard, 212n93
Smith, James, 54
Smith, Robert C., 2, 56, 106, 167–168
Smith, Rogers, 33–34
Sontany, Janis, 98
Soss, Joe, 24
South, the: complexity of, 4–6, 59; polarization in, 66–68, 198; racial politics in, 1–2, 6, 69, 76, 85, 183–186
Southern Christian Leadership Conference (SCLC), 139, 142, 187
Southern Manifesto, 49, 212n93
Southern Politics (Key), 66–67, 198
Spencer, Theodore L., 49
sponsorship networks, 81, 82–86, 89–99
Stanberry, Artemesia, 26–27
Starling, A. J., 70
stealth reconstruction model, 26–27
Stonecash, Jeffrey, 4–5
Strolovitch, Dara, 28
Student Nonviolent Coordinating Committee (SNCC), 52
subsponsorship/sponsorship, 81, 82–86, 89–99
Sugarman, Russell, 49, 58
Sundquist, Donald: state income tax proposals, 7, 80, 105, 107, 109–110; TennCare program and, 130–131
Supreme Court (U.S.), decisions, 23, 163, 184, 186, 189; consent decrees monitoring TennCare curtailments, 135–138. *See also Baker v. Carr*; Tennessee Supreme Court
surplus politics concept, 10, 66, 68–72. *See also* politics
Sykes, Elizabeth, 185

Tate, Katherine, 167
tax and spending policies, 105–123, 225n48; budget issues, 107–108, 128, 131; poll taxes, 47–48, 49, 209n39; racial differences in attitudes toward, 112–122, 123; reform proposals, 108–112. *See also* income tax, state; sales taxes, state
Tedin, Kent, 115
TennCare/Medicaid program, 109, 124–162, 226n4, 230n75, 238n39; attitudes toward, 133, 144, 145–148; Bredesen's reform measures, 7, 125–126, 127, 131–145, 145–149; consent decrees regarding, 135–138, 144; debate over, 1, 129–145, 156; Economic Disadvantage Index measuring impact of, 150–152, 155; field experiment regarding, 149–153, 159–162; origins of, 127, 128, 130; polarization over, 11, 126–128, 140, 144, 145–149, 156; timeline for, 157–159. *See also* blacks: impact of TennCare cuts on
TennCare Saves Lives Coalition, 11, 126, 138–139, 142, 226–227n12
Tennessee: constitutional amendment of 1870, 48, 108, 109; Fair Practices Code of 1964, 51, 62; poorest counties in, 68; as swing state, 65, 196, 198; territorial expansions, 34–35
Tennessee Black Caucus of State Legislators (TBCSL), 58, 180, 182; agenda of, 10–11, 88–89, 123; involvement in public sphere, 83–84; ratified resolutions, 100–101; rise of, 85–89; tax reform proposals, 80–81, 106, 108–112, 123; TennCare reforms and, 133, 139–140. *See also* black lawmakers; black politics
Tennessee Colonization Society (TCS), 35
Tennessee Federation of Democratic Leagues, 51
Tennessee General Assembly: biracial coalitions in, 84–85; blacks elected to, 39, 57–59; disenfranchisement laws passed by, 40–41; Free Negro Bill, 36–37; partisan/political realignment in, 1, 2–3, 78, 85, 196, 197–198; racial politics in, 82–83; resolutions, 222n54; sentencing reform laws, 184–185. *See also* Democratic Party / Democrats: lose majority in Tennessee General Assembly; Republican Party / Republicans, supermajority in Tennessee General Assembly
Tennessee Justice Center (TJC), consent decrees monitoring TennCare curtailments, 135–138
Tennessee Regulatory Authority, black representation on, 110–111
Tennessee Sentencing Commission, collapse of, 183, 185

Tennessee State Convention of Colored Citizens, 33
Tennessee Supreme Court (TSC): consent decrees monitoring TennCare curtailments, 135–138; death penalty decisions, 189; overseeing prison reform, 240n21; poll tax ruling, 48; slavery disputes, 37–38; tax cases, 108–109. *See also* Supreme Court (U.S.), decisions
Tent City movement, 54
Terrell, Mary Church, 43, 44
terrorism, racial, 30, 32–33, 39. *See also* lynchings
Tindell, Harry, 98
Todd, Curry, 163, 164, 167, 178
Towns, Joe, 89
Traughber, Charles, 181
Trump, Donald J., 198–199
Turner, Brenda, 98, 99
Turner, Johnnie, 83, 90–91
Turner, Larry, 88, 90, 95
Turner, Mike, 98
Twenty-First Amendment, U.S. Constitution, 59
Tyree, Hiram, 41

unemployment, 68, 73, 76–77
Union Transportation Company, 42
urbanization, 49, 57, 86

Valentino, Nicholas, 21
van Zeller, Mariana, 163
Vaughn, Nathan, 18, 87, 95, 97
Vickers, Jill, 24
Villegas, Juana, 171
Volunteer Party, 49
voters/voting rights, 31, 84; black struggle for, 1, 33–34, 46, 53–55, 57; county voting patterns, 9, 72–76, 79; exclusions from, 43, 209n29, 209n32; for felons, 181, 239n7; Reconstruction-era, 38–41; Voting Rights Act of 1965, 27, 54–55, 56, 69, 87. *See also* civil rights movement; whites: voter intimidation by

Walters, Ronald, 30, 44–45
Walton, Hanes, 1, 5
Washington, Booker T., 42, 43
Wathers, William C., 49, 56
Welch, William, 125
welfare: child, 80; social, 23, 25–26, 27–28, 33, 60, 99, 145
Wells-Barnett, Ida B., 43, 61
West Tennessee Civic and Political League, 44–45
Wharton, A. C., 57, 132
whites: anti-immigration views of, 167, 170, 176–177, 179; backlash against civil rights, 41, 50, 67, 68; bills sponsored by, 82; conservative, 25, 44, 60; criminal justice reform views, 190, 192, 193; in Democratic Party, 22, 27–28, 31, 69; moderate, 17, 20, 50, 67; political comity with blacks, 27, 28, 29; in Republican Party, 22, 73–74; TennCare reform views, 150–153; voter intimidation by, 44, 46–47, 48–49, 54, 183–184
white supremacists / white supremacy, 34, 39, 44, 168, 186. *See also* Jim Crow era; racism/racists; segregation/segregationists
Wilder, Douglas, 143
Wilder, John S., 2
William H. Mercer, Inc., study of TennCare, 228n39
Williams, Avon, 58, 59
Williams, Kent, 90
Williamson County, conservatism of, 68
Willis, Archie "A. W.," 49, 51, 57–58, 86
Withers, Dedrick "Teddy," 57
Wood, Eliza, 40
Wunderlich, Gordon, 150
Wyman, Linda, 44, 45

Yardley, William F., 56
Young, William Henderson, 40

zero-sum game, of party politics, 20, 26
zero-tolerance policies, 180, 183, 184, 185

Printed in the USA
CPSIA information can be obtained
at www.ICGtesting.com
LVHW030254211223
766976LV00004B/166